LUXOR

ILLUSTRATED

WITH ASWAN, ABU SIMBEL, AND THE NILE

First published in 2009 by
The American University in Cairo Press
113 Sharia Kasr el Aini, Cairo, Egypt
420 Lexington Avenue, Suite 1644, New York, NY 10170
www.aucpress.com

This revised and updated edition published in 2024

ISBN 978 1 649 03338 3

Photograph of Tutankhamun's sarcophagus on page 53 by Sherif Sonbol. Photograph of the tomb of Nefertari on page 75 courtesy of the Yorck Project. Aerial photograph of the Theban hills on page 74 by Stanislaw Zurek. The cleared sphinx avenue on page 33; Luxor Museum, stela of Nehemsubastet, head of Senwosret III, statue of Senwosret I, and canopic lid of Tuy on pages 46–47; Silsileh on page 83; and Temple of Khnum at Elephantine on page 99 by Aidan Dodson. All other photographs by Michael Haag.

Library of Congress Cataloging-in-Publication Data

Names: Haag, Michael, 1943–2020 - author. | Dodson, Aidan, 1962- editor.
Title: Luxor illustrated : with Aswan, Abu Simbel, and the Nile / written and photographed by Michael Haag ; revised and updated by Aidan Dodson.
Other titles: With Aswan, Abu Simbel, and the Nile
Identifiers: LCCN 2023033562 | ISBN 9781649033383 (trade paperback) | ISBN 9781649033390 (adobe pdf)
Subjects: LCSH: Thebes (Egypt : Extinct city)--Description and travel. | Thebes (Egypt : Extinct city)--Pictorial works. | Luxor (Egypt)--Description and travel. | Luxor (Egypt)--Pictorial works. | Aswān (Egypt)--Description and travel. | Aswān (Egypt)--Pictorial works. | Abū Sunbul (Egypt)--Description and travel. | Abū Sunbul (Egypt)--Pictorial works.
Classification: LCC DT73.T3 H29 2023 | DDC 932/.30222--dc23/eng/20230812

1 2 3 4 5 28 27 26 25 24

Designed by Sally Boylan

LUXOR ILLUSTRATED

WITH ASWAN, ABU SIMBEL, AND THE NILE

REVISED, UPDATED, AND WITH A NEW INTRODUCTION
BY AIDAN DODSON

MICHAEL HAAG

THE AMERICAN UNIVERSITY IN CAIRO PRESS
CAIRO NEW YORK

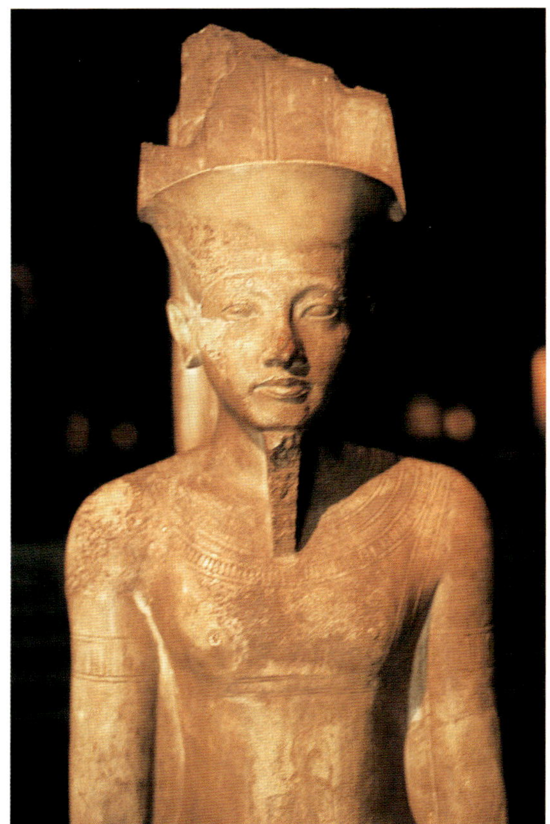

Above: Tutankhamun portrayed as the god Amun. The statue was found at the Temple of Amun at Karnak and is now on view at the Luxor Museum.

I dedicate this book to
Miomir and Aleksandra Milovanovic.

CONTENTS

ABOUT THE AUTHORS

Michael Haag (1943–2020) was a London-based writer and photographer. He is author and photographer of *Alexandria Illustrated* (AUC Press, 2004) and *Cairo Illustrated* (AUC Press, 2006), and author of *Alexandria: City of Memory* and *Vintage Alexandria: Photographs of the City, 1860–1960* (AUC Press, 2008). His long-in-the-making biography of Lawrence Durrell is scheduled to appear in 2024.

Aidan Dodson is honorary full professor of Egyptology at the University of Bristol. He is the author of over twenty-five books, including *Monarchs of the Nile, Amarna Sunrise, Amarna Sunset, Poisoned Legacy,* and *Afterglow of Empire*, as well as *Sethy I, Rameses III, Nefertiti, The First Pharaohs, Tutankhamun,* and *The Nubian Pharaohs*, in the Lives and Afterlives series, all published by the American University in Cairo Press.

INTRODUCTION TO NEW EDITION

Aidan Dodson

Michael Haag was born in New York in 1943, the son of George Michael Haag and Maureen Veronica Maguire. Having been brought up in New York, he briefly attended Boston University before later moving to London, UK, where he completed his undergraduate and master's degrees at University College London. He spent much of the rest of his life in Belsize Park and became a traveler and a writer, especially on travel, in Egypt and Greece, but also on a wide variety of historical topics, including the Knights Templar. He also republished long-neglected classics of travel literature. As far as Egypt was concerned, he wrote a number of guidebooks, as well as a book on the city of Alexandria that is a classic in itself.

Haag was also a photographer, and this book is essentially a photographic evocation of the key sites of the southern part of Egypt. This is of course that stretch of the Nile best known to tourists, especially through the classic cruise between Luxor and Aswan, with the potential for side trips—upstream to Abu Simbel; downstream to Dendera and Abydos. As such, it represents an ideal souvenir of such a trip.

In revising this new edition of the book, I have endeavored to adjust the text to provide the reader with the most up-to-date views on historical matters. Egyptology is a subject where "history" can quite literally change overnight through one new archaeological discovery—or simply a fresh look at old finds. Thus, while some firm fixed points exist (or at least we think they do!), a large proportion of ancient Egyptian history is really, to a greater or lesser degree, only a "working hypothesis." Keeping track of the regular adjustments is hard enough for professional Egyptologists, still less for other specialists. Thus, in a number of cases,

Haag's original text included some ideas that had actually passed out of Egyptological consensus, but which have continued to exist in the popular literature. As well as updating views on such matters, I have also tweaked some statements to embrace certain subtleties that Haag may not have been aware of at that time, and also to highlight things in the photographs that I thought deserved to be pointed out or enlarged upon.

The core of the book is of course these photographs, and they have been left almost entirely untouched, except for two where the caption and the image in the original edition were mismatched. These have been replaced with images of my own that reflect what is actually being described in the caption. I have also made substitutions where objects described as in the Luxor Museum have now been removed to Cairo, and added one new image. The latter reflects a fundamental change in one of the locations: the opening-up of the great avenue of sphinxes between the temples of Luxor and Karnak, much of which was still buried when the book was originally published.

This excavation has greatly changed the whole aspect of the city of Luxor, destroying many buildings, and splitting a neighborhood in two, with only the occasional bridge joining the sundered parts. This conflict between a desire to reveal and display the past of a place, and the current life of the place, is a very real one, not just in Egypt, but also in many other parts of the world, and it is important to recognize the symbioses—and conflicts—between the past and the present in such places. Accordingly, I have twinned with Haag's view of sphinxes half-buried in a lush field a view of part of the cleared avenue, now in a deep, steep-sided, and distinctly sterile cutting below street level. In addition, the map of Luxor has had to be partly redrawn to show the sphinx avenue, while some changes in road layouts on the west bank of the Nile have been incorporated. The opportunity has also been taken to add some additional detail to various features of the map directly relevant to locations dealt with in the book.

The Nile between Abydos and Abu Simbel embraces some of the greatest artistic and architectural works of humankind; it is also in itself a monument to nature. The journey between these two points presents scenery that ranges from arid desert to the lushest of greenery—sometimes within only a few kilometers, or even on opposite sides of the river. Monuments as well range from structures so broken down that their nature can only be discerned by the expert, to others that seem like they were built only yesterday—rather than millennia ago. It is hoped that the new edition of this book will prove a useful companion to those undertaking such a journey—whether in person or vicariously!

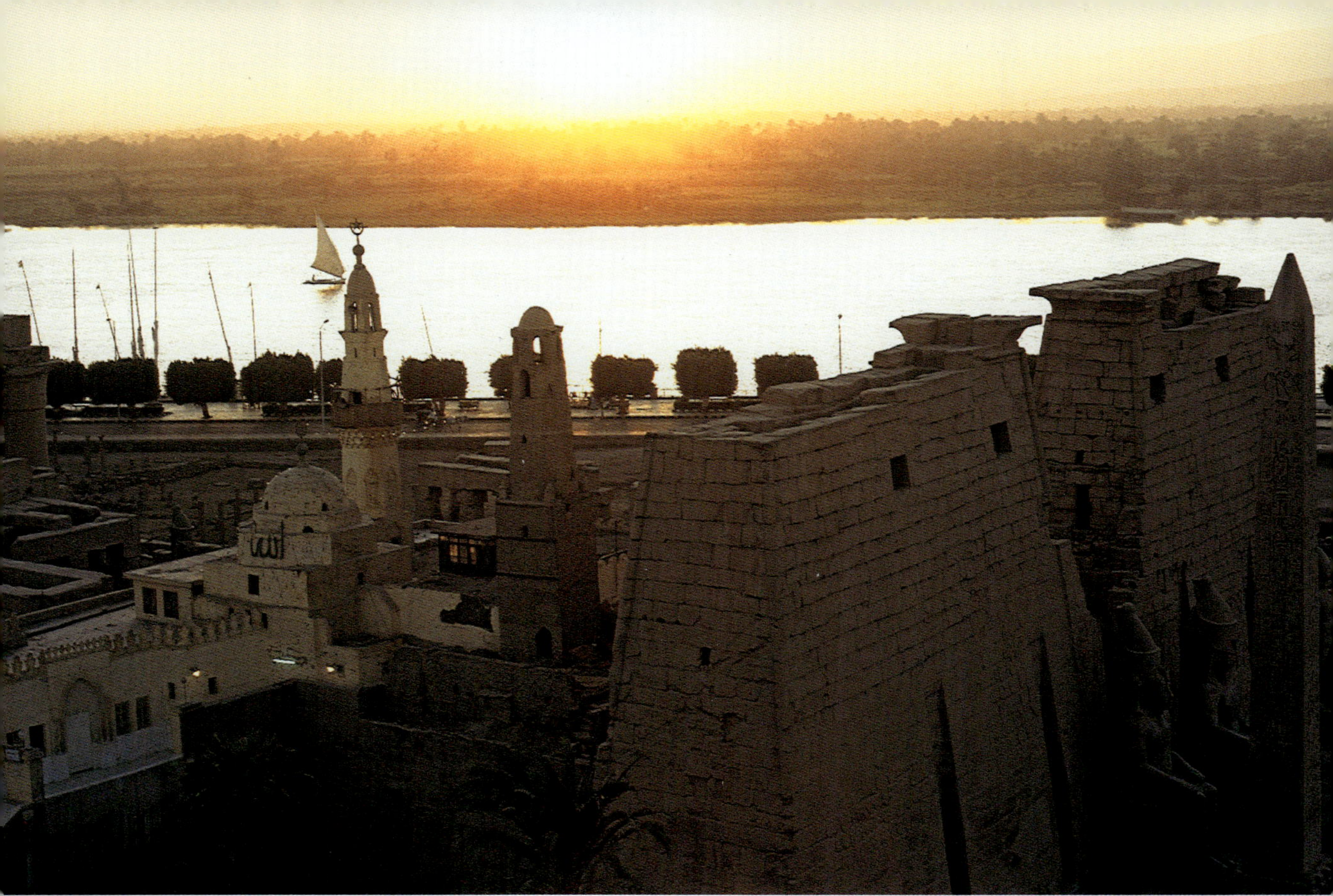

AN OUTLINE OF PEOPLE AND EVENTS

3050–2660 BC: Early Dynastic Period (First and Second Dynasties)

Upper and Lower Egypt are united by king **Menes** (probably identical with **Narmer**), who establishes his capital at Memphis. There is civil conflict during the second half of the Second Dynasty, before reunification by **Khasekhemwy**.

2660–2200 BC: Old Kingdom (Third to Eighth Dynasties)

Following the reunification, **Djoser** builds the first pyramid, followed by the Fourth Dynasty pyramids of **Khufu, Khaefre,** and **Menkaure** at Giza, which mark the apogee of the Pyramid age and of Old Kingdom pharaonic authority.

2200–2010 BC: First Intermediate Period (Ninth to Eleventh Dynasties)

Low Niles, bad harvests, foreign incursions, and a weakened royal authority lead to the collapse of the central administration, and a north–south split, finally resolved by civil war. The Temple of Amun at Thebes is founded in about 2050 BC.

Above: The Temple of Luxor at sunset; across the Nile lies the vast Theban necropolis with its funerary monuments, noble tombs, and Valley of the Kings. The temple was begun in the mid-14th century BC by Amenhotep III, who dedicated it to Amun and the Royal Ka, the spiritual embodiment of kingship. A century later, Rameses II added the great pylon, and placed in front of it two obelisks and six colossal statues of himself. One of the obelisks has been taken off to Paris where it graces the Place de la Concorde. In Roman times, the temple was used as a fortified camp; the Christians then built a church within the temple precincts, and in the thirteenth century the mosque of Abu al-Haggag was built atop the temple walls. The Temple of Luxor has been a sacred site for over three thousand years.

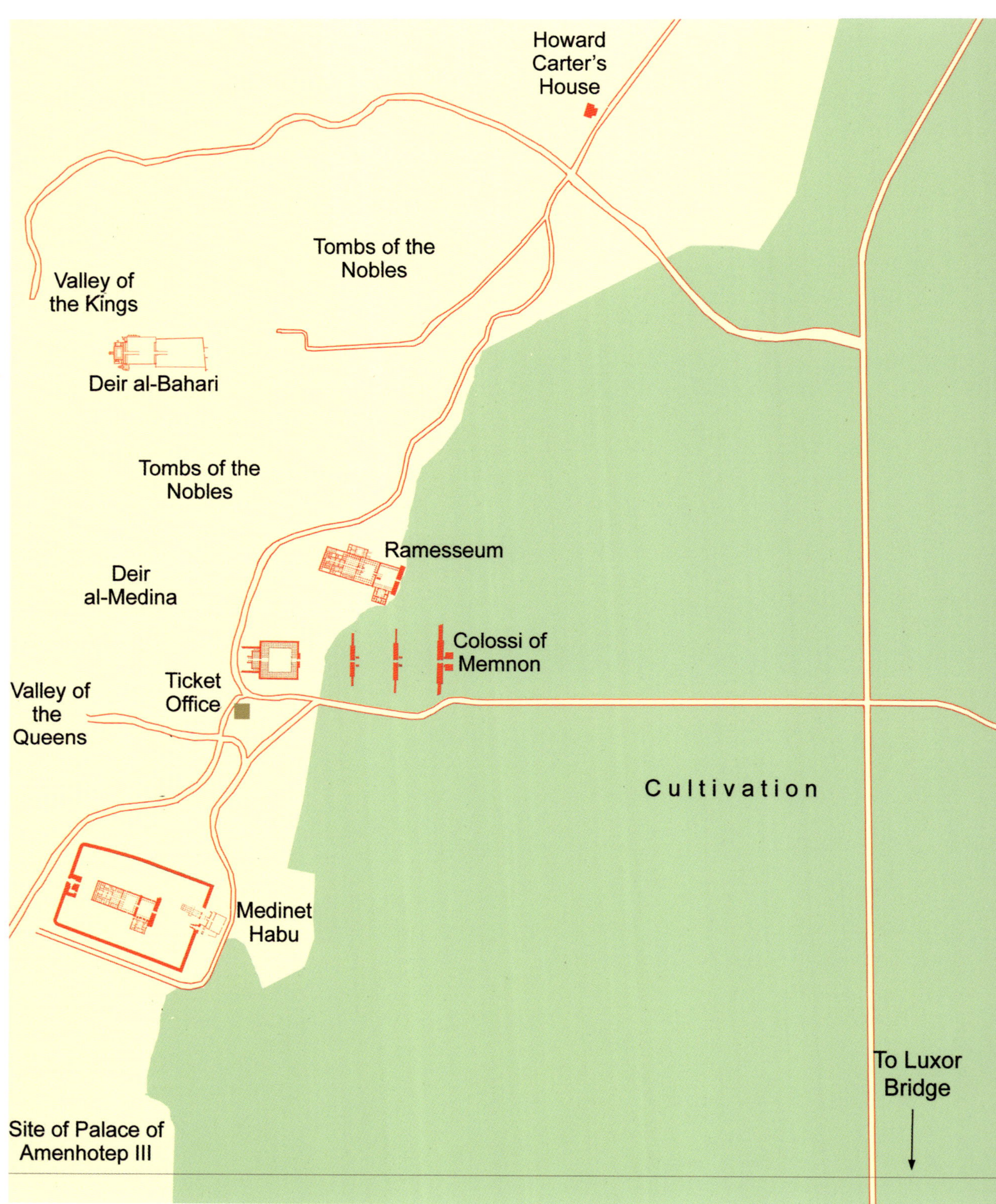
Howard Carter's House
Tombs of the Nobles
Valley of the Kings
Deir al-Bahari
Tombs of the Nobles
Ramesseum
Deir al-Medina
Colossi of Memnon
Ticket Office
Valley of the Queens
Cultivation
Medinet Habu
To Luxor Bridge
Site of Palace of Amenhotep III

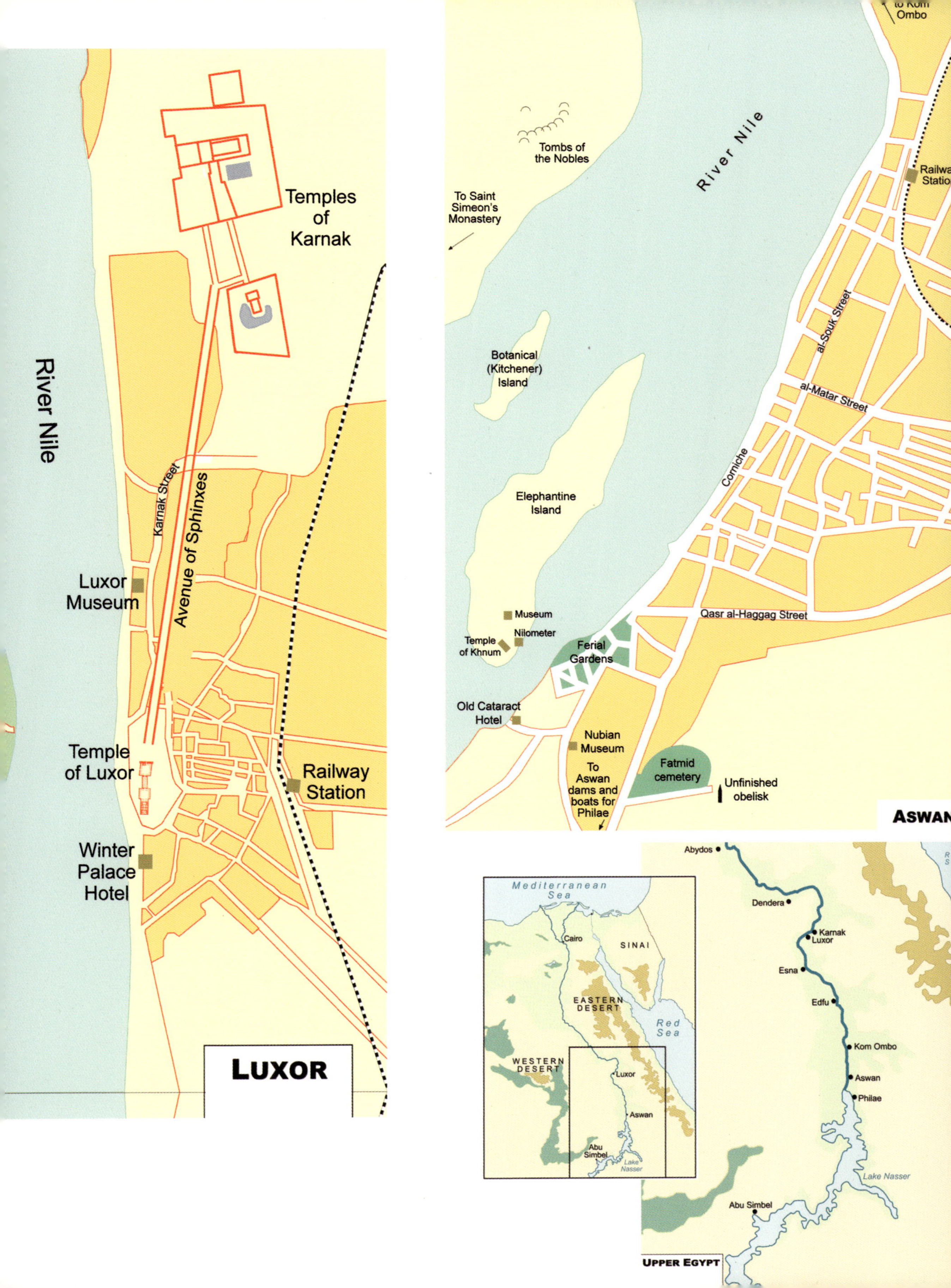
Temples
of
Karnak
River Nile
Karnak Street
Avenue of Sphinxes
Luxor
Museum
Temple
of Luxor
Railway
Station
Winter
Palace
Hotel
LUXOR
to Kom
Ombo
Tombs of
the Nobles
To Saint
Simeon's
Monastery
River Nile
Railway
Station
Botanical
(Kitchener)
Island
al-Souk Street
al-Matar Street
Corniche
Elephantine
Island
Museum
Nilometer
Temple
of Khnum
Ferial
Gardens
Qasr al-Haggag Street
Old Cataract
Hotel
Nubian
Museum
To
Aswan
dams and
boats for
Philae
Fatmid
cemetery
Unfinished
obelisk
ASWAN
Mediterranean
Sea
Cairo
SINAI
EASTERN
DESERT
Red
Sea
WESTERN
DESERT
Luxor
Aswan
Abu
Simbel
Lake
Nasser
Abydos
Dendera
Karnak
Luxor
Esna
Edfu
Kom Ombo
Aswan
Philae
Lake Nasser
Abu Simbel
UPPER EGYPT

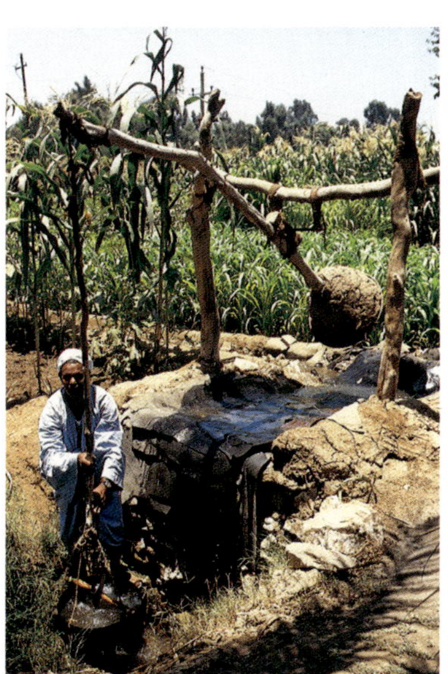

Above: The *shaduf*, a simple device for lifting water to irrigate the fields, was already in use by the New Kingdom and is still occasionally to be seen in Egypt today.

2010–1650 BC: Middle Kingdom (Eleventh to Thirteenth Dynasties)

The capital is initially at Thebes (Luxor), but soon moves to near Lisht in northern Egypt. The kings of the Twelfth Dynasty (all named **Amenemhat** and **Senwosret**) expand Egyptian control into Lower Nubia, building fortresses and trading posts at the Second Cataract to ensure control over gold supplies and trade with Africa. Central authority decays during the Thirteenth Dynasty, with the loss of control over Nubia.

1650–1540 BC: Second Intermediate Period (Fourteenth to Seventeenth Dynasties)

The northeastern part of Egypt becomes independent under Palestinian rulers of the Fourteenth Dynasty, who are then replaced by the "Hyksos" Fifteenth Dynasty. They introduce the horse and chariot to Egypt and then conquer much of the country, leaving a rump Egyptian regime (Sixteenth and Seventeenth Dynasties) in Thebes. Rulers of the latter finally begin the liberation of the country.

1540–1078 BC: New Kingdom (Eighteenth to Twentieth Dynasties)

The expulsion of the Hyksos is completed by **Ahmose I** (1540–1516 BC), and he and his successors initiate a new foreign policy that includes the conquest of Syria-Palestine and tight control over its rulers. In the south, the whole of Nubia is taken over and made a direct dependency of Egypt. The greatest extent of Egyptian control is reached under **Thutmose III** (1468–1415 BC) who, together with his aunt and co-ruler **Hatshepsut** (1462–1447 BC), is responsible for a major expansion of the temple of Karnak. The latter's father, **Thutmose I** (1496–1481 BC) begins the practice of royal burials in the Valley of the Kings. Under **Amenhotep III** (1377–1337 BC), who built most of the temple of Luxor, the New Kingdom reaches its apogee of opulence. His son **Amenhotep IV**, later **Akhenaten** (1337–1321 BC), establishes a short-lived monolatrous cult of the sun god Aten, but traditional religion is re-established during the reign of the young pharaoh **Tutankhamun** (1321–1312 BC). **Tutankhamun** marks the end of the dynastic bloodline, and three army generals rule after him, the last of whom, **Rameses I**, marks the beginning of the Nineteenth Dynasty. His son, **Sethy I** (1276–1265 BC), and grandson, **Rameses II** (1265–1200 BC), restore royal prestige by means of their campaign into Syria-Palestine. Rameses is a prodigious builder, adding to the temples at Luxor and Karnak, and constructing a huge number of temples, including his memorial temple, the Ramesseum, and the rock-cut temples at Abu Simbel in Nubia. His reliefs often advertise his valor against the Hittites at the battle of Qadesh; he later signs a peace treaty with them. Conflict flares within the royal family within a decade of Rameses's death, leading to the beginning of a new dynasty.

Its second king, **Rameses III** (1172–1140 BC), builds his memorial temple at Medinet Habu and repels an invasion by the Sea Peoples, whose depredations had previously caused the collapse of many eastern Mediterranean cultures, but his reign ended with his assassination, and a steady decline in Egypt's economic and political state under his successors **Rameses IV through XI**.

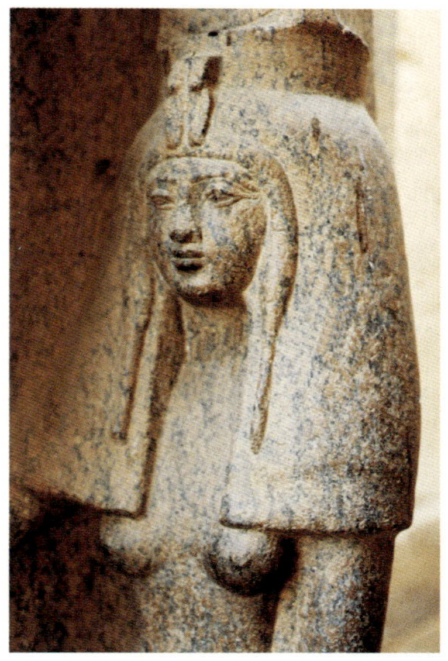

Above: Nefertari was the chief wife of Rameses II. The king had a fair number of women in his harem, but he described Nefertari as "more than comparable with the palace beauties."

1078–664 BC: Third Intermediate Period (Twenty-First to Twenty-Fifth Dynasties)

The Twentieth Dynasty ends on political and economic collapse, and for much of the next few centuries Egypt often falls into two or more separate political units. Unity is restored by the Nubian Twenty-fifth Dynasty (755–664 BC), but their rule culminates in Assyrian invasions.

664–525 BC: Saite Period (Twenty-sixth Dynasty)

Unity and prosperity is restored by **Psamtik I** (664–610 BC), who builds links with the Greek world. However, the dynasty ends with the absorption of Egypt into the Persian Empire.

525–332 BC: Late Period (Twenty-seventh to Thirty-first Dynasties)

Egypt remains under Persian rule until 404 BC, when independence is restored. **Nakhtnebef** (380–362 BC), founder of the Thirtieth Dynasty, builds at Philae and donates land for the temple of Horus at Edfu. The Persians return in 340 BC and remain until **Alexander the Great** enters Egypt in 332 BC.

332–30 BC: Ptolemaic Period

At **Alexander**'s death in 323 BC, his empire, which extends as far east as India, is divided among his generals, with **Ptolemy** taking Egypt. As **Ptolemy I Soter** (323–282 BC), he establishes a dynasty at Alexandria that rules Egypt for 300 years. Egypt is colonized by Greeks, many of whom adopt a culture that merges elements of their own with that of the Egyptians. **Ptolemy III Euergetes** (246–221 BC) builds at Karnak and begins the temple at Edfu. The temples at Dendera, Esna, Kom Ombo, and Philae are also begun during Ptolemaic times. The last of the Ptolemies is **Cleopatra VII** (51–30 BC), who with her Roman partner Mark Antony attempts to create a new Hellenistic empire, but when **Octavian** (the future **Augustus**) invades Egypt in 30 BC they are defeated and commit suicide.

30 BC–AD 642: Roman and Christian Periods

Egypt is incorporated into the Roman Empire. The Romans complete and add to many of the temples begun by the Ptolemies. The dominant culture of the country remains Greek. Christianity comes to Egypt in the first century AD, and in about AD 330 the first monasteries are founded in Egypt's deserts. By the end of the fourth century the majority of Egyptians are Christian (Copts). The last pagan shrine, the Temple of Isis at Philae, is closed in 543.

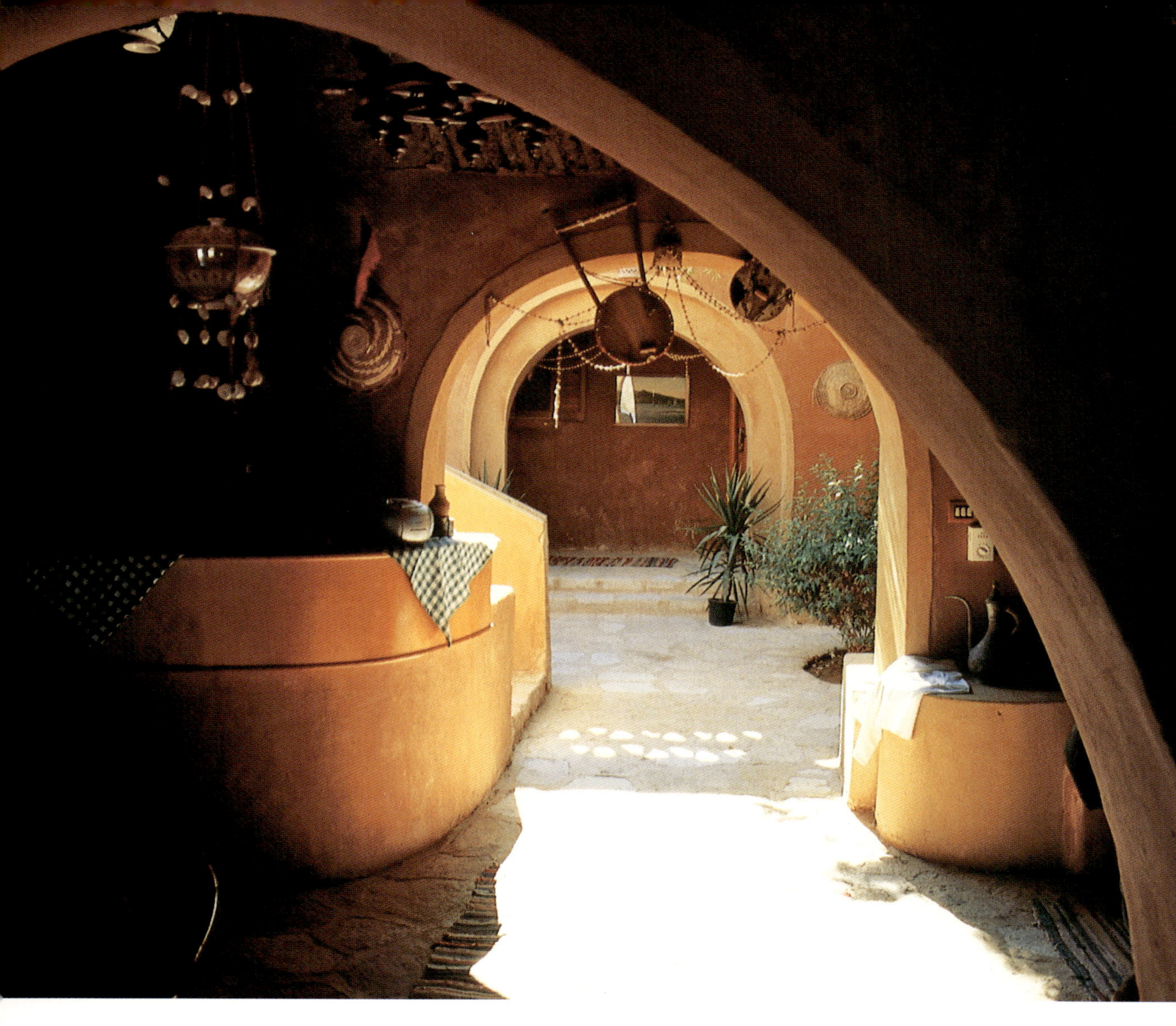

Above: Eskaleh, also known as Beit al-Nubi, meaning the Nubian House, is a cultural center cum restaurant and hotel at a quiet spot on the shore of Lake Nasser close to the Abu Simbel temples. Built in traditional Nubian style with domed rooms set around a central courtyard, the interior is always shady and cool. The place is the dream-child of Fikry Kachif, a musician known throughout Egypt, who often plays Nubian music with his friends here. With so much of Nubia lost beneath the waters of the lake, Eskaleh is Fikry Kachif's personal effort to preserve something of his people's culture.

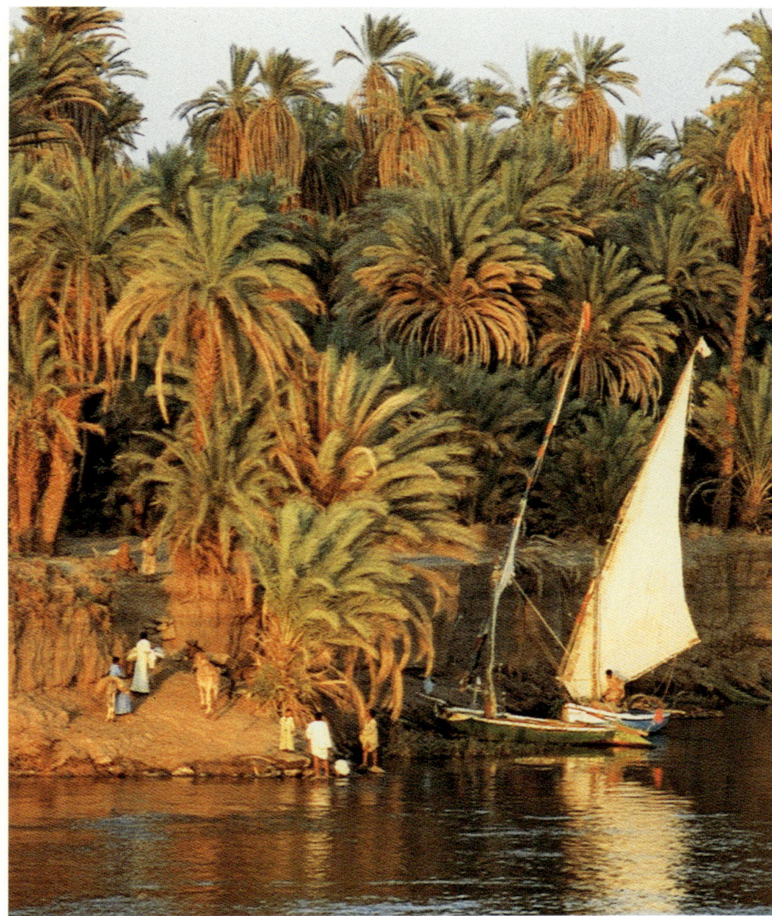

Left:. The Nile is central to the everyday life of Egypt. It provides water for animals, people, and fields, and it is a livelihood for fishermen who sail upon the river in their graceful feluccas.

AD 642–Present: From the Arab Invasion to the Present Day

In 642 an Arab army invades Egypt. Some Egyptians convert to Islam, but the majority remain Christian until at least the eleventh century. Initially part of the wider Caliphate, in 1250 Turkish slave-warriors known as the Mamluks overthrow the last Arab dynasty in Cairo and rule Egypt for themselves. In 1517 Egypt becomes part of the Ottoman Empire.

In 1798 **Napoleon Bonaparte** invades Egypt, opening Egypt to western curiosity and learning; modern Egyptology is born in 1822 when **Jean-François Champollion** deciphers the hieroglyphic script.

Muhammad Ali, a westernizing Ottoman commander, becomes governor of Egypt in 1805 and begins modernizing the country. His descendants become hereditary viceroys, and later kings, of Egypt. The Suez Canal opens in 1869 and, concerned for its strategic interests, Britain occupies Egypt in 1882. Egypt becomes a nominally independent kingdom in 1922, but remains under British military occupation until after the 1952 revolution, which overthrows the monarchy. The Aswan High Dam is constructed in the 1960s; Philae and Abu Simbel are saved from the rising waters of Lake Nasser.

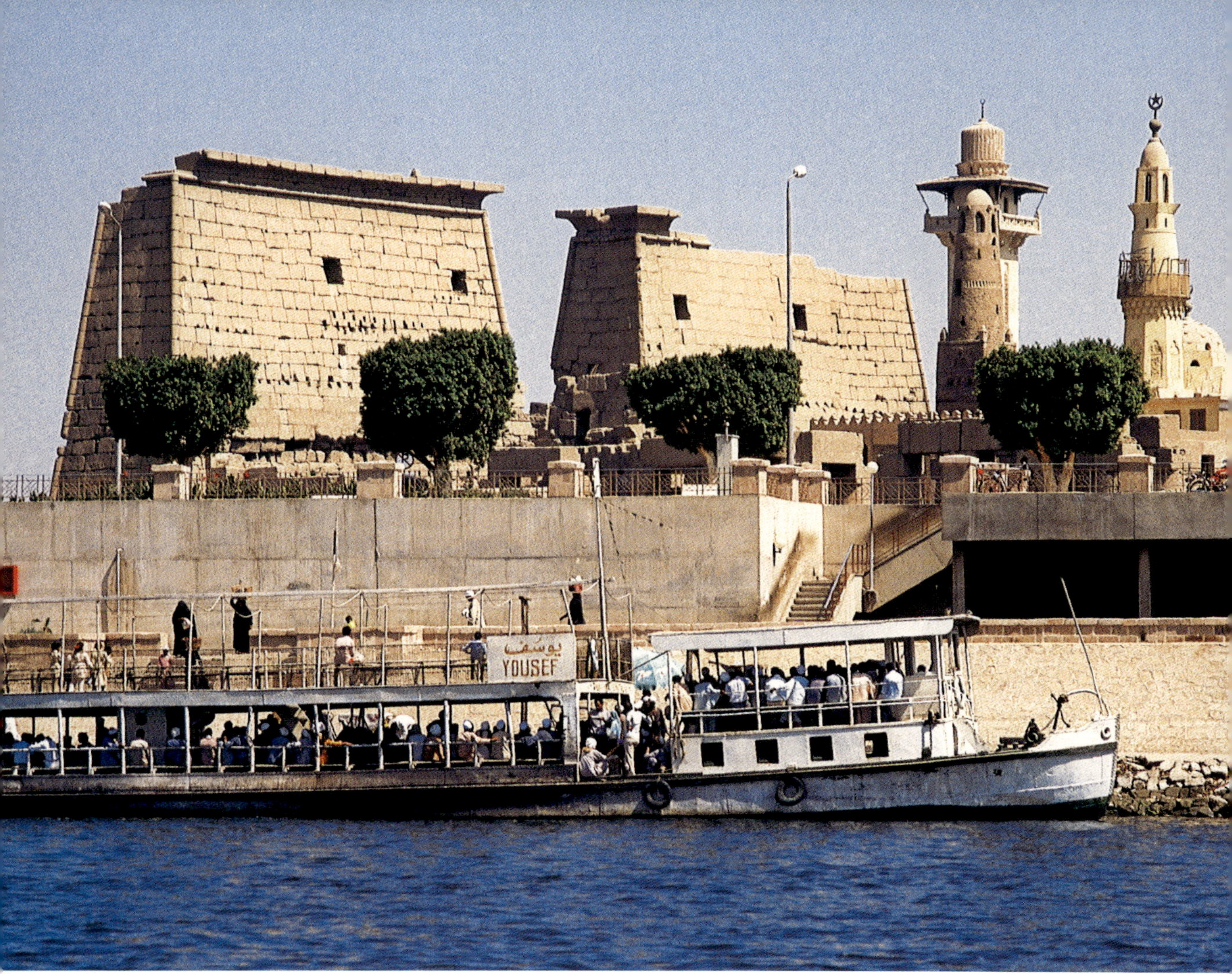

Above: Luxor temple stands close by the Corniche. Ferries take passengers across the Nile to the west bank with its great funerary temples such as Medinet Habu, the Ramesseum, and Deir al-Bahari, and also the royal tombs in the Valley of the Kings.

Top right: Feluccas glide along the broad and placid Nile at Luxor.

Bottom right: The traditional way of getting about Luxor is by horse and carriage.

Luxor

Luxor derives from the Arabic al-Uqsur, meaning "palaces," and refers to the appearance of the town until the end of the nineteenth century when it lay largely within the remains of the palace-like Temple of Luxor. The ancient Egyptians called their city Waset, although it is best known as Thebes, the name given to it by ancient Greek historians. The city embraced both sides of the Nile, the eastern being essentially the domain of the living, and the western that of the dead and those who provided for them. On the east bank, Thebes encompassed both the Temple of Luxor to the south and the immense Temple of Amun at Karnak, four kilometers to the north. It extended for many kilometers along the west bank of the river, where were constructed the memorial temples of the kings of the New Kingdom, and the tomb-chapels of many of their officials. Hidden within the rugged folds of the barren range of the Theban hills was the Valley of the Kings, where the pharaohs and some exceptionally favored associates had their burial places.

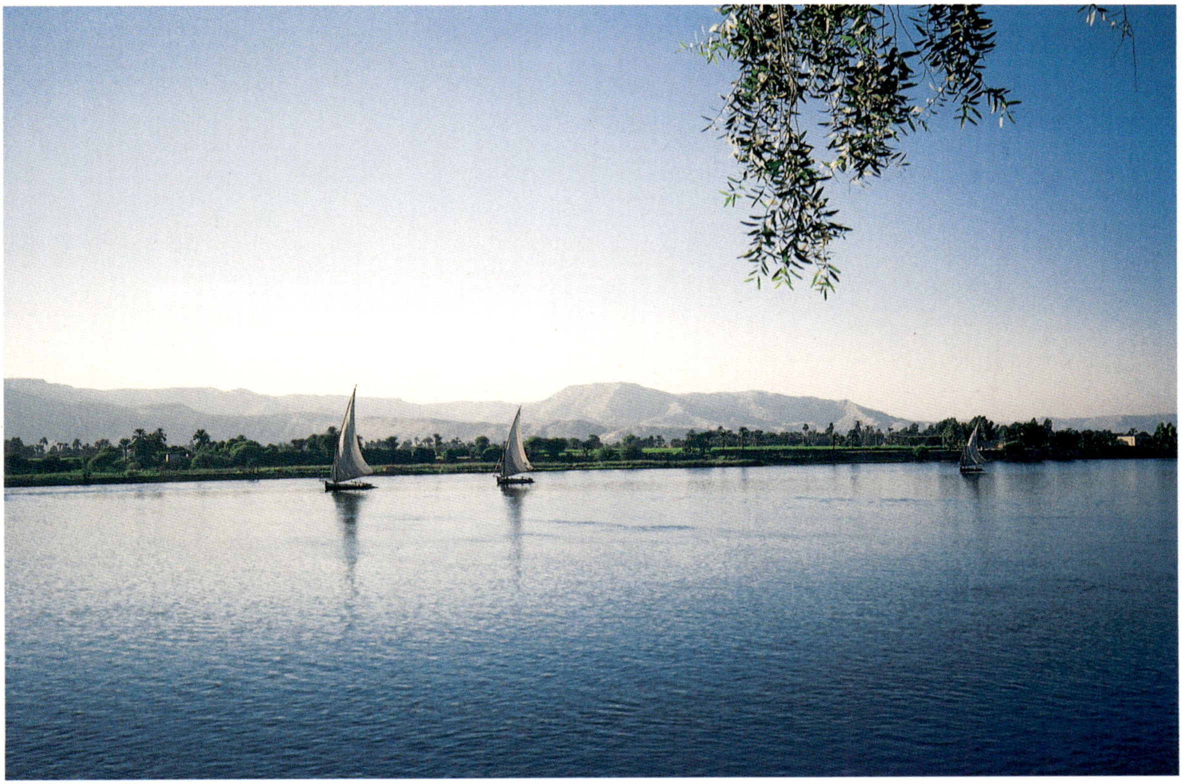

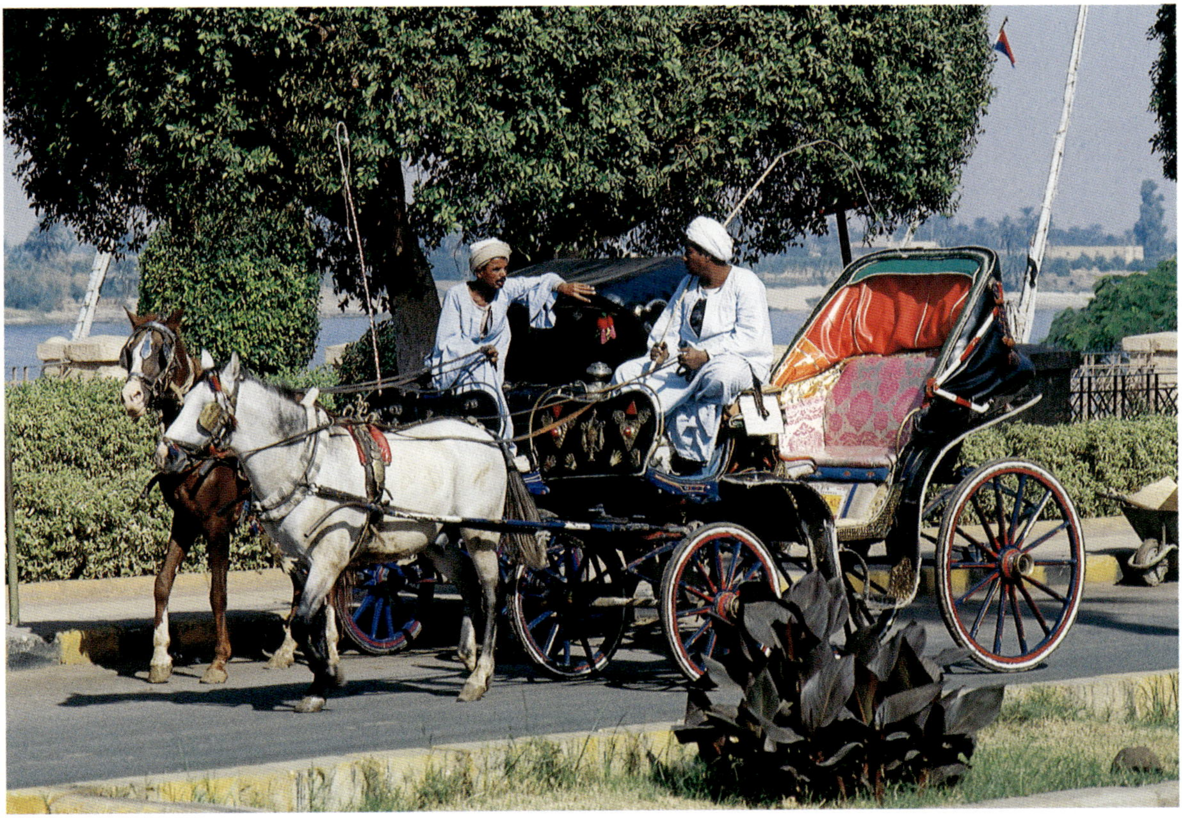

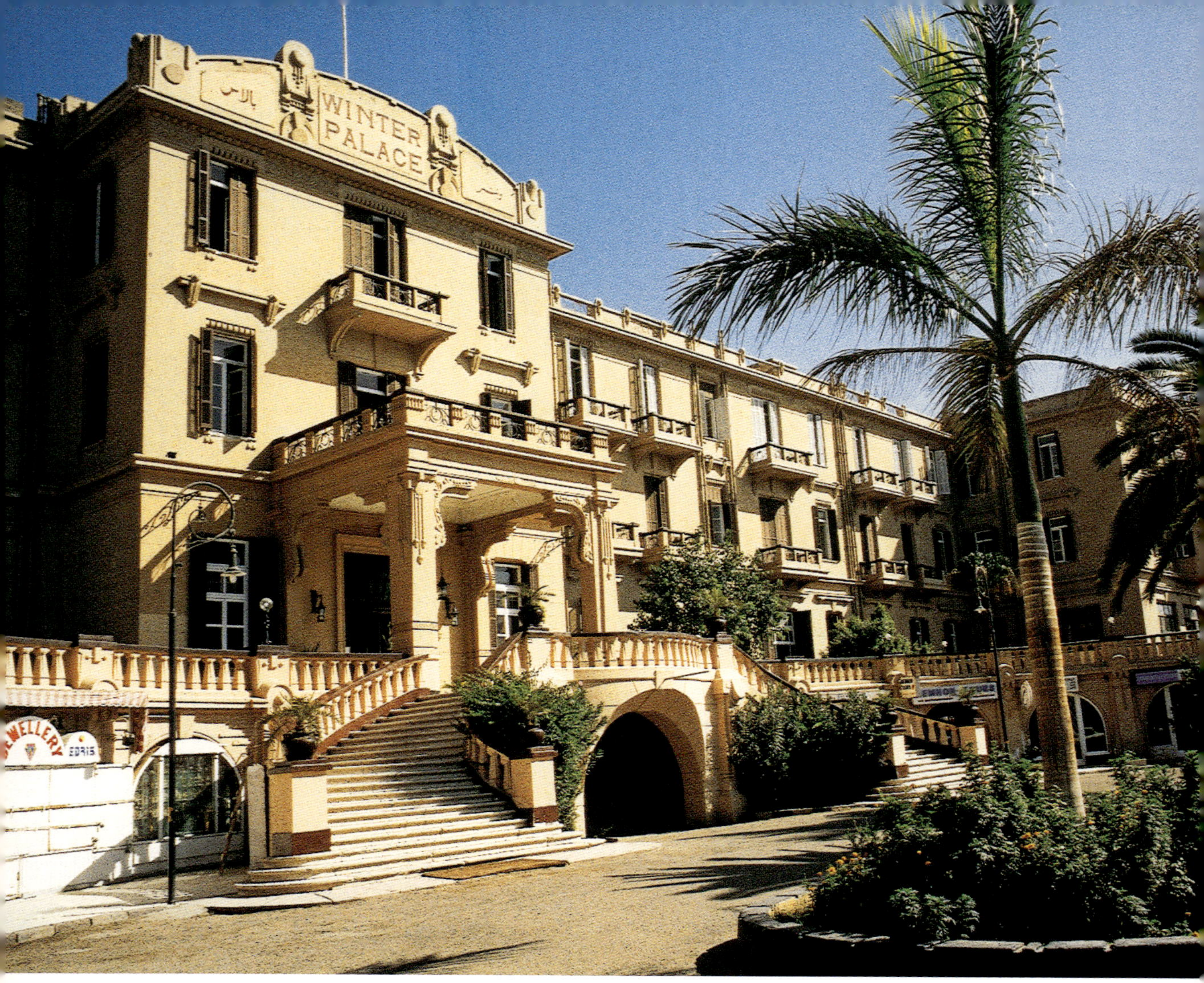

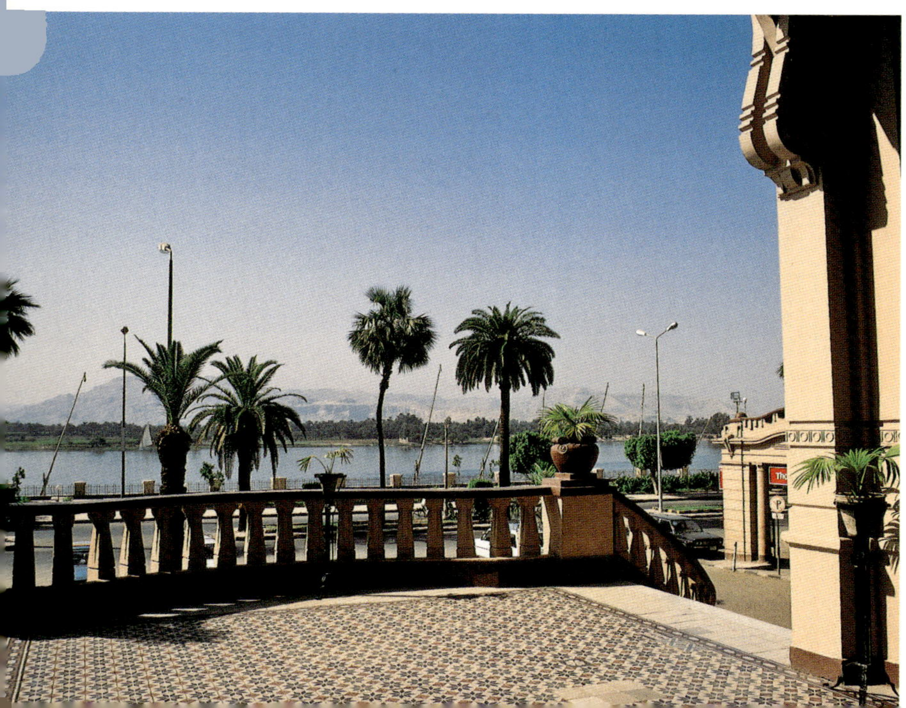

Top: During the search for Tutankhamun's tomb, Lord Carnarvon stayed at the Winter Palace, and Howard Carter posted announcements to the press here.

Left: View of the Nile from Luxor's Winter Palace Hotel. The Theban hills are in the distance.

Thanks to the imperial conquests of Egypt's warrior kings the wealth and talent of the world poured into Thebes, which was a cosmopolitan and universal city. Ships from Phoenicia and Nubia tied up at its quays to unload their precious cargoes from the Mediterranean and Africa, including annual tributes of silver, gold, ebony, ivory, slaves, and grain from Egypt's dependencies. Horses and the finest produce from the vineyards, orchards, and pastures of Asia were imported. The Egyptians thought of Waset, filled with color and spectacle, as the prototype of all cities and as the very spot where mankind first came into being. But if the royal dynasties were the driving force in this success, two other institutions became major beneficiaries of the imperial system—the army and the priesthoods, especially of Amun-Re, King of the Gods. The empire required a standing army, which if not on active service was kept employed in other ways, such as on major construction works, while army men increasingly filled many of the most important positions in the administration. Amun, as the local god of Thebes, had grown in prominence with the rising fortunes of the town during the Middle Kingdom, and by the New Kingdom he was grafted onto the solar Re as Amun-Re, king of the gods. Amun means "hidden," and being an unseen god he took on the quality of being immanent, a suitably embracing and universal quality for a cosmopolitan and imperial age. The military conquests in Nubia and Syria-Palestine provided endowed lands for supporting Amun's priesthood and for building, enlarging, and maintaining his temples, and those of other gods, in Egypt.

The great pharaohs of the New Kingdom responded, sometimes sensitively, sometimes grandiosely, to the special beauty of the place and the architectural possibilities of the landscape, which is placid and horizontal, a broad and richly cultivated plain on either side of the river. The desert to the east rises gently to the Arabian plateau, while to the west the Theban hills interpose themselves between the cultivation and the Libyan Desert. The Nile is majestic, at sundown an implacable lava flow. By day, feluccas seem to stride upon its surface like pond insects, and distant palms rise from the level stillness, distinct and exactly outlined in the clear air and brilliant light. For the ancient Egyptians, the richness and never-failing fertility of this landscape was a source of wonder. As a regular residence of the New Kingdom pharaohs, and effectively the national religious capital, it was the focus of an architectural activity so grand, and still so well preserved, that it can lay just claim to being the world's greatest outdoor museum.

Ever since the nineteenth century, tourists have followed in the footsteps of Egyptologists to explore the magnificent antiquities of Luxor. Nowhere in Egypt have there been such exciting discoveries of the past. Luxor's fascinating history, the beauty of its situation, and its benevolent climate continue to attract visitors from around the world.

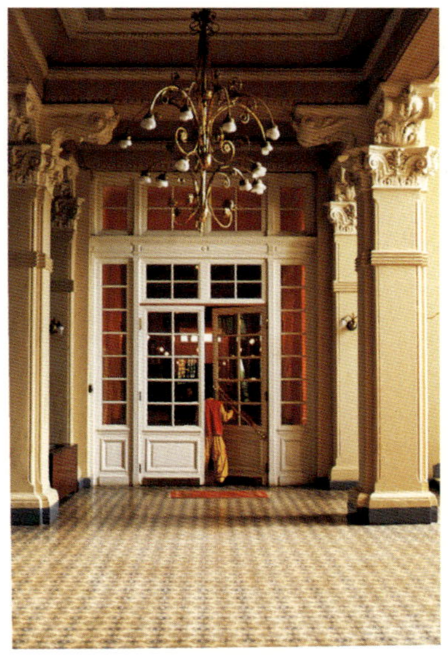

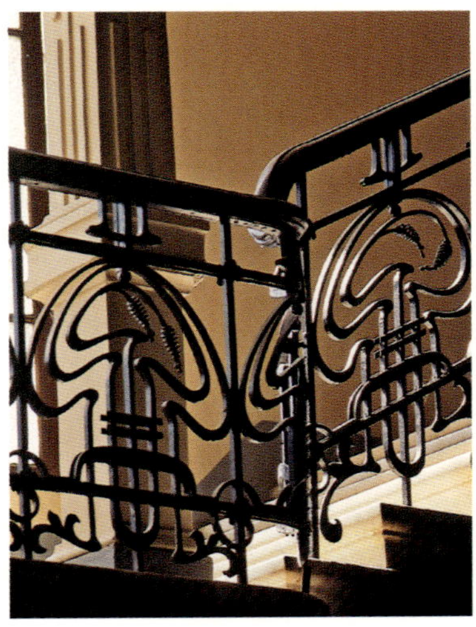

Above: The elegant Winter Palace, opened in 1907 (not 1886 as it claims!), is a living monument to the heyday of leisured travel.

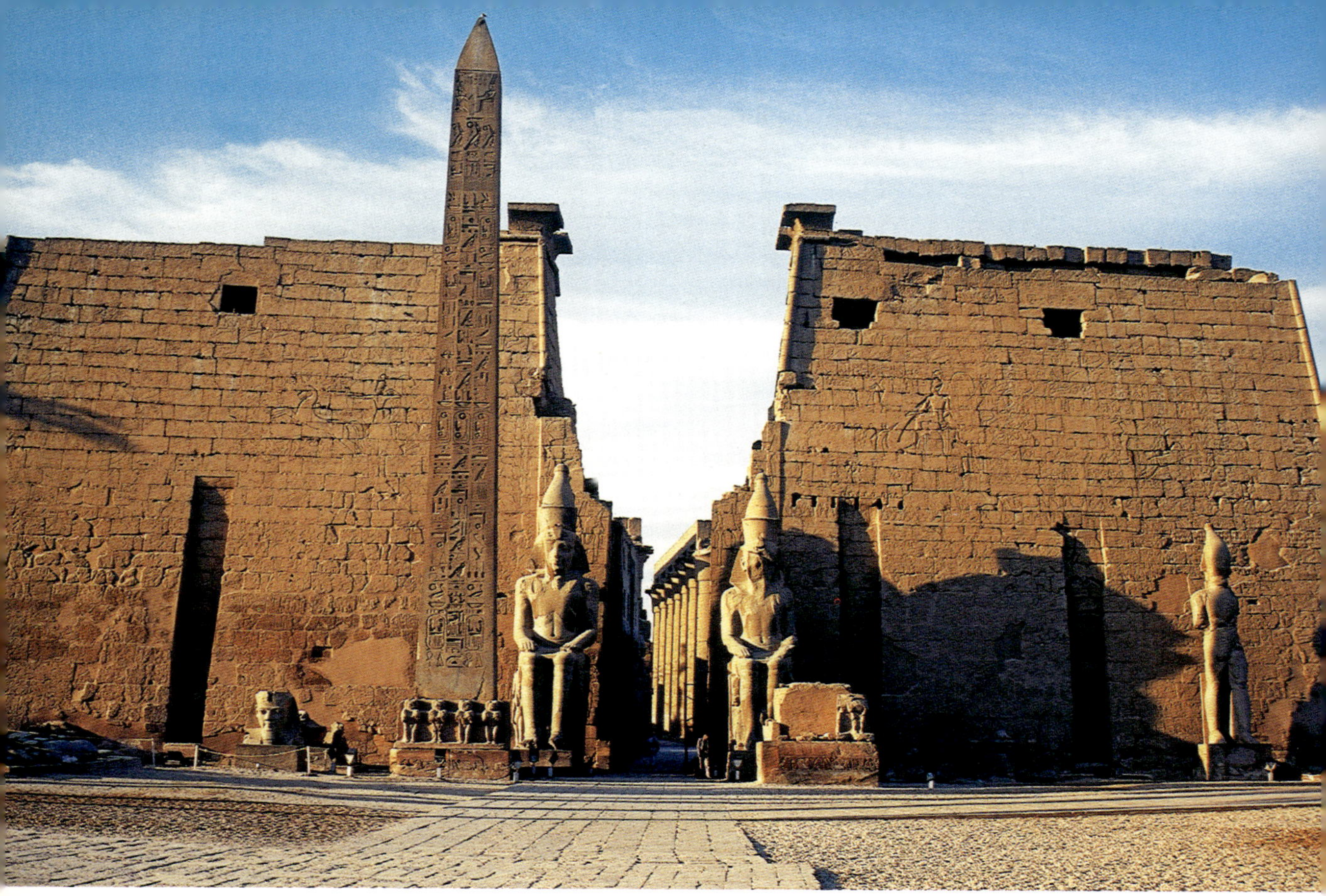

Above: The pylon was added to the Luxor Temple by Rameses II.

Below: A fallen head of Rameses in front of the pylon.

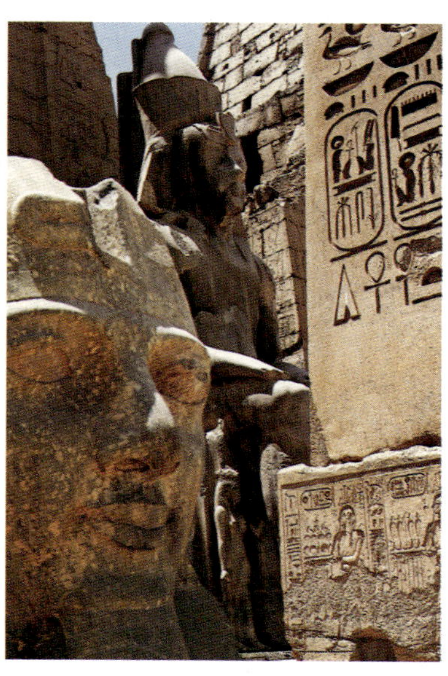

The Temple of Luxor

The Temple of Luxor was built largely under Amenhotep III and dedicated to Amun, and also to the Royal Ka, the ultimate spirit of kingship. Later kings embellished the temple, among them Tutankhamun and Alexander the Great, but the most significant additions were made by Rameses II, who built the massive entrance pylon, engraved with scenes of his victory in the battle of Qadesh, and the first court. In front of the entrance pylon were six statues of Rameses: two sitting, four standing, some of which have been the subject of restoration and re-erection. There were once two obelisks in front of the gateway, standing on plinths decorated with baboons. However, Muhammad Ali gave the west obelisk to the French, who in 1836 erected it in the Place de la Concorde in Paris.

Excavations to clear the temple began in 1885, gradually removing the village that had grown up in its midst. Sitting above the northeast corner of Rameses's first court is the one survival from that time, the mosque of Abu al-Haggag, a Sufi sheikh born in Baghdad, who spent the last fifty years of his life at Luxor, dying here in his nineties in 1243. The present mosque, however, is only nineteenth century, although the north minaret is eleventh century.

Below: The remaining obelisk in front of the pylon; the other stands in the Place de la Concorde in Paris. The base is decorated with baboons adoring the rising sun. The colossal figure behind is of Rameses II.

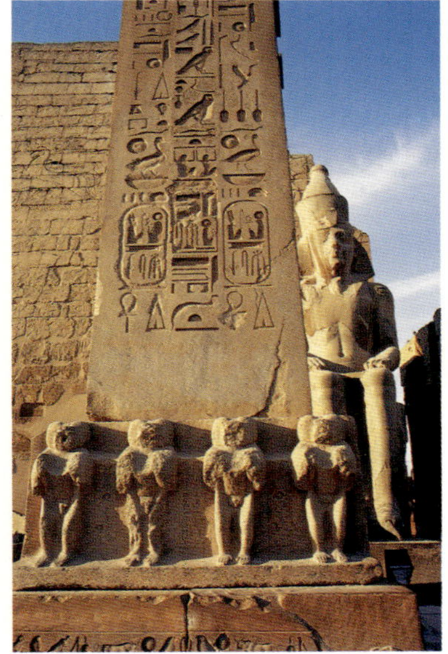

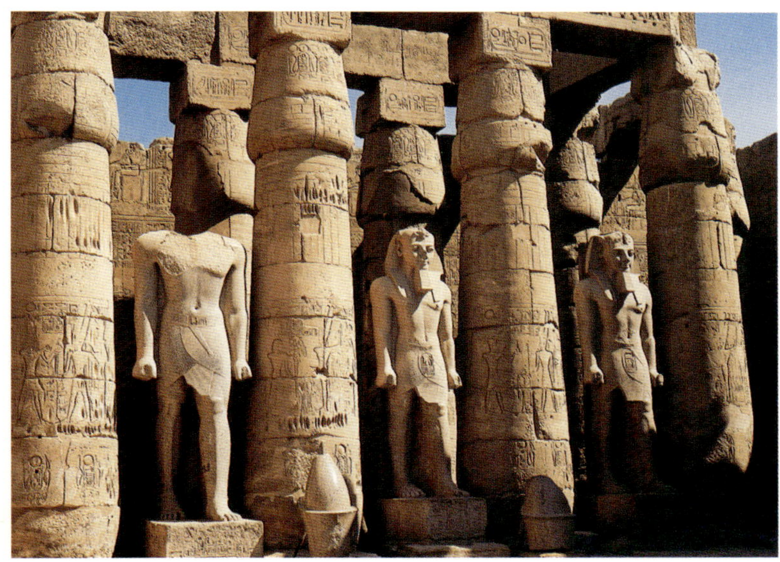

Above: Colossal statues of Rameses II in the first court.

Below: When the temple was excavated, the mosque of Abu al-Haggag was left in place. Its original doorway now overhangs Rameses's court, where shrines housing the sacred boats of Amun, Mut, and Khonsu can be seen on the left.

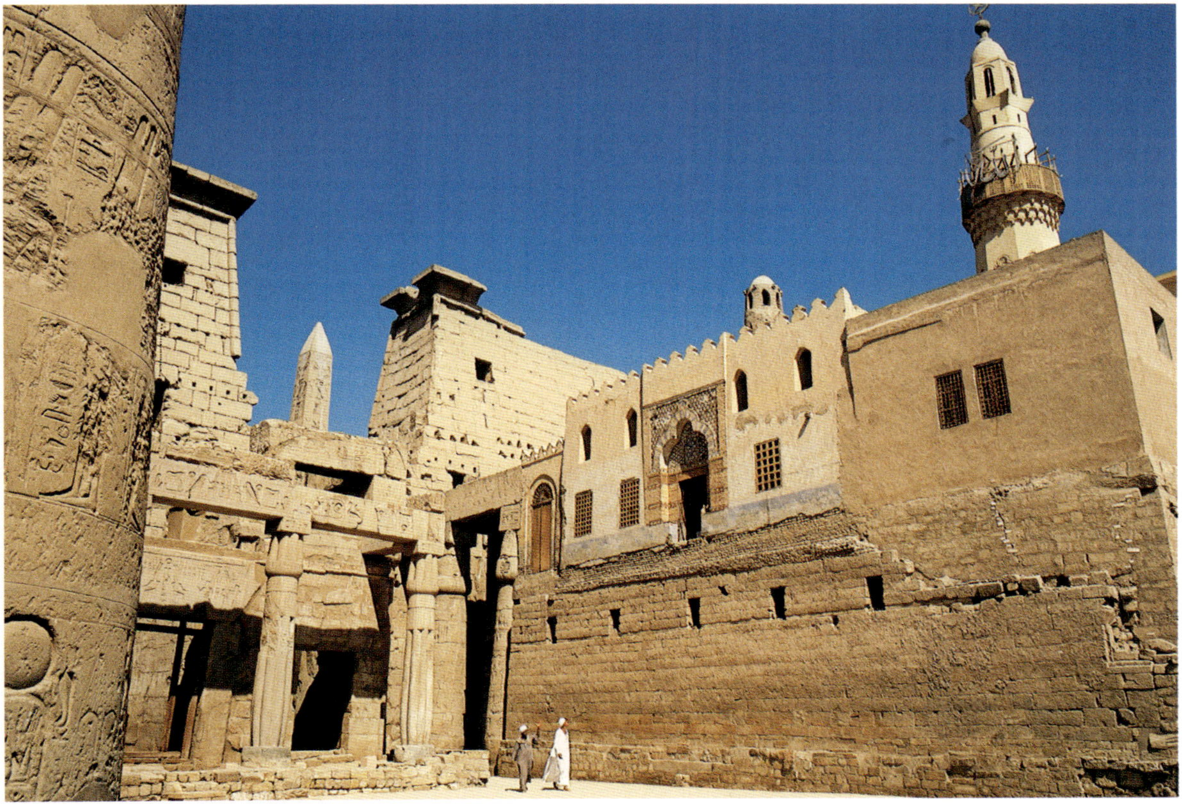

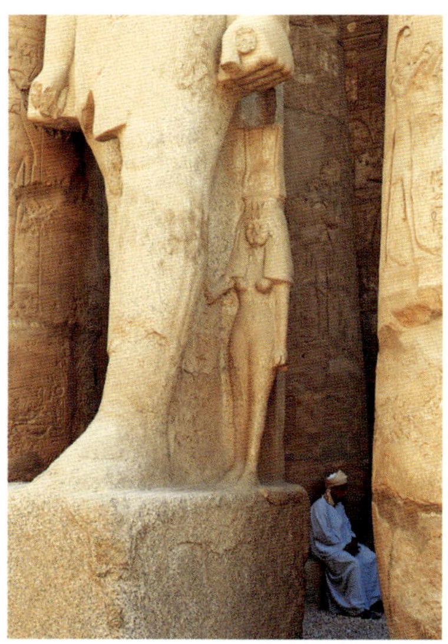

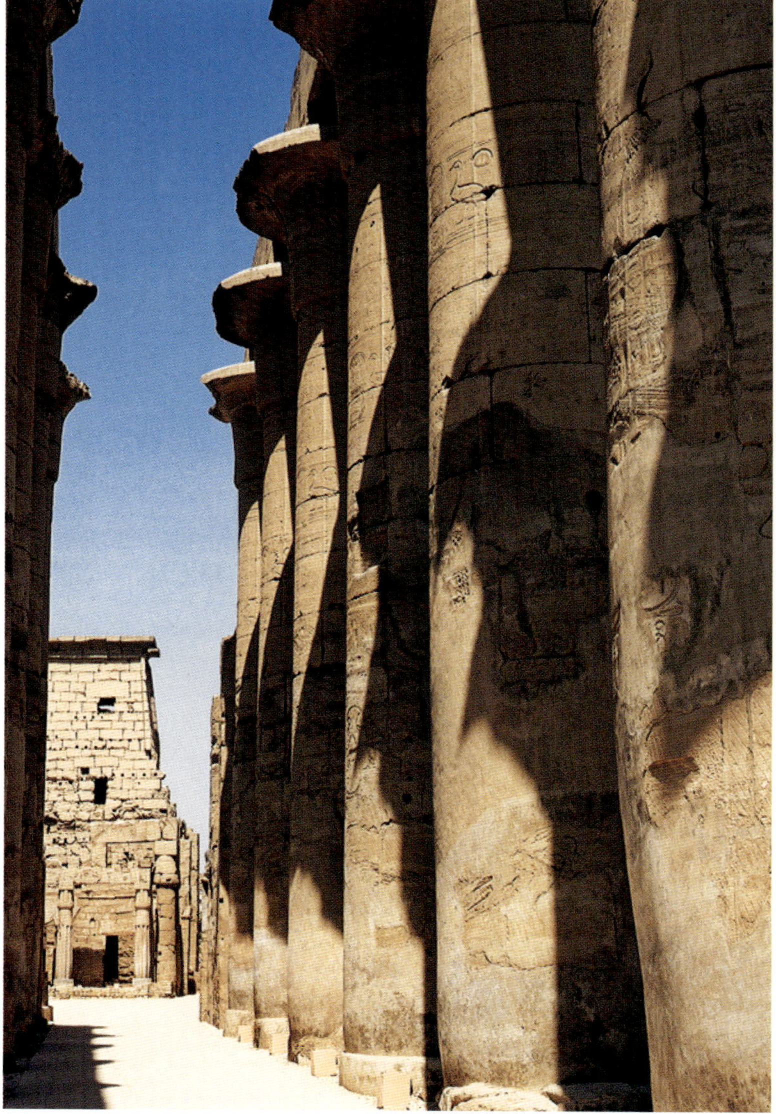

Above: Nefertari stands beside her husband, Rameses.

Near right: The imposing colonnade hall of Amenhotep III. The stylized papyrus columns are nearly 16 meters high.

Top Right: The upper portion of the flanking walls of the colonnade of Amenhotep have collapsed, but the lower courses bear fine and fascinating reliefs from the reign of Tutankhamun depicting in realistic detail the Opet Festival, when Amun, Mut, and Khonsu voyaged from Karnak to the Temple of Luxor at the height of the inundation period. This relief shows the priests carrying one of the sacred boats to the Nile.

Bottom Right: The figure on the left is Tutankhamun, shown before Amun.

Beyond the first court are the colonnade hall, peristyle court, hypostyle hall, and inner temple built by Amenhotep III. It lay at the end of a processional way leading from Karnak, and may have been constructed on the site of an earlier shrine of Hatshepsut. Amenhotep also created a new royal area on the west bank of the Nile that included a temple and a palace (now known as Malqata), an enormous artificial lake (Birket Habu), and his own memorial temple (Kom al-Hetan). This was guarded by colossal statues of his divinized self, those at the entrance being known to future generations as the Colossi of Memnon. The purpose of his works was to create an immense ceremonial stage for religious pageantry on both sides of the Nile that comprised the great Festival of Opet. During this, Amun traveled on his golden barge with

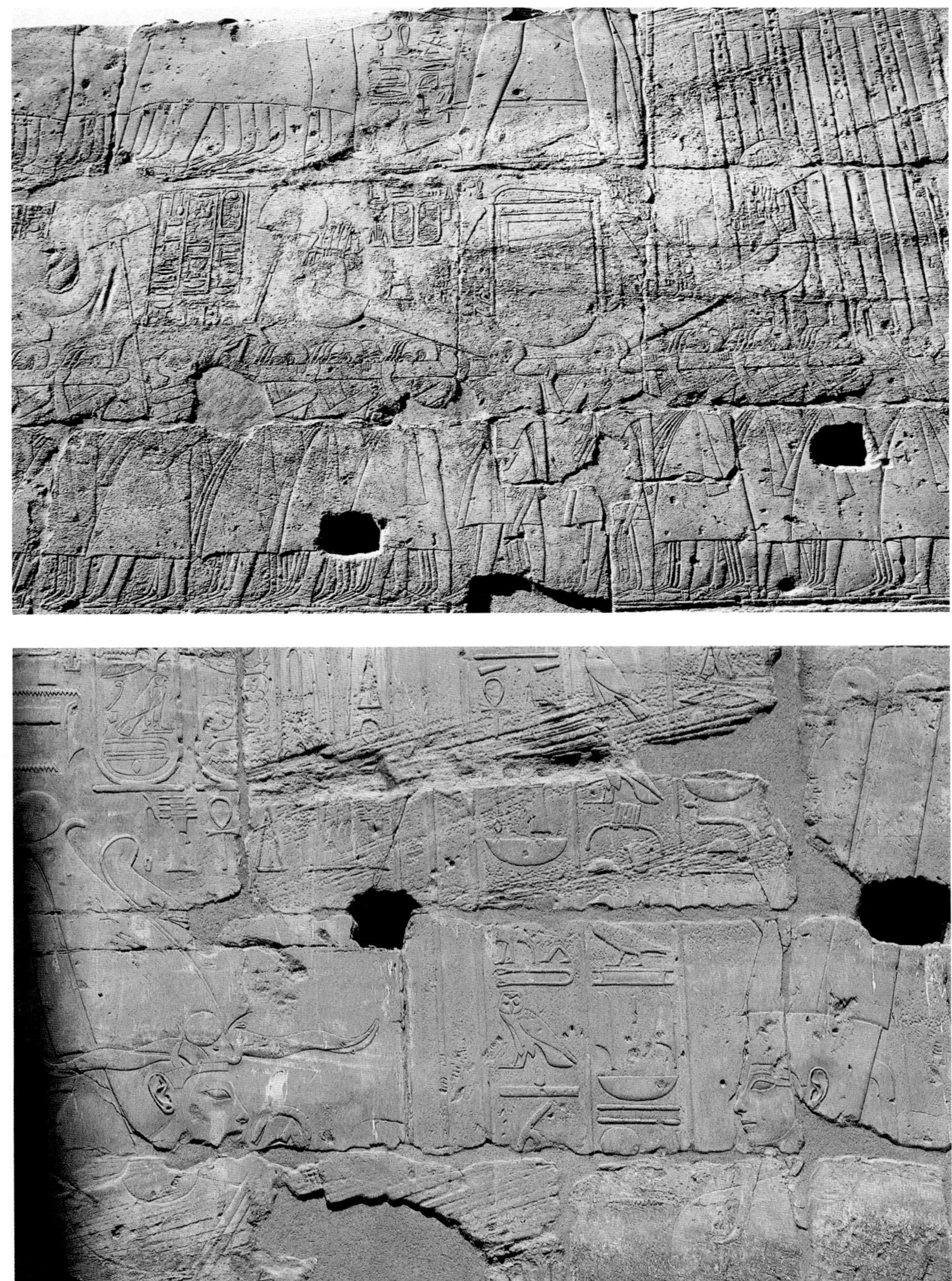

Near rlght: Crowds of common folk followed the procession by land amid scenes of rejoicing, music, and dancing. This relief shows dancers performing.

Below: Beyond the colonnade of Amenhotep III is his open court and then his hypostyle hall of thirty-two columns.

Top far right:. Painted column bases in the hypostyle hall.

Bottom middle: The hypostyle hall gave access to the inner temple where the walls are decorated with scenes of ritual, sacrifice, divine birth, and so on. Here we see an animal is bound for sacrifice.

Bottom right: In the hall chamber beyond the hypostyle hall the original reliefs were whitewashed over and covered with painted figures, which relate to the Roman imperial cult.

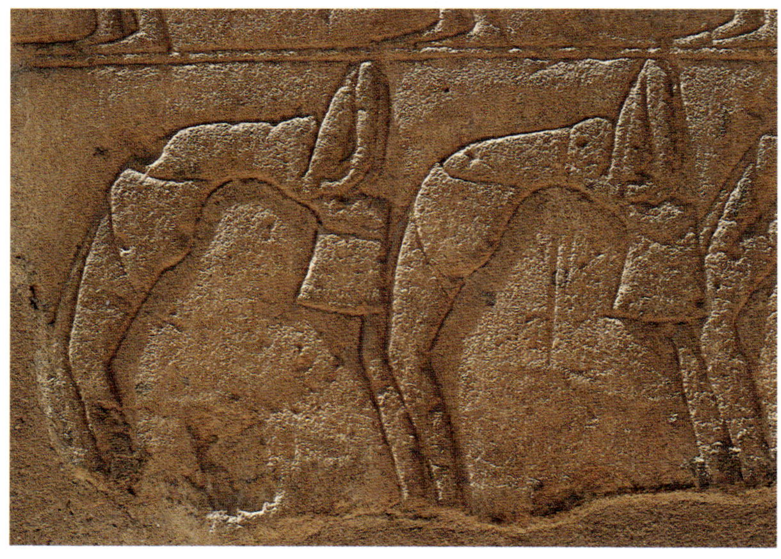

his wife Mut and their son, the moon god Khonsu, in a floating procession of great splendor from Karnak to Luxor, returning to Karnak in refreshed glory some three weeks later.

Once a year also, Amun crossed the Nile in his golden barge to celebrate the Beautiful Festival of the Valley at one of the royal funerary temples, while the families of Thebes held overnight feasts in the tomb chapels, amid the music of harps, lutes, lyres, and double pipes, the living and the dead united in one celebration.

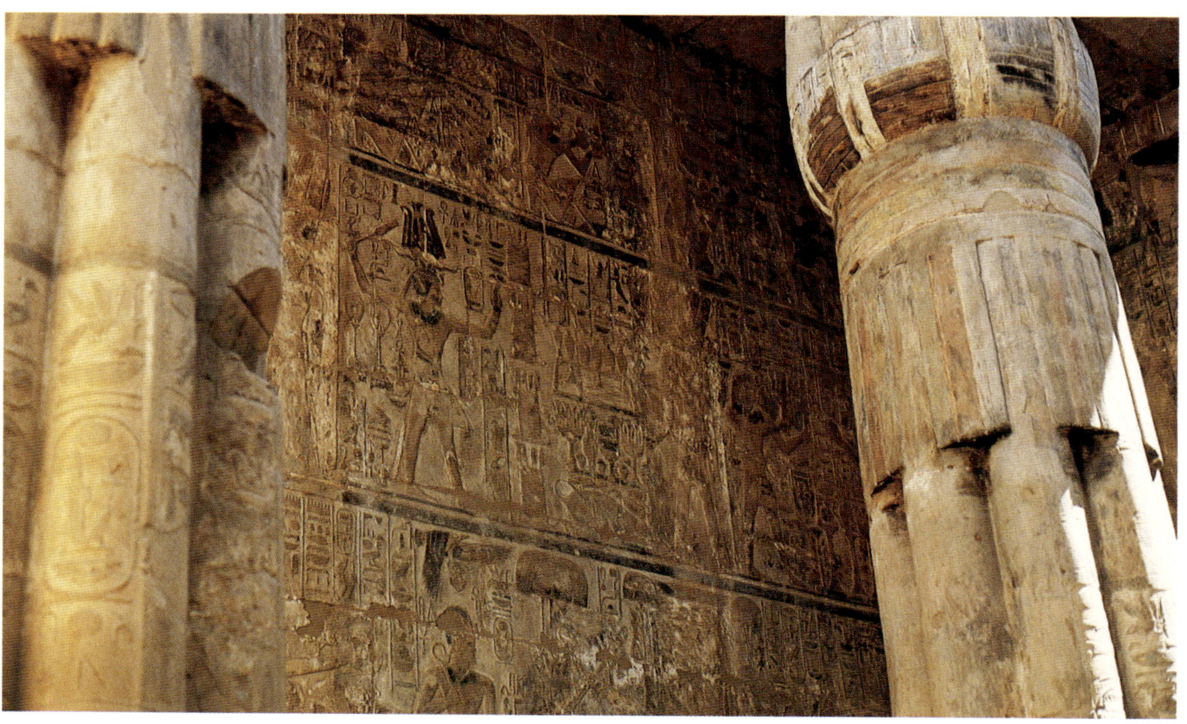

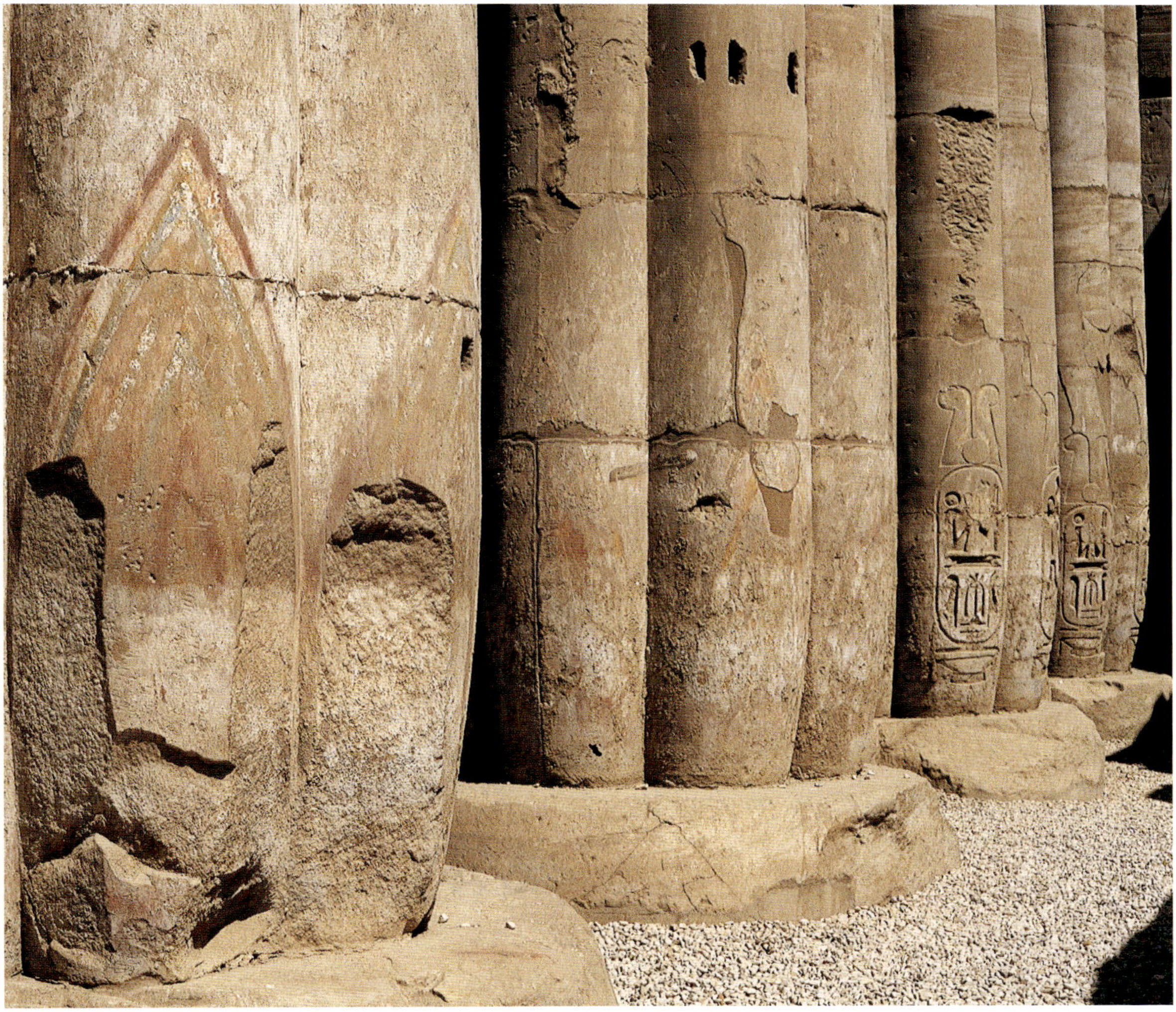

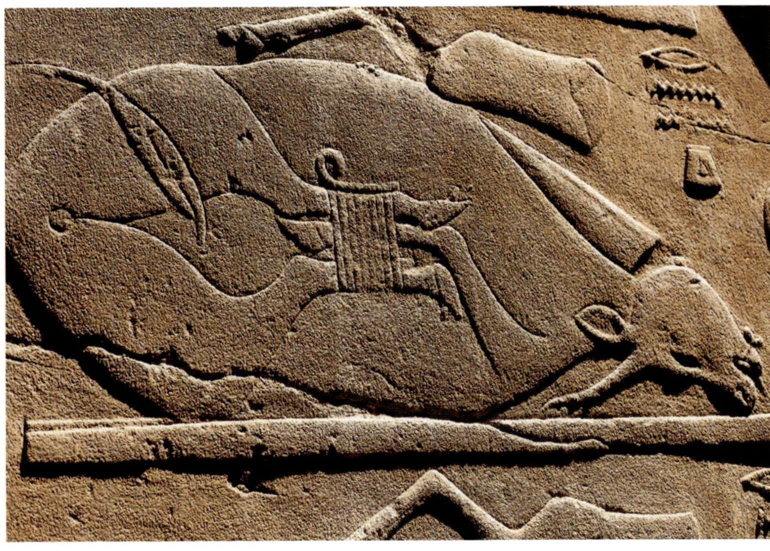

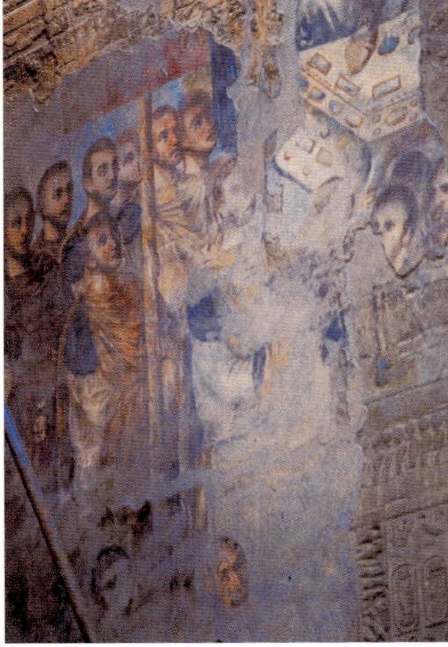

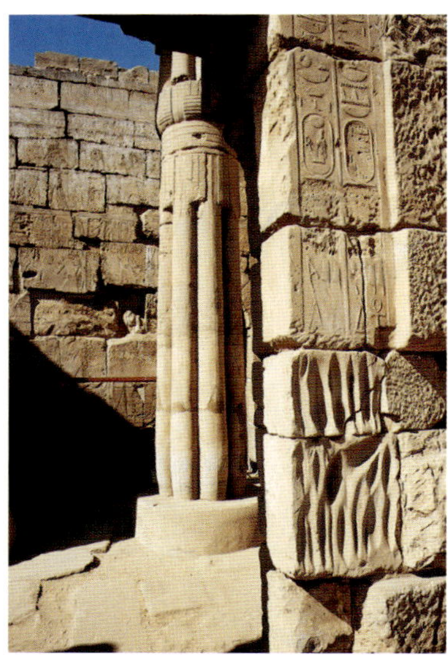

Above: These deep grooves were made by ancient visitors seeking to obtain stone dust from this sacred place for use in magical charms.

RIght: Amun-Min was a composite of Amun and Min, the god of sexual potency, who was accordingly represented with an erect penis. He is shown here receiving offerings from Amenhotep III. The figure of Amun and the second cartouche of the king were erased under the "heretic king" Akhenaten, and recarved under a later king.

Far right: Looking back along the length of the temple from within the shrine of the sacred boat of Amun, which was entirely replaced by Alexander the Great.

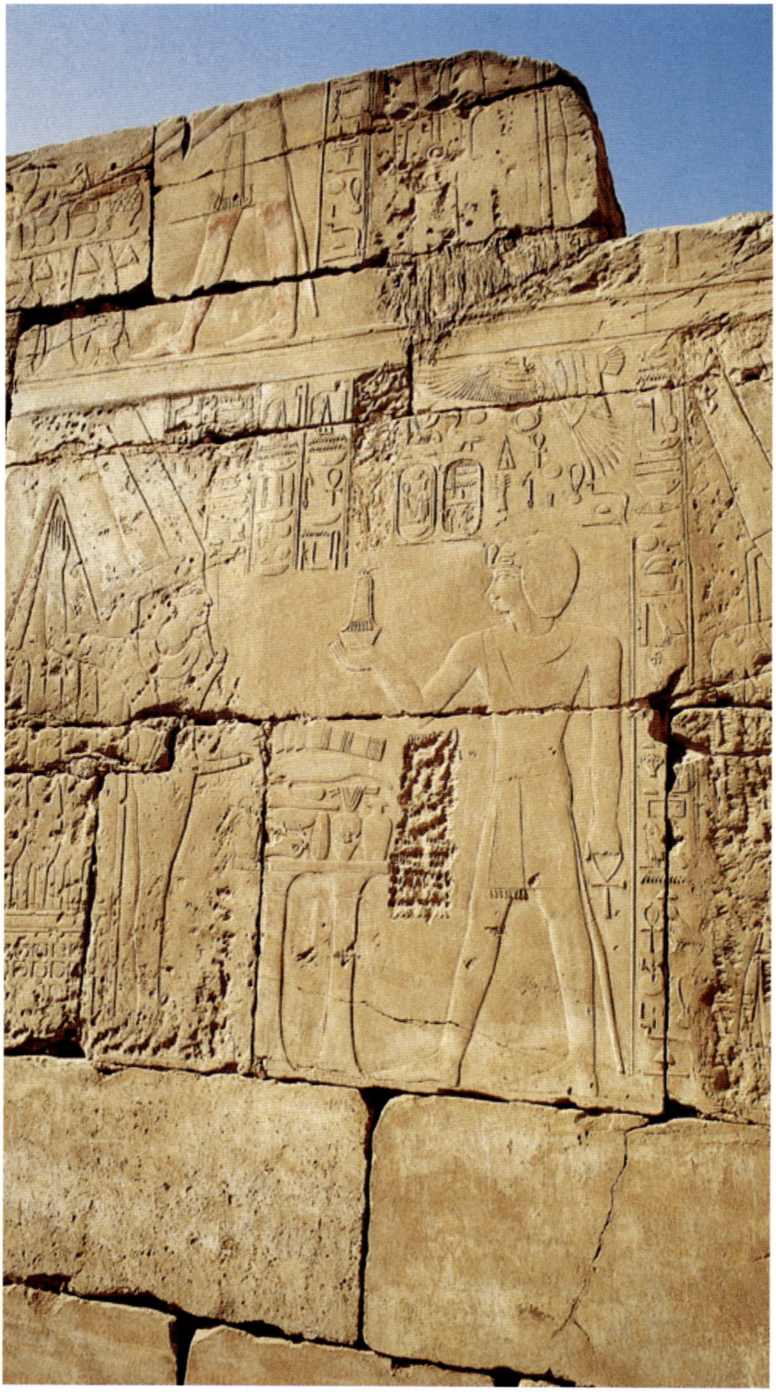

In a curious continuity with the ancient past, the mosque of Abu al-Haggag, which sits atop the Temple of Luxor, celebrates the saint's moulid, his feast day, which is the biggest in Upper Egypt, with a great procession in which the faithful carry aloft a boat, just as priests carried Amun's sacred boat during the Opet Festival over 3,000 years ago.

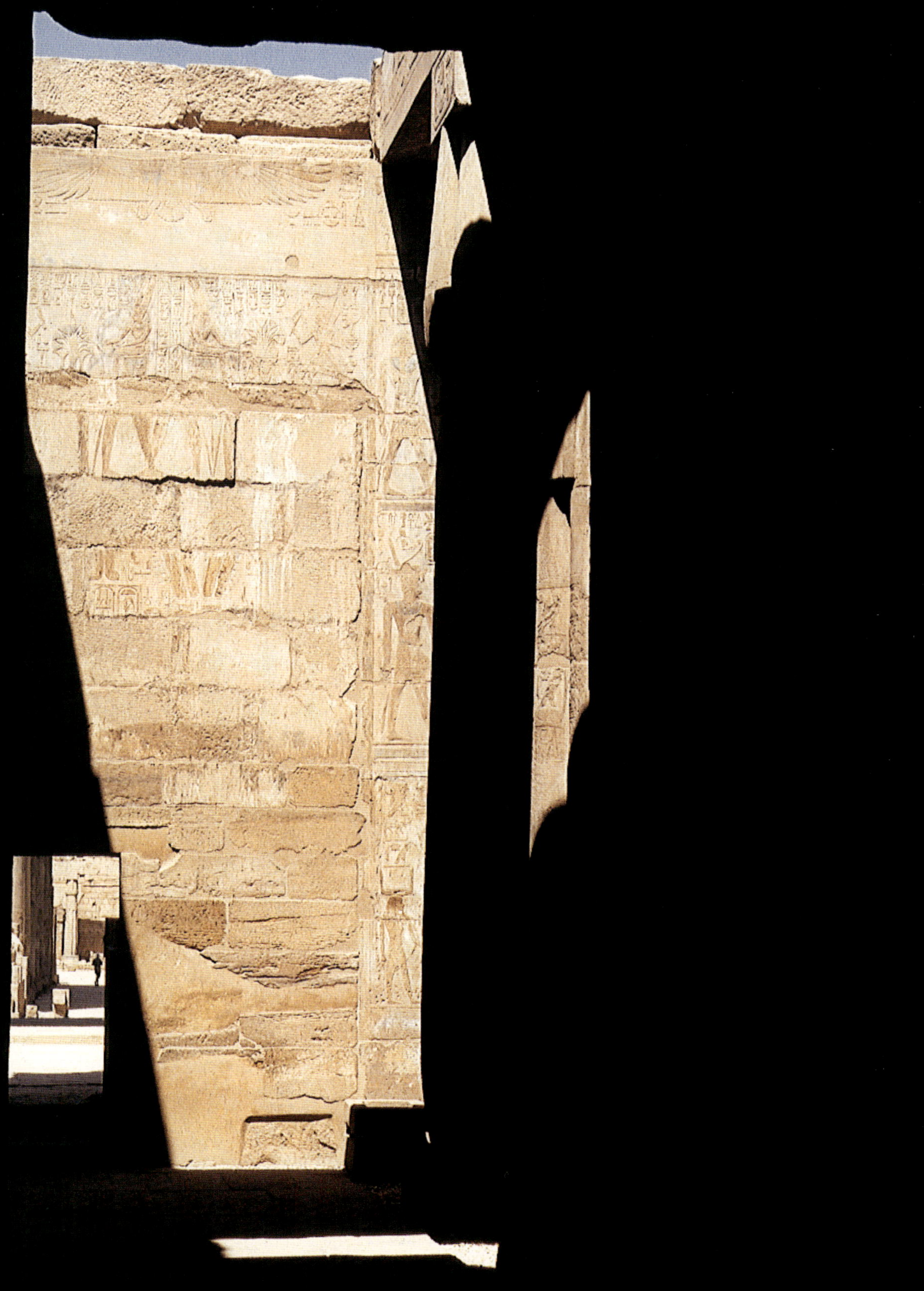

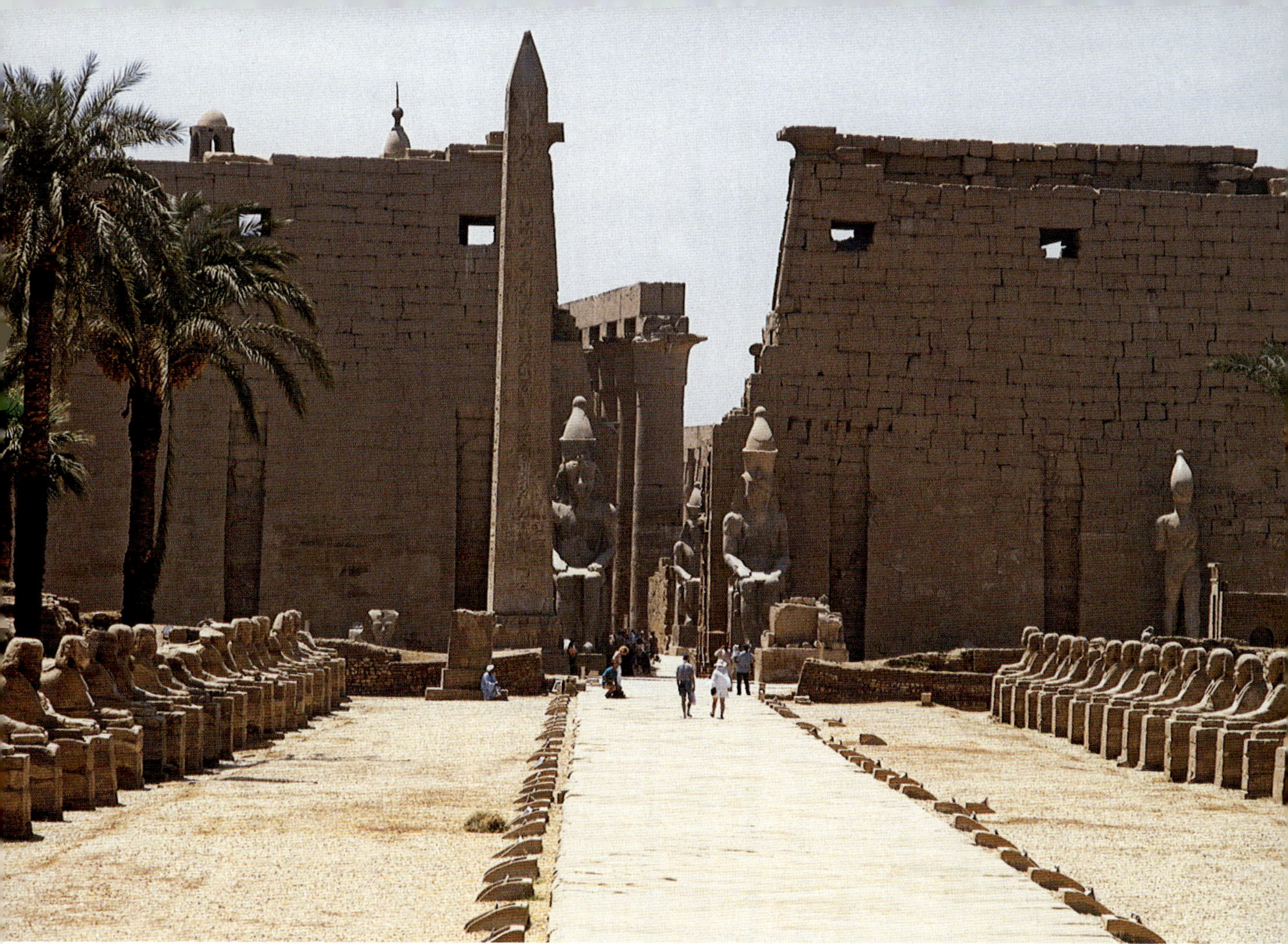

Above: The avenue of sphinxes leads from the Temple of Luxor toward Karnak.

The avenue of sphinxes

A processional avenue had existed between the Temple of Luxor to the great temple at Karnak since before the time of Hatshepsut. During the Opet Festival, when Amun, Mut, and Khonsu sailed from one temple to the other along the Nile, their ships were followed by celebrants along this sacred way. The section of the avenue between the temples of Amun and Mut was adorned with ram-headed sphinxes under Tutankhamun, but a thousand years later, Nakhtnebef lined the rest of the avenue with sphinxes bearing his own face, running from the gateway of Ptolemy III Euergetes in front of the temple of Khonsu. The whole route was opened up during the 2010s, carving what some have seen as a great scar through the modern city of Luxor.

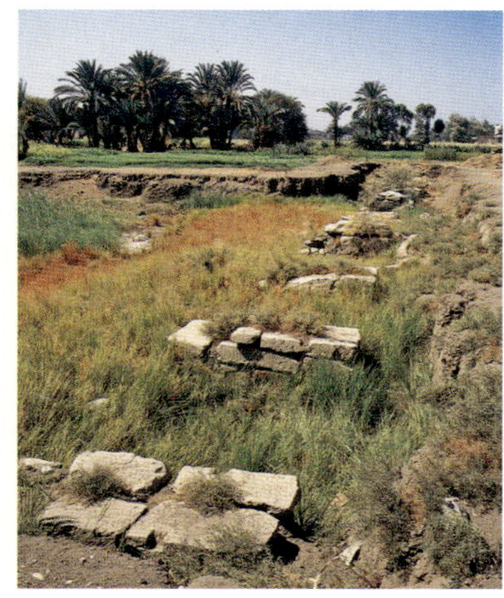

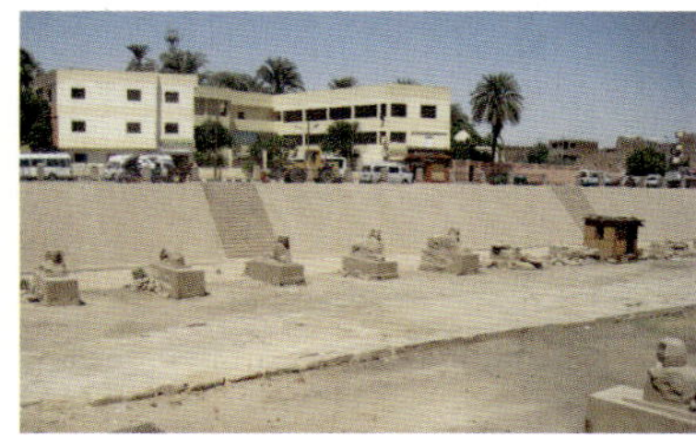

Above: The bases of sphinxes formerly ran across a field, but now the whole avenue has been cleared, and it is possible to walk unimpeded between the temples of Luxor and Karnak.

Top right: The avenue formerly disappeared beneath a mosque (now demolished) but surfaced on the other side.

Center and bottom right: The final approach toward Ptolemy III Euergetes's southern gateway at Karnak was not flanked with sphinxes, but much earlier recumbent rams, dating to the time of Amenhotep III.

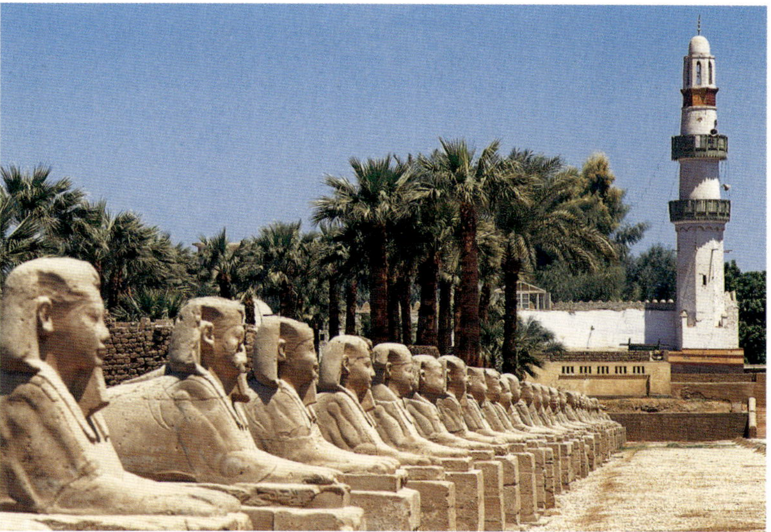

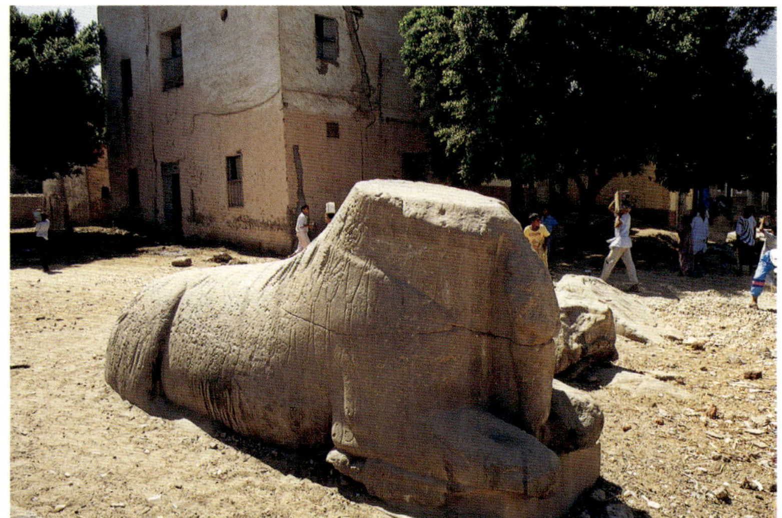

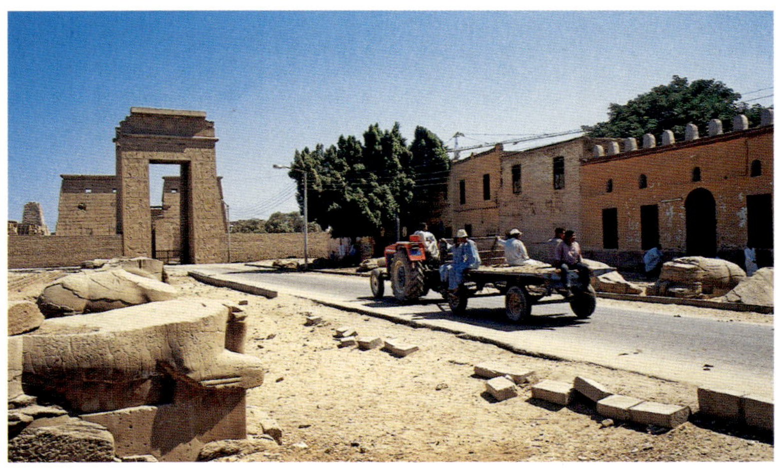

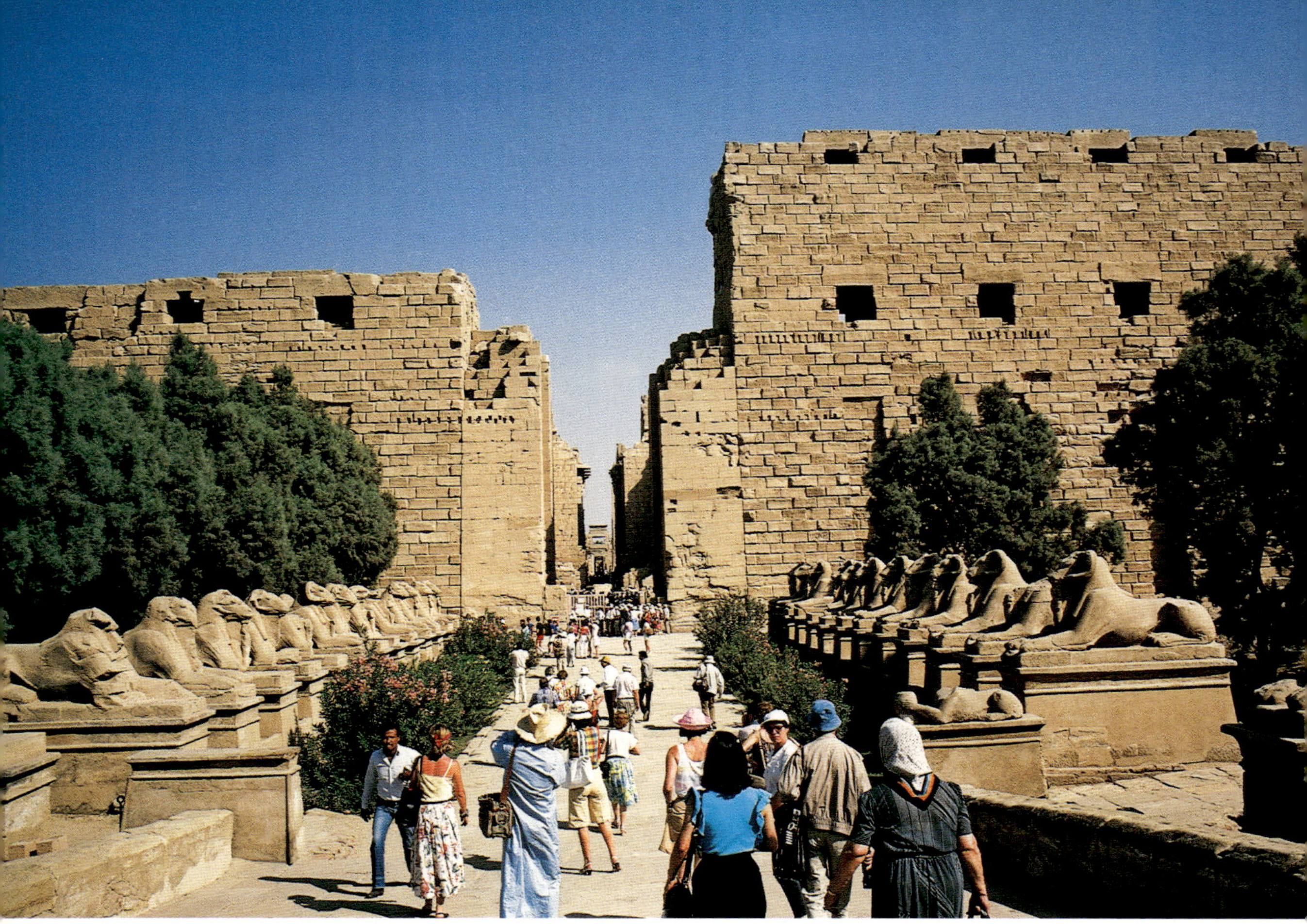

Above: Karnak takes its name from the nearby village of that name, but the ancient Egyptians called the site *Iput-isut,* "the most select of places," as befitted the home of Amun, the supreme god of the New Kingdom. As visitors approach the Temple of Amun they are dwarfed by the immense first pylon, which opens onto vast receding vistas toward the innermost sanctuary. The pylon is the largest in Egypt and nearly twice the size of the entrance pylon at the Temple of Luxor, but it was never completed; the south tower is higher than the north and neither bears any decoration. The date of the pylon is uncertain, but it was probably the responsibility of the fourth century BC king Nakhtnebef (Nectanebo I) of the Thirtieth Dynasty, who built the oldest part of the Temple of Isis at Philae.

Karnak

The Karnak site covers an enormous area and embraces several temples and shrines, most famously the great Temple of Amun, founded early in the Eleventh Dynasty and repeatedly enlarged over the following 1,300 years. At the height of the New Kingdom, when Egypt ruled over a vast empire and Thebes ruled over Egypt, and when Amun was supreme over all, the god's temple here possessed scores of ships, hundreds of thousands of cattle and slaves, owned perhaps as much as a third of Egypt's land, and received an annual income of gold, silver, copper, and semi-precious stones from sixty-five cities and towns of Africa and Asia.

When you enter the Temple of Amun, you pass through its newest and largest feature, the massive first pylon, built or rebuilt possibly as late as the fourth century BC. Beyond this lies the first court, laid out in the tenth century BC by the Twenty-second Dynasty pharaoh Shoshenq I (943–922 BC), and shrines from the time of Sethy II of the Nineteenth Dynasty and Rameses III of the Twentieth. From here you pass through the second pylon, not as big as the first, and built by Horemheb (1308–1278 BC) at the end of the Eighteenth Dynasty, and advance through

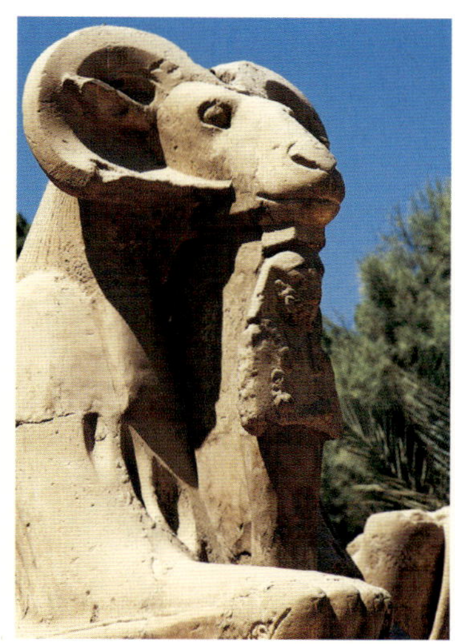

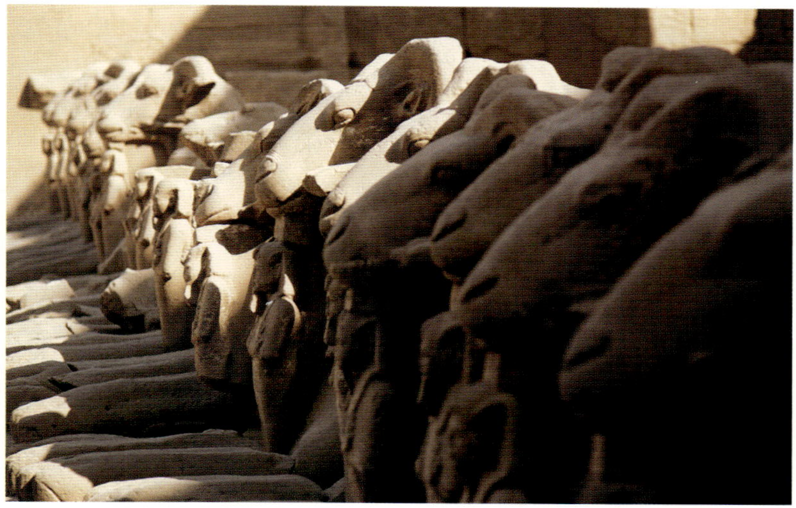

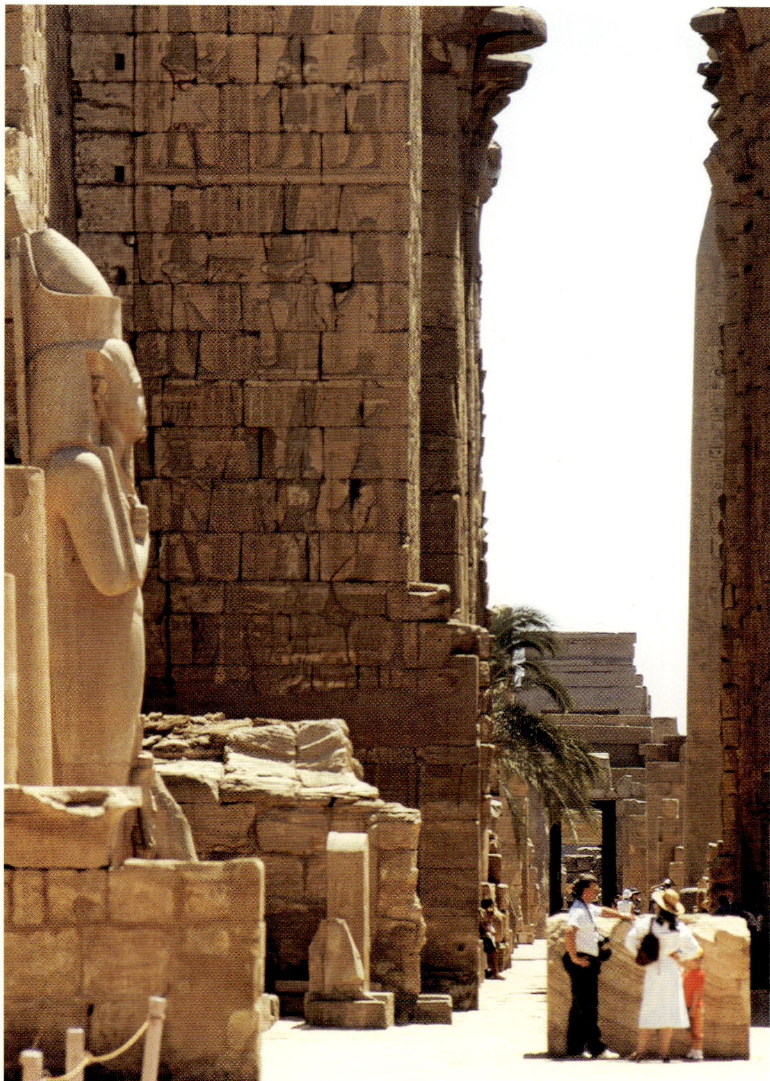

Above left and right: The temple is approached along a short processional way lined with ram-headed sphinxes with sheathed figures of Rameses II between their forelegs. Most of them were later usurped by Panedjem I of the Twenty-first Dynasty.

Left: Looking across the first court toward the hypostyle hall. A colossal statue of the Twenty-first Dynasty High Priest of Amun, Panedjem I (mid-11th century BC), is on the left. He was a man of exceptional power, and was depicted as a king even while still High Priest. Still later he gained the royal names and titles as well.

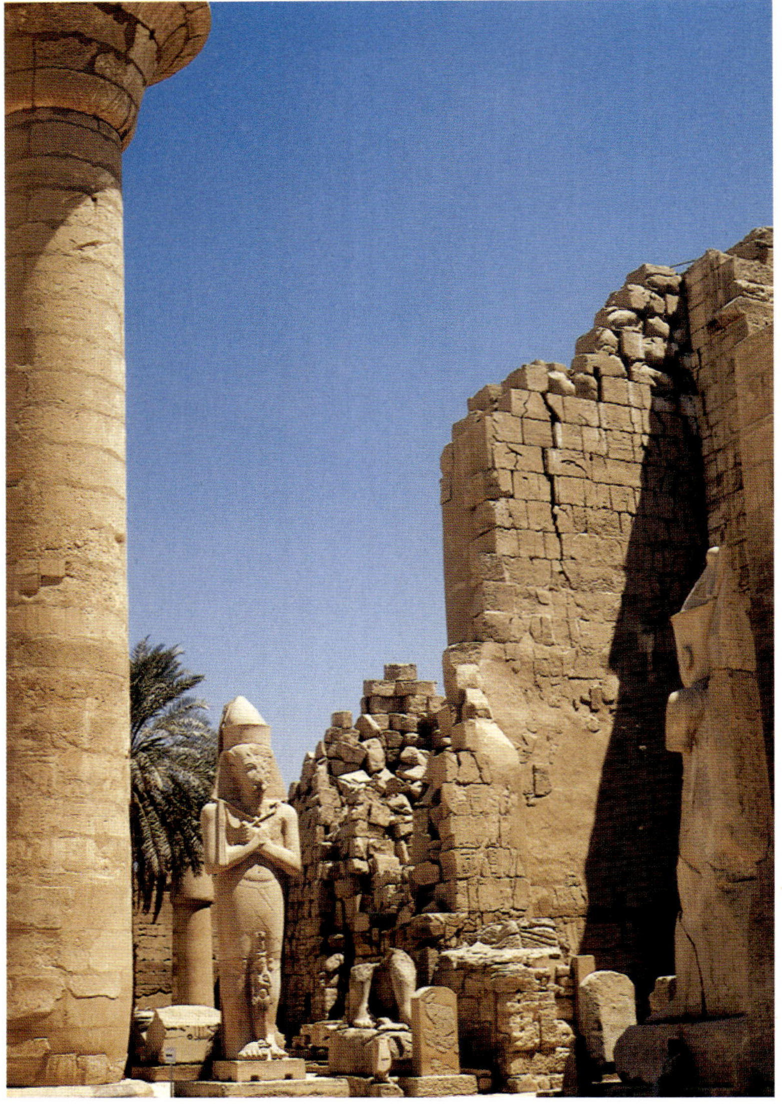

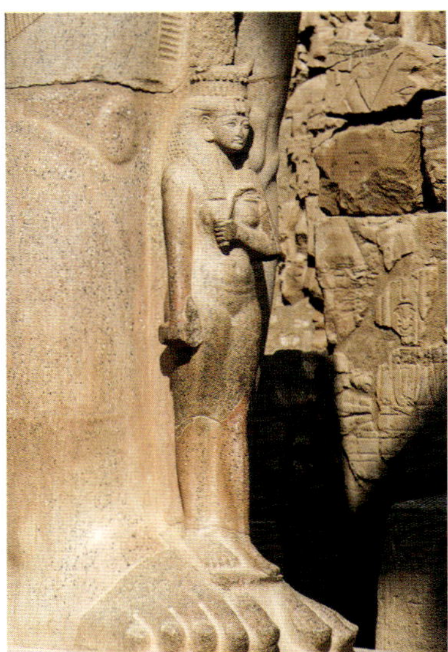

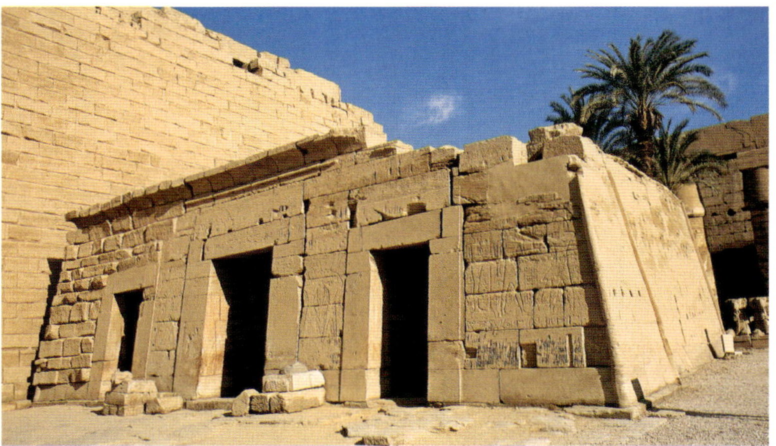

Left: The colossal statue of Panedjem I; his wife, Henttawy, stands upon his feet.

Above: Henttawy, Panedjem I's wife.

Bottom left: The chapel of Sethy II within the first court consists of three chapels which served as way stations for the sacred boats of Amun (center), Mut (left), and Khonsu (right) as they were carried in stages from the innermost sanctuary to the Nile before sailing to the Temple of Luxor during the Opet Festival, or crossing the Nile for the Beautiful Feast of the Valley.

Near right: Looking east along the central aisle of the hypostyle hall, lined with papyrus columns bearing open-bud capitals.

Top right: The hypostyle hall of immense papyrus columns was originally roofed over and sunlight filtered in through lattice clerestory windows of stone, which created the intended impression of a primeval swamp, the waters of Chaos, from which Amun created himself.

Bottom right: The hypostyle hall is a forest of stone filled with 134 papyrus columns, the twelve taller columns along the central aisle with open capitals, the remaining 122 with closed capitals.

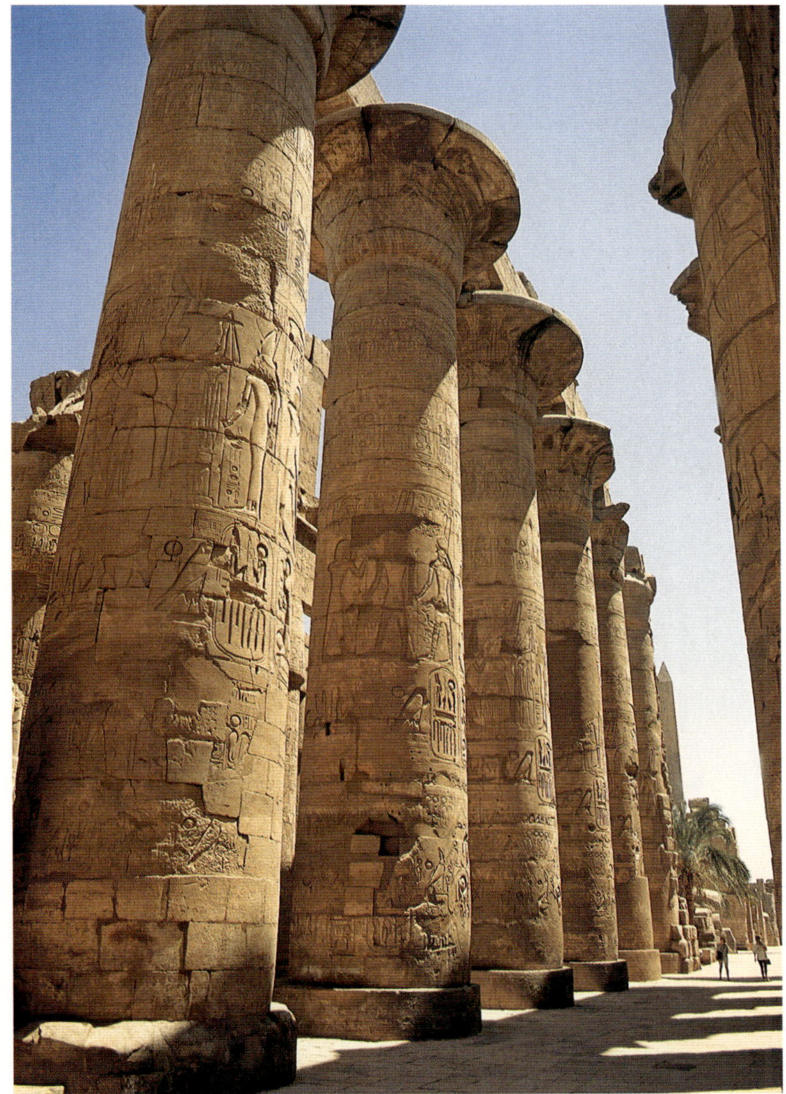

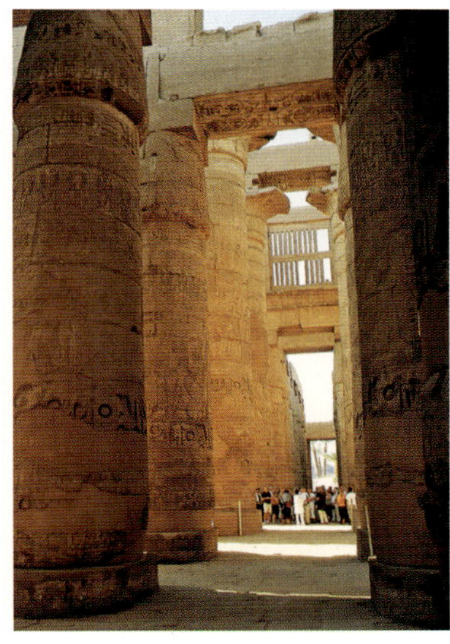

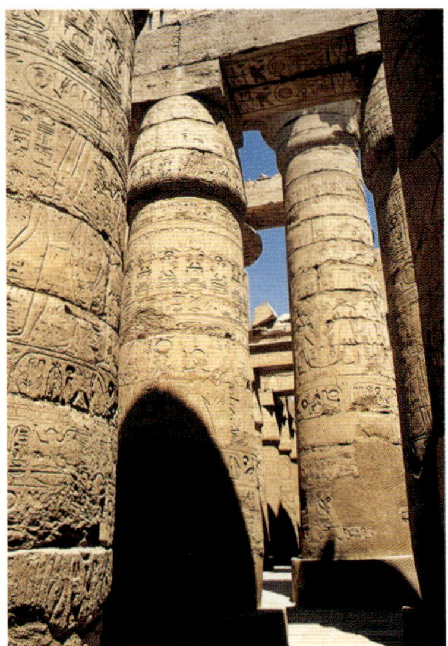

the magnificent hypostyle hall, built by the Nineteenth Dynasty pharaoh Sethy I around 1275 BC, but with its decoration completed by his son, Rameses II. The temple becomes more ruinous beyond this point, but there are the great obelisks of Hatshepsut and Thutmose I to see, and the Festival Hall of Thutmose II, all dating from the Eighteenth Dynasty, as well as the sacred lake, home to the geese of Amun and where the priests performed their ablutions.

A temple of this great size and age has many stories to tell. One is that of the great heresy of Akhenaten, the son of Amenhotep III. Whereas Amenhotep and all Egypt worshiped a pantheon of gods of whom Amun was supreme, his son honored only the sun disc, the Aten, ignoring most gods and violently attacking Amun. Akhenaten built a new capital down the Nile at Amarna, but in his early days he built a number

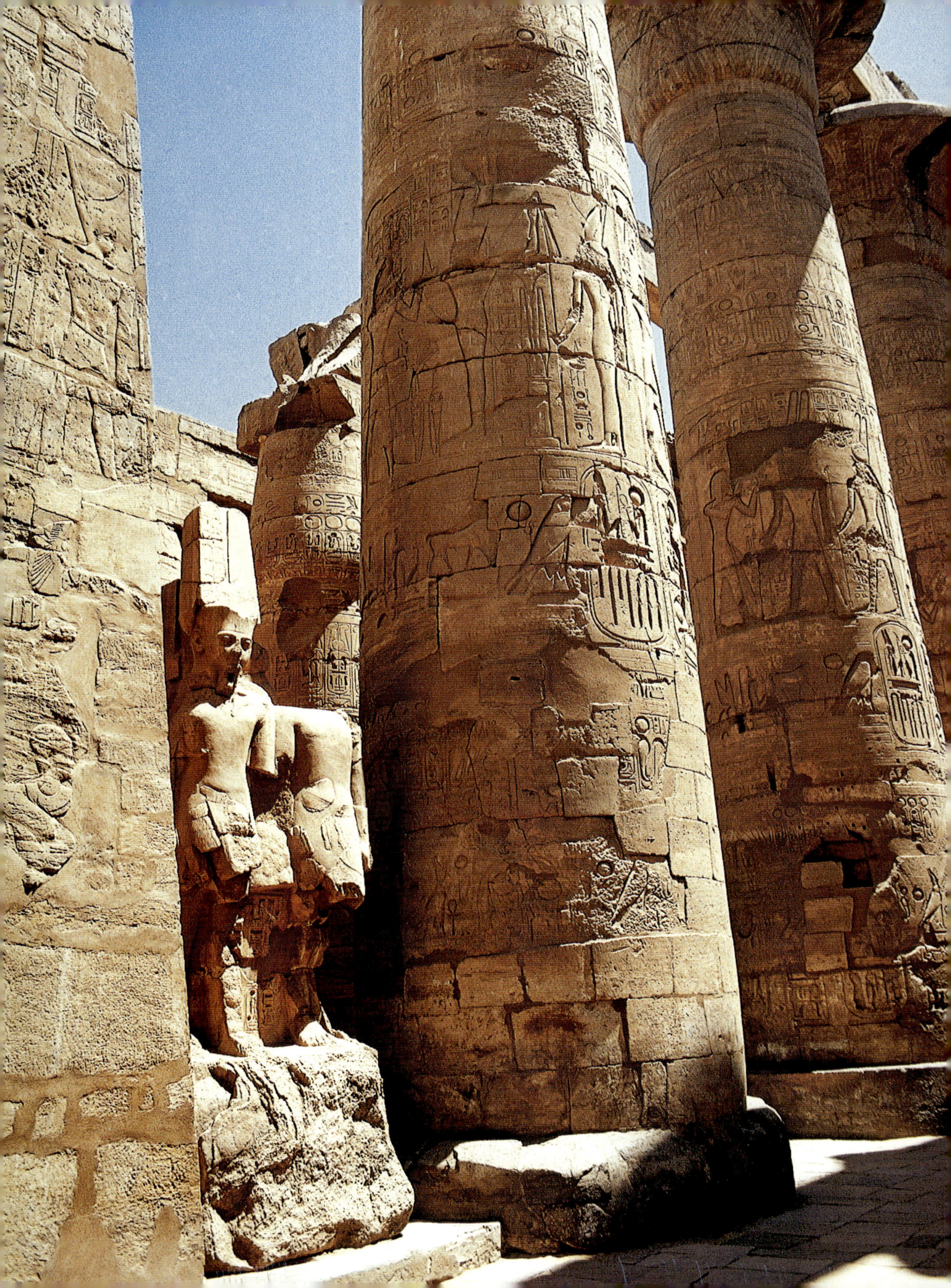

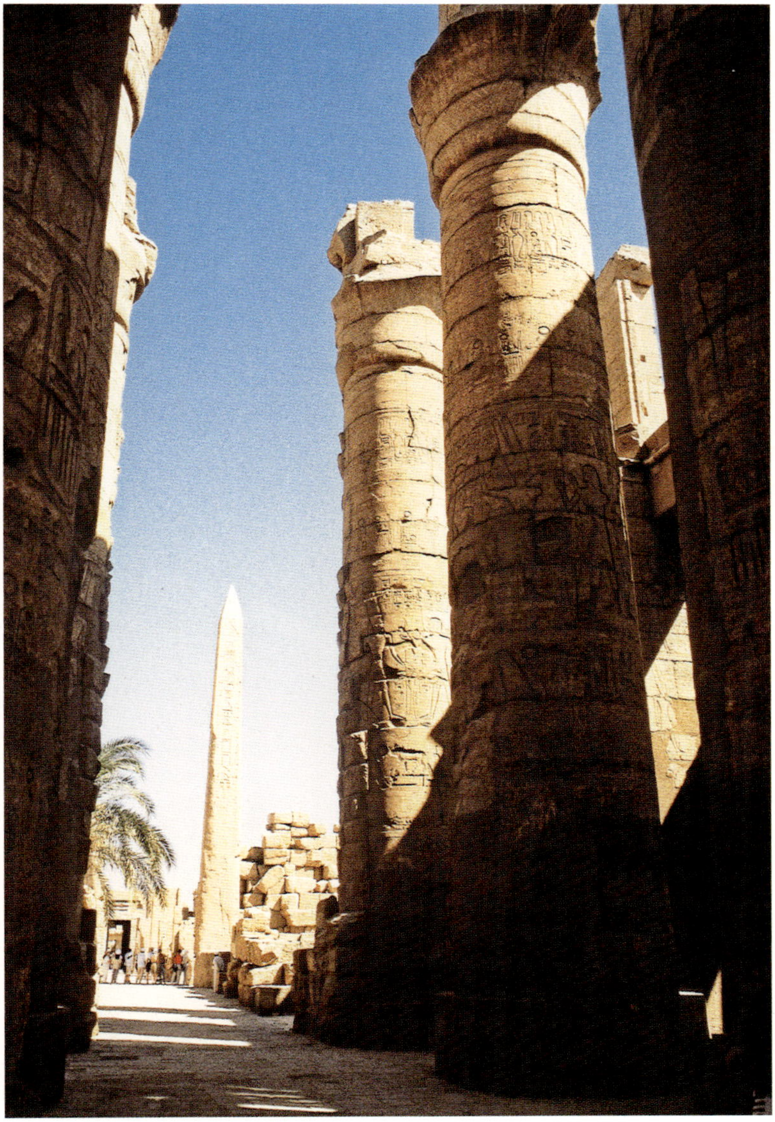

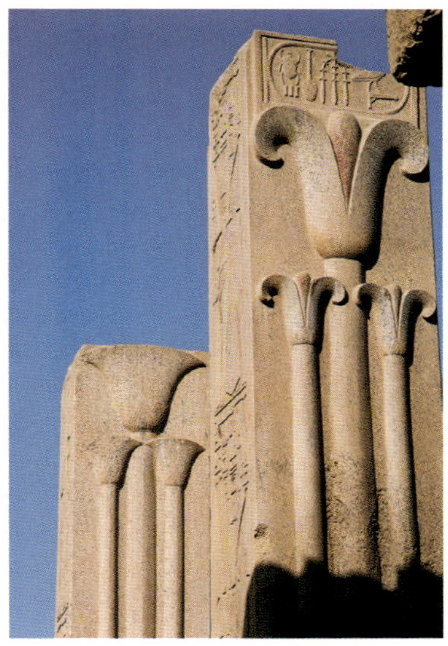

Far left: A statue of Amun in the hypostyle hall; many of the spaces between the columns were once filled with statues of gods and kings.

Top left: Beyond this obelisk raised by Thutmose I stood the inner temple, much of it ruinous today.

Above: Two rose granite pillars, erected by Thutmose III, grace this court of the inner temple. Carved in beautifully stylized high relief are three lilies on the south pillar and three papyri on the north pillar, the heraldic plants of Upper and Lower Egypt.

Bottom left: The upper part of Hatshepsut's other obelisk by the sacred lake; she is depicted being crowned by Amun, identifiable by his double-feathered headdress.

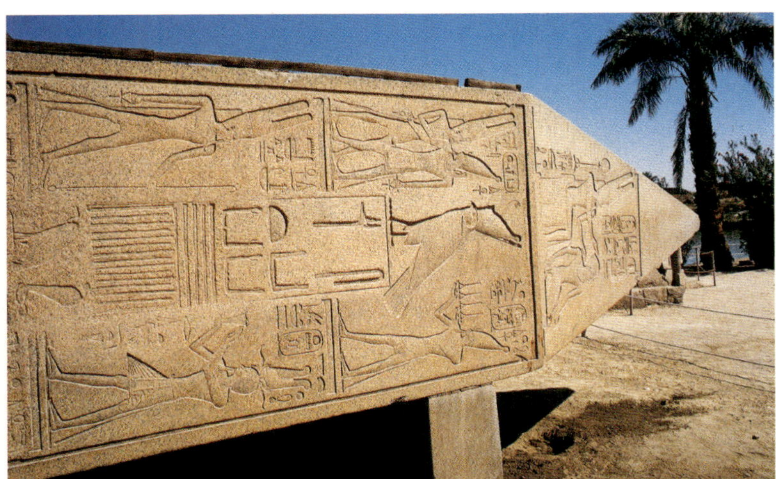

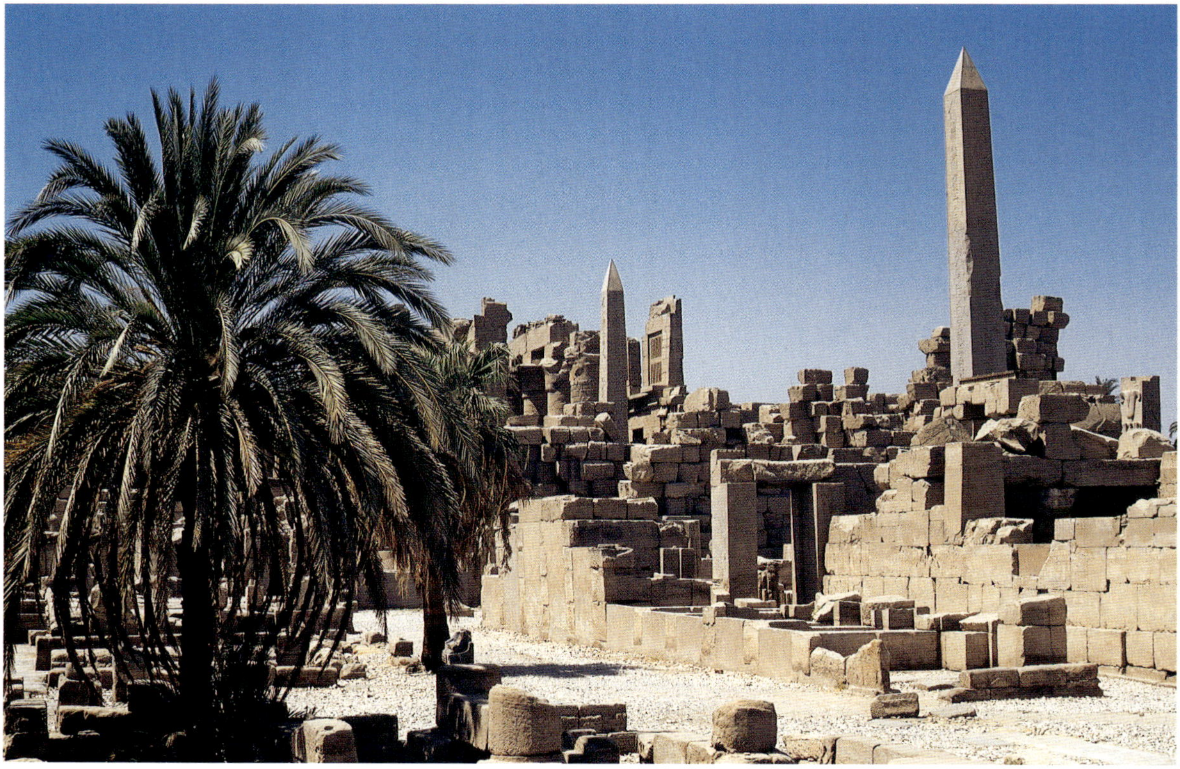

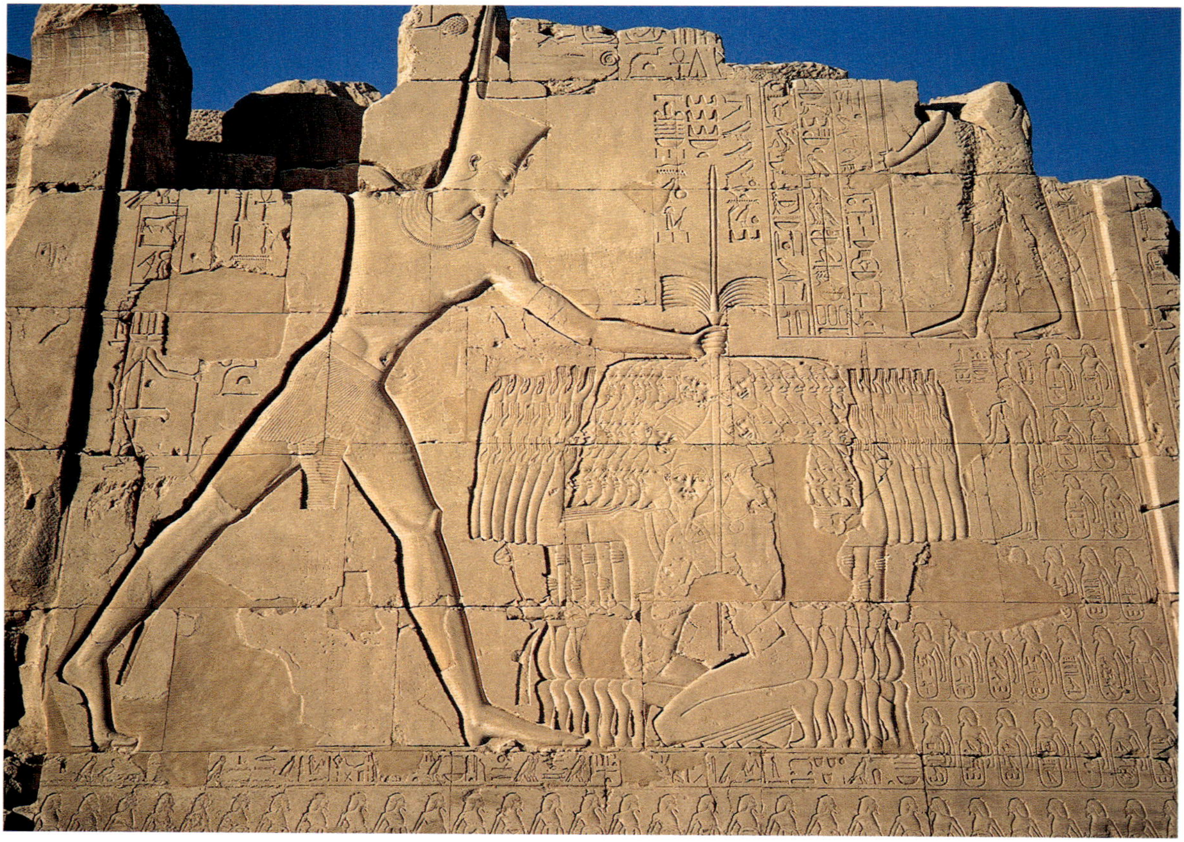

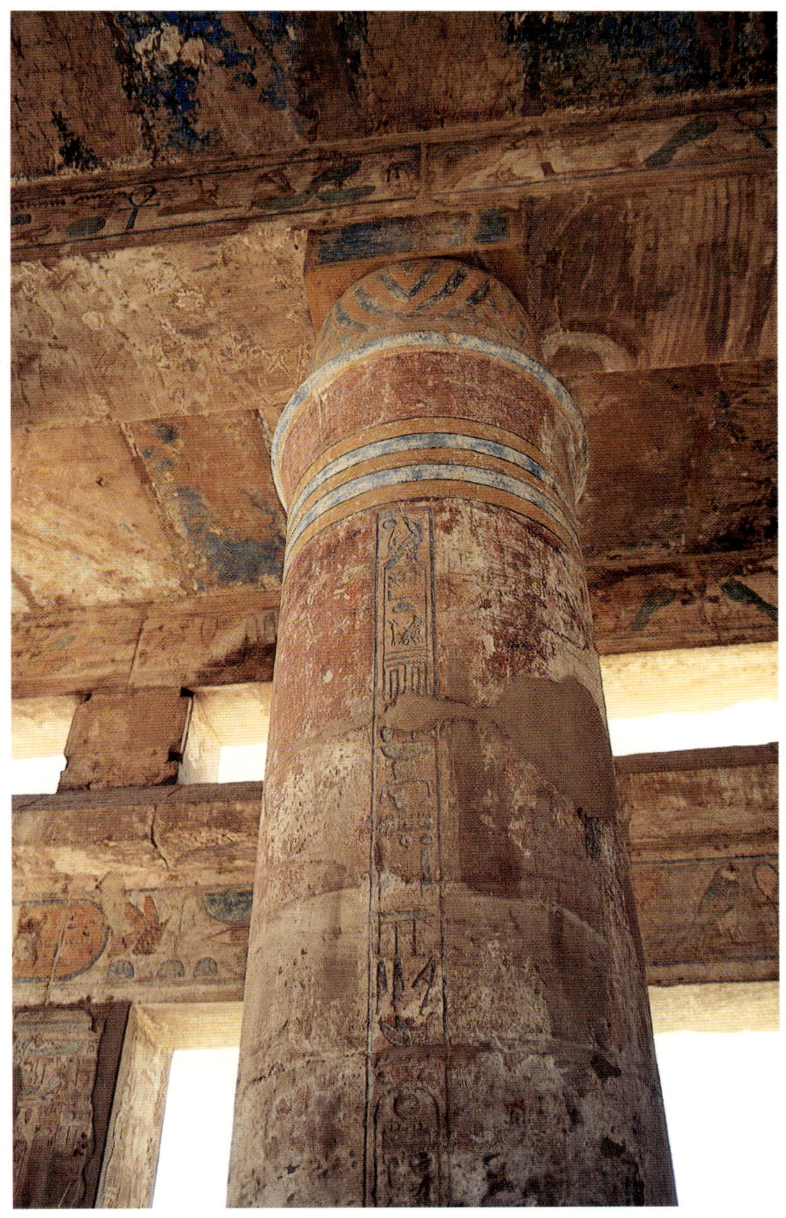

Top left: The obelisk of Thutmose I is on the left; on the right is the obelisk of Hatshepsut, the tallest completed obelisk still in situ.

Bottom left: Thutmose III shown in relief on the Seventh Pylon seizing Asiatic prisoners by the hair and bashing out their brains. Following Hatshepsut's death, Thutmose spent much of his time on campaign in Syria-Palestine, beginning with the defeat of a coalition of Syrian princes at Megiddo, also known as Armaggedon, whose name later became a byword for cataclysmic events. Over the course of seventeen annual campaigns he consolidated Egyptian dominance over Syria, and brought great wealth into Egypt from tribute, as well as control of the overland and maritime trading routes of the Levant. Thutmose especially lavished the proceeds from his conquests on the Temple of Amun at Karnak.

Near left: Thutmose III celebrated his jubilees, those reinvigorations of temporal power and divine spirit, in his Festival Hall complex, which stands to the east of the inner temple at Karnak. Many of its columns, in an unusual form recalling the poles of a tent, and their capitals still retain their painted colors.

of sanctuaries to his god at Karnak. Akhenaten's revolution did not long survive his death, however, and the reign of his son Tutankhamun marked the beginning of the counterrevolution. Akhenaten's buildings were soon dismantled and their blocks were reused in the foundations of later structures, including pylons built by Horemheb, and the hypostyle hall. The king's statues were broken and buried. Many of these have been recovered and can be seen in a number of museums, including the Luxor Museum. Akhenaten and his immediate successors were written out of history, and official lists of kings jumped straight from Amenhotep III to Horemheb.

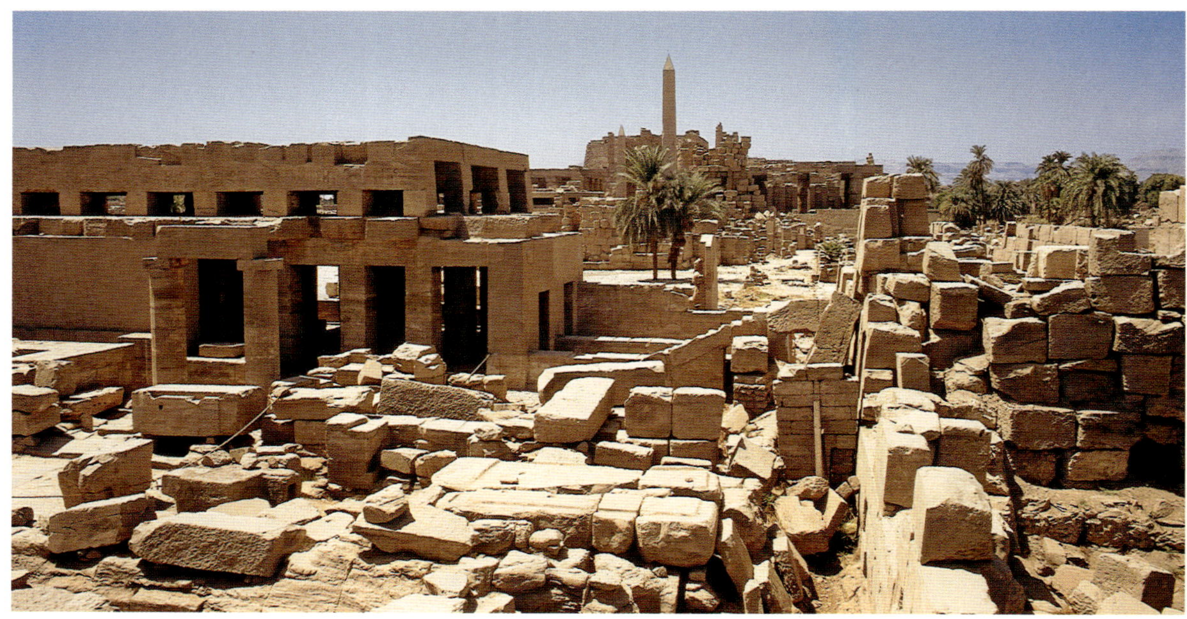

Above: The Temple of Amun seen from the east, with the Festival Hall on the left; a great deal of the Karnak site remains an unreconstructed jumble.

Right center: At the heart of the inner temple stands the sanctuary of Amun's sacred boat, built during the time of Philip Arrhidaeus, half-brother of Alexander the Great, replacing an earlier one of Thutmose III. This exterior relief shows the boat of Amun carried by priests led by the pharaoh.

Bottom right: The east gateway to the Karnak complex set in a mud brick enclosure wall and built by Nakhtnebef. In this area outside the main temple lay one of the temples of Akhenaten.

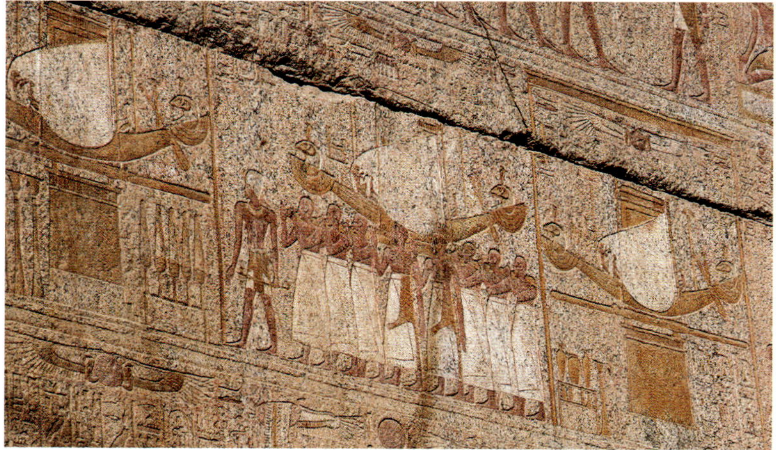

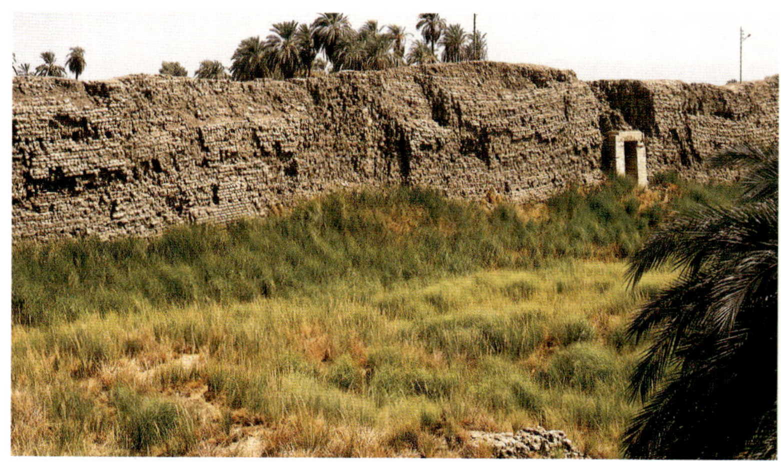

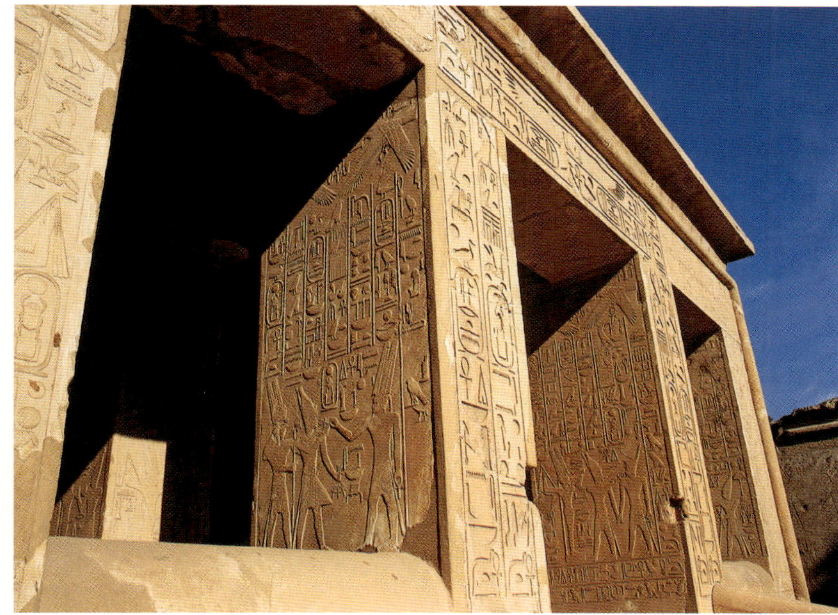

Left: The beautifully decorated White Chapel, a shrine built by the Twelfth Dynasty king Senwosret I as a resting place for the sacred boat of Amun, has been rebuilt in the Open Air Museum on the north side of the Temple of Amun.

Below left: Sekhmet, the lion goddess, in the Temple of Ptah against the northern enclosure wall.

Below: The sacred lake where the priests performed their ablutions and where sacred boats might be sailed.

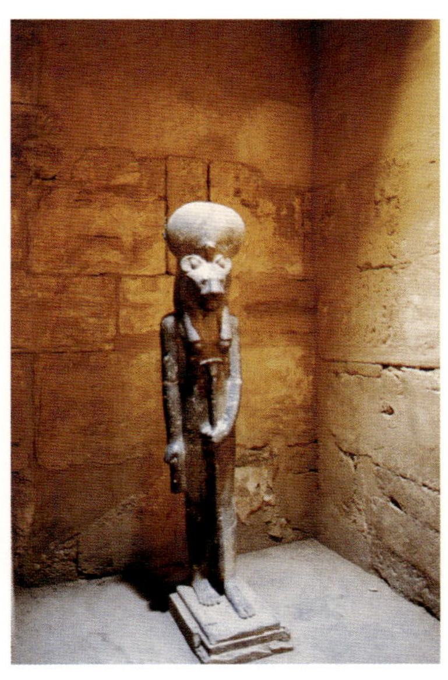

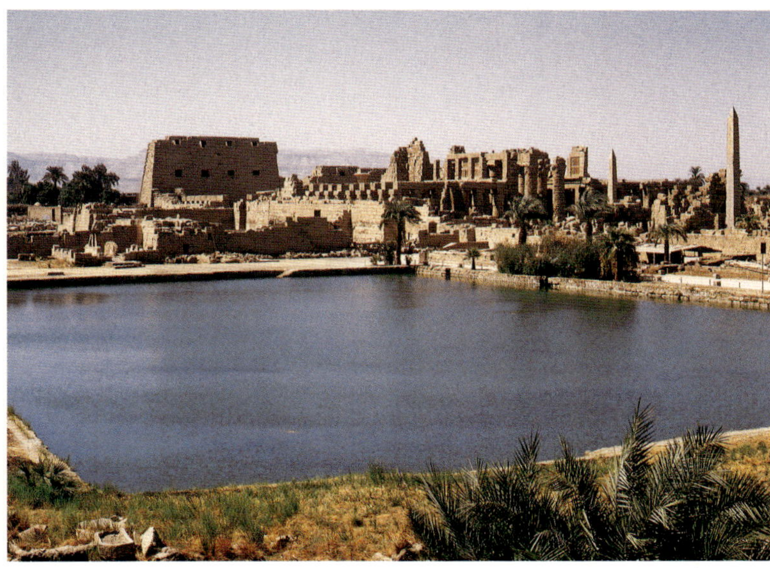

Although work was still being carried out at Karnak in Ptolemaic times, the New Kingdom rulers were responsible for the vast majority of structures visible at Karnak today. The main later additions were the first court in the tenth century BC, the first pylon in the fourth century, and a series of propylon gateways added in the enclosure walls by Ptolemy III. The original Middle Kingdom temple seems to have been demolished in preparation for the construction of a new structure in Ptolemaic times, but this was never carried through, probably as a result of the Great Theban Revolt of 206 to 186 BC. As a result, the area in front of the Festival Hall now appears as an empty space.

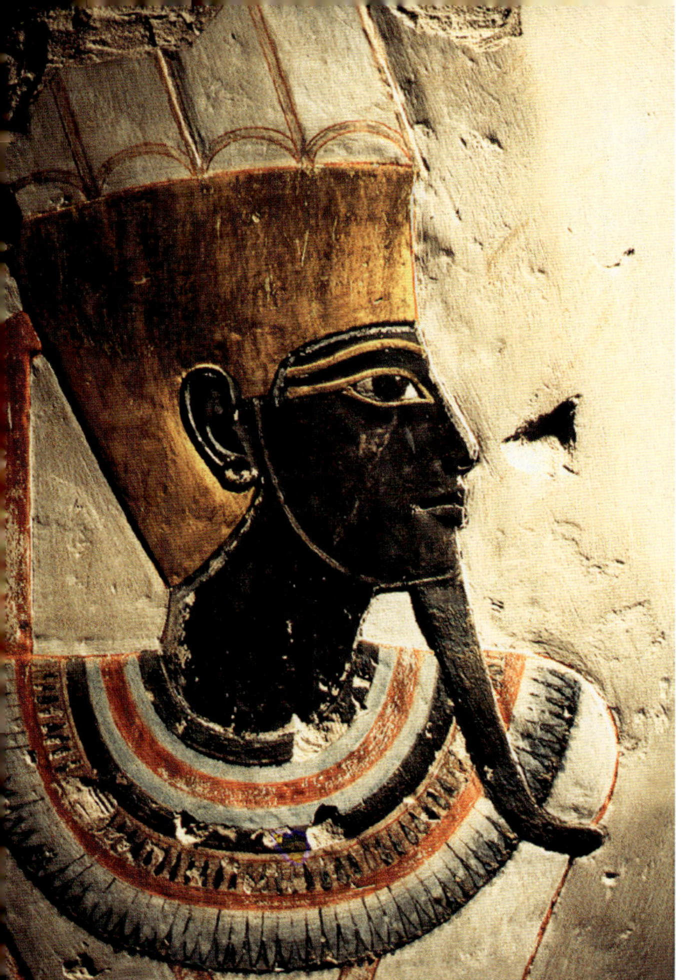

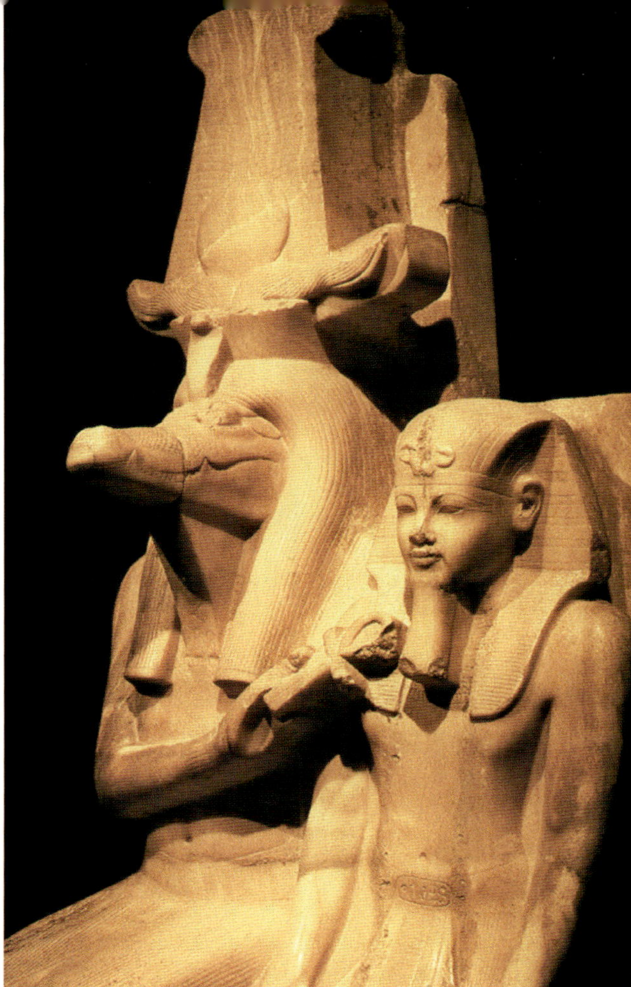

Above: Amun, who began as the local god of Thebes, became the supreme deity during the New Kingdom. Shown here in the composite form Amun-Min, he is identified by his double-feathered crown.

Above right: Amenhotep III with the crocodile god Sobek representing royal prowess. He built the colonnade hall at the Temple of Luxor. His son was the heretic king Akhenaten, and his grandson was Tutankhamun.

Bottom right: Akhenaten worshiping the Aten, a disembodied sun globe whose rays reach out to the king offering him an *ankh*, the sign of life.

Luxor Museum

The **Museum of Ancient Egyptian Art**, to give it its proper name, stands along the Corniche about midway between the Temple of Luxor and the Temple of Amun at Karnak (open daily; admission charge.) This is the perfect place to make the acquaintance of the great kings and queens of Thebes and their various gods. Purpose-built in 1975 and subsequently extended, the presentation of the museum is superb, its well-chosen objects lit to best advantage. The collection is almost entirely from the pharaonic period and includes jewelry, pottery, and furniture, as well as several exquisite objects from the tomb of Tutankhamun. There are many magnificent stone sculptures, among them figures of the divine Theban triad, Amun, Mut, and Khonsu; the Eighteenth Dynasty kings Thutmose III and Amenhotep III; and the Middle Kingdom pharaoh Senwosret III, of the Twelfth Dynasty, who is recognizable by his big ears. One gallery houses a cache of twenty-two magnificent New Kingdom statues, including from the times of Amenhotep III and Tutankhamun, unearthed in 1989 at the Temple of Luxor where they had been buried, perhaps as part of a "tidying-up" of the temple in Ptolemaic times.

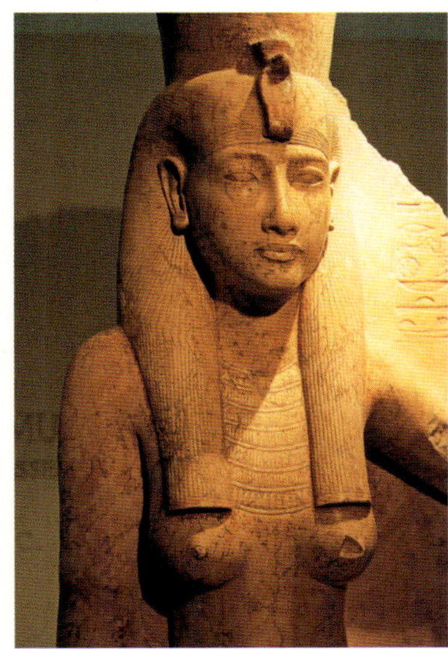

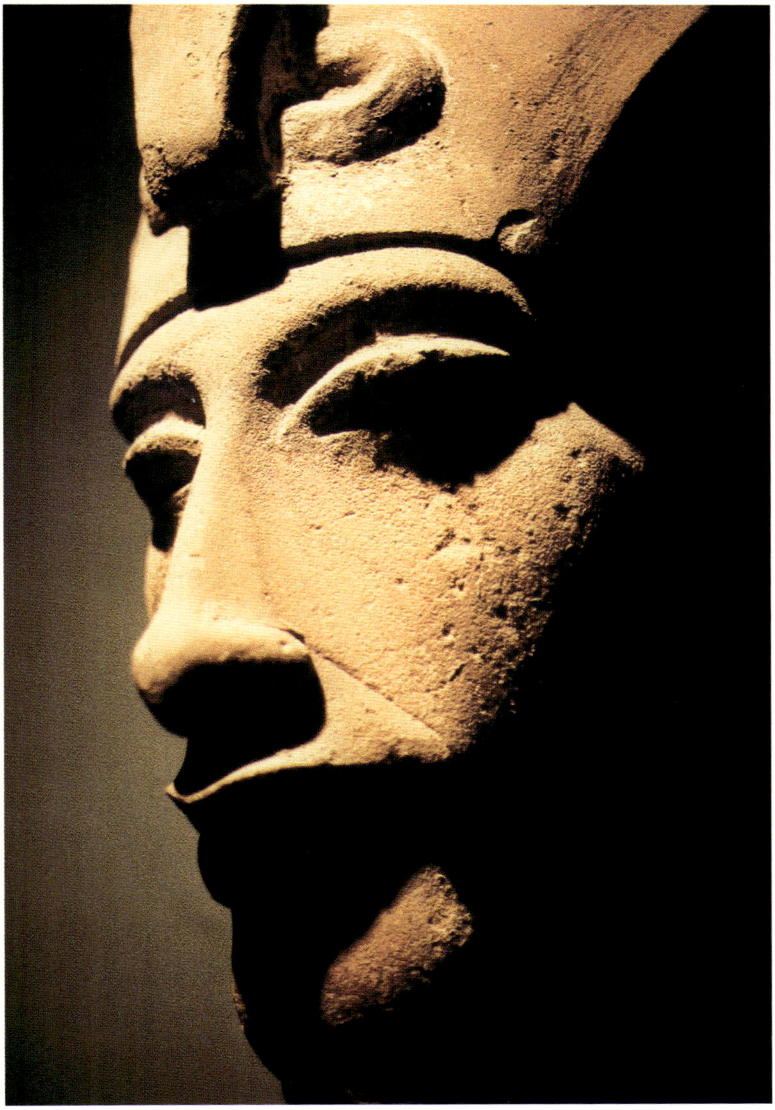

Above: The goddess Mut, wife of Amun, depicted with the facial features of Ankhesenamun, wife of Tutankhamun. This statue was found at the Temple of Luxor, and is now in Luxor Museum.

Top right: The worship of a single god was first introduced to history by Akhenaten, or Amenhotep IV, as he was known when he first came to the throne. In place of the traditional forms of the sun god, he gradually came to worship a disembodied solar globe called the Aten. Then in the fifth year of his reign he changed his name from Amenhotep to Akhenaten, that is, from "Amun is Content" to the "Effective Spirit of Aten." The king and his family now became the sole intercessor between mankind and the god. Revenues were withdrawn from the temples of all other gods, who were then ignored. The exception was Amun, whose images, names, and titles were destroyed wherever they were found, and to some extent his wife Mut and son Khonsu. This may have been owing to Amun's claim to be "King of the Gods," which contradicted the Aten's divine supremacy. Akhenaten's religious revolution did not outlast his death, and under his son Tutankhamun the worship of Amun and all the other gods was restored.

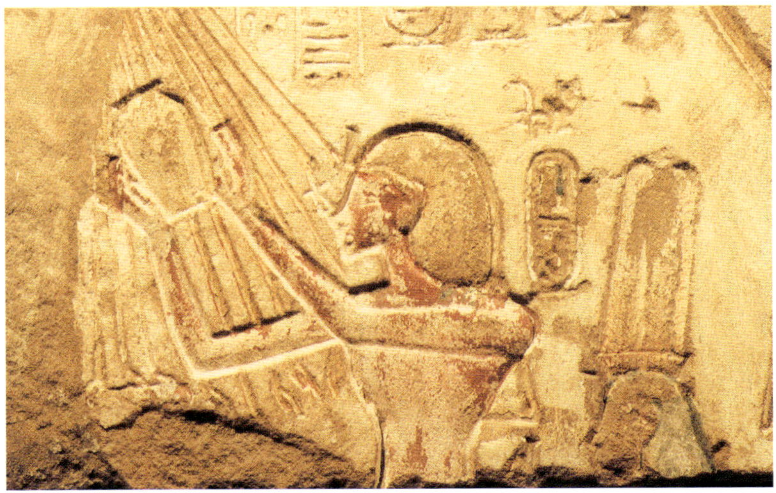

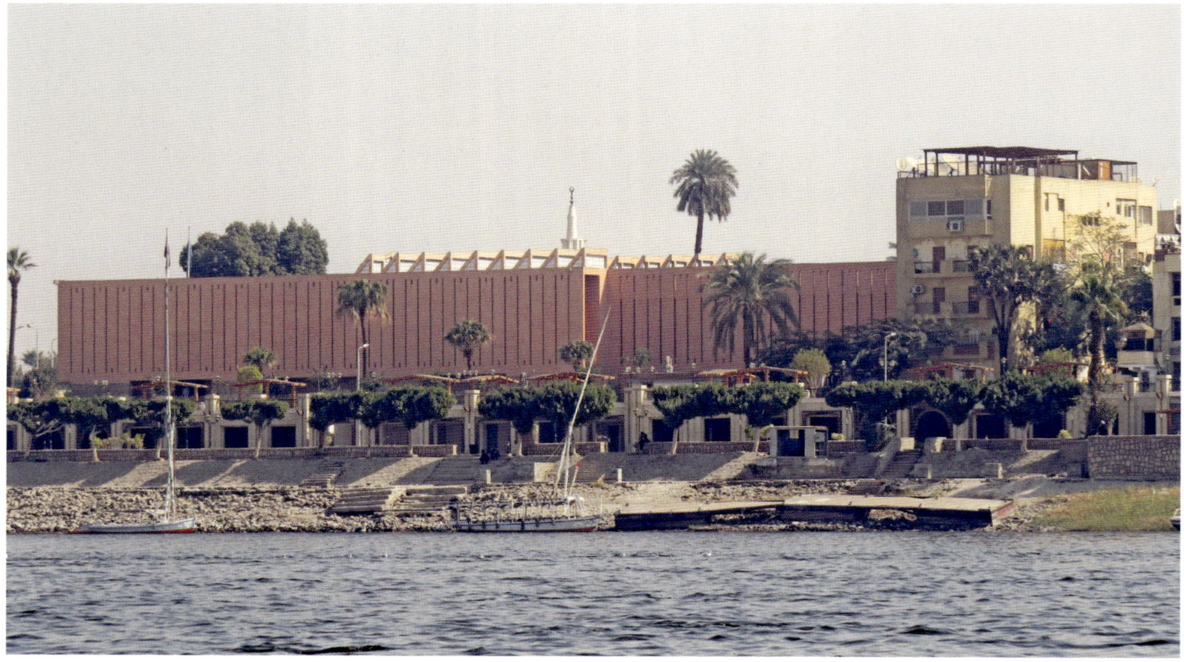

Above: Luxor Museum as seen from the Nile.

Right: Stela of the Lady Nehemsubastet, found in the Valley of the Kings in 2011, in an Eighteenth Dynasty tomb that was reused for Nehemsubastet some five centuries later. It shows the dead woman adoring the god Ra-Horakhty

Below: A priest presents the Thebian triad: Khonsu, Amun, and Mut.

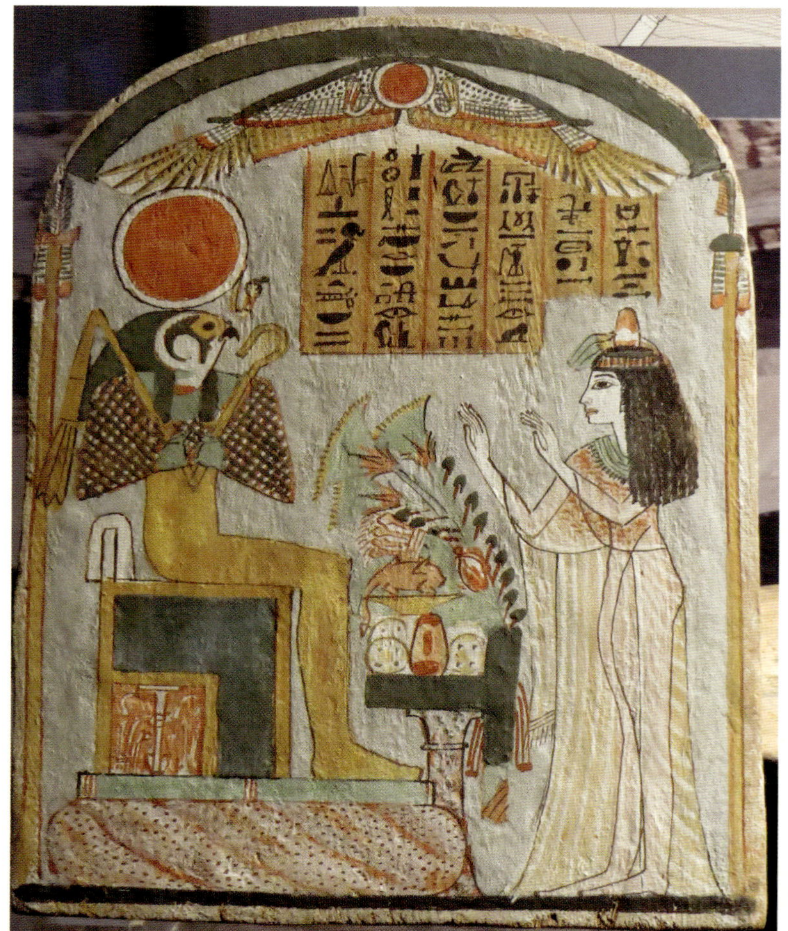

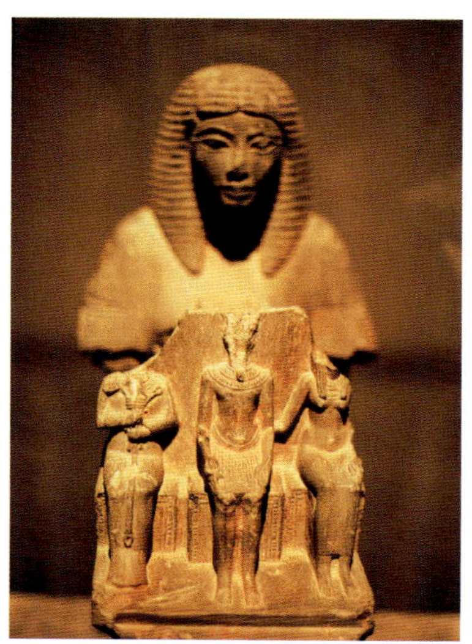

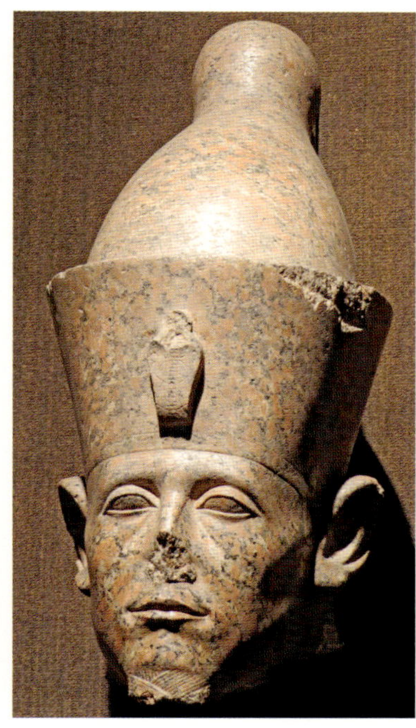

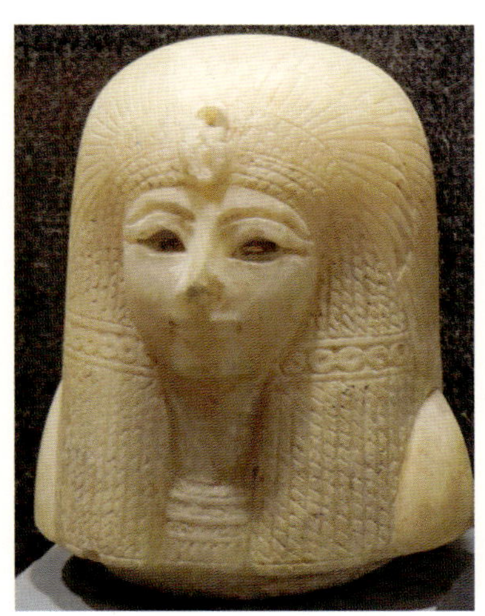

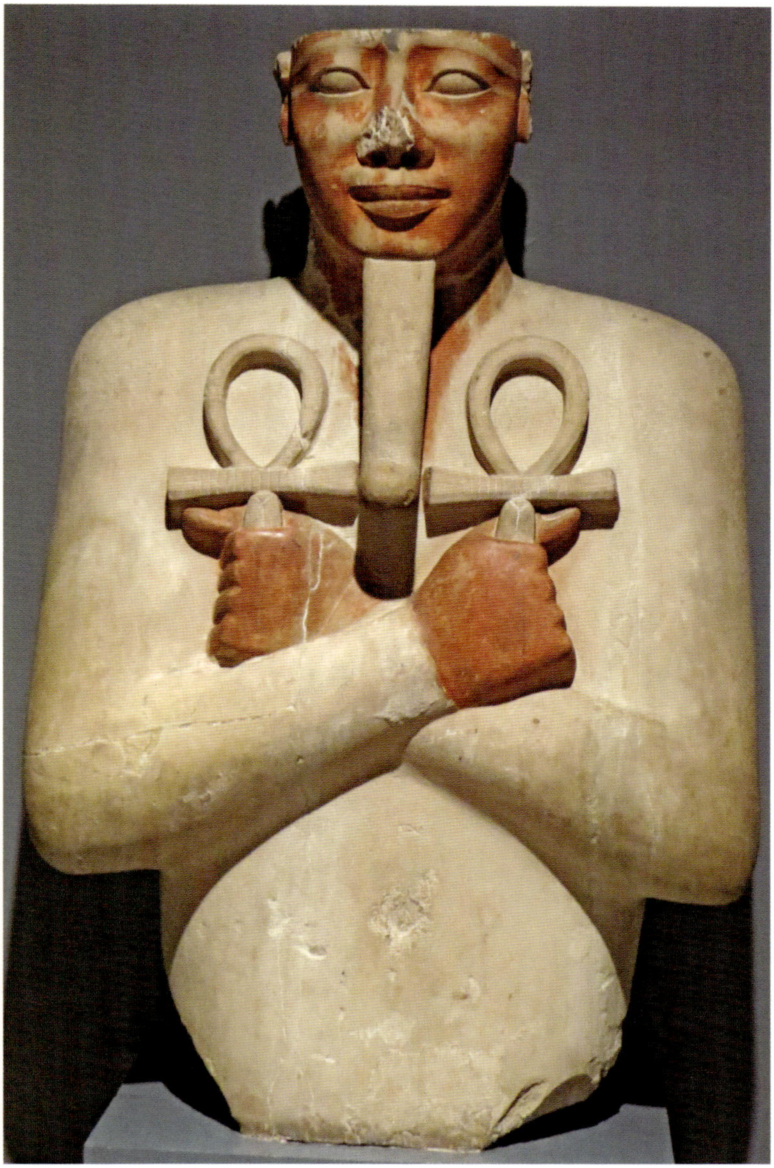

A similar, but vastly larger, cache was found at Karnak in 1904. The craftsmanship of the sculptors working in granite, basalt, and alabaster is marvelous, and the enjoyment of working with the sensuous curves of crowns, necks, and waists is clear.

A section of wall from a destroyed temple of Akhenaten at Karnak has been reconstructed in the museum; the limestone blocks are decorated with scenes in sunk relief showing Akhenaten and Nefertiti worshiping their god Aten, whose cult briefly overthrew Egypt's traditional pantheism. The mummy of Ahmose I, founder of the Eighteenth Dynasty, is on also on display, together with another which some have suggested is Rameses I, founder of the Nineteenth Dynasty,

Top left: Granite head of Senwosret III from Karnak, showing his distinctive facial features.

Bottom left: One of the alabaster canopic jar lids of Tuy, the mother of Rameses II, found in her tomb in the Valley of the Kings.

Above: A painted limestone statue of Senwosret I. It was found at Karnak, where he was responsible for some of the earliest building, including the innermost sanctuary.

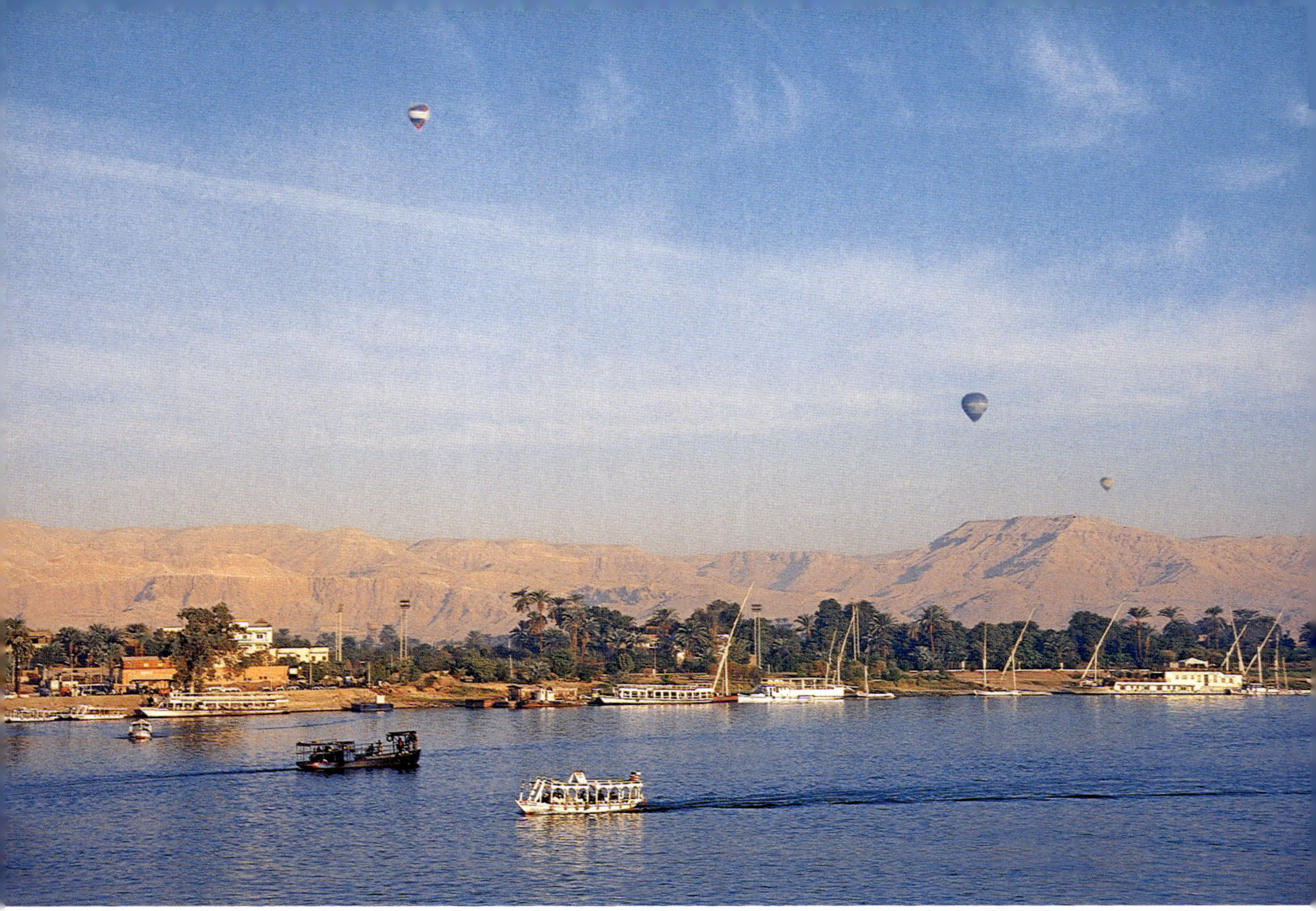

Above:. Ferries from the quayside near the Temple of Luxor take you to the west bank of the Nile. In the early morning, visitors can take soaring balloon flights over the plain of the Theban necropolis and high above the Valley of the Kings.

Below: Howard Carter's house on the west bank of the Nile; for a long time it was allowed to deteriorate but has now been turned into a museum.

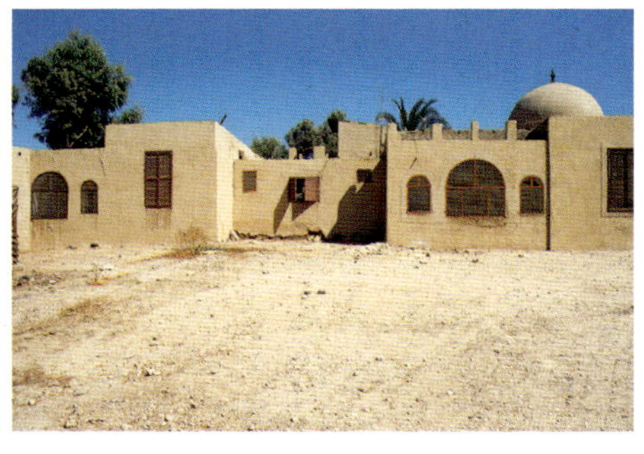

The West Bank

The opulence of Thebes during the New kingdom extended to both sides of the Nile. Amenhotep III had a great palace on the west bank at Malqata, decorated with painted birds and water plants, and where a vast lake was dug on which he sailed in his pleasure barge with his wife Queen Tiye or with one of the several hundred women in his harem. Not surprisingly he called his palace the House of Joy. Barely a trace of that palace, and its surrounding complex, survives today, and instead we know the west bank better as a necropolis—though there is plenty of village life and agricultural activity on the west bank today.

The great monuments in the plain on the west bank are memorial temples. These combined the worship of Amun and the sun god Ra-Horakhty with rituals that were performed to help sustain the pharaoh who owned the temple in the afterlife. In earlier periods, the latter were carried out in temples directly attached to royal pyramids, below which the king was buried. However, at the beginning of the New Kingdom, pyramids were abandoned for royal burials, and the temple separated from the actual burial place, probably for reasons of security. From the reign of Thutmose I onward, the burial place of pharaohs was the Valley of the Kings, over a kilometer away from the temples, but still tightly linked with them conceptually.

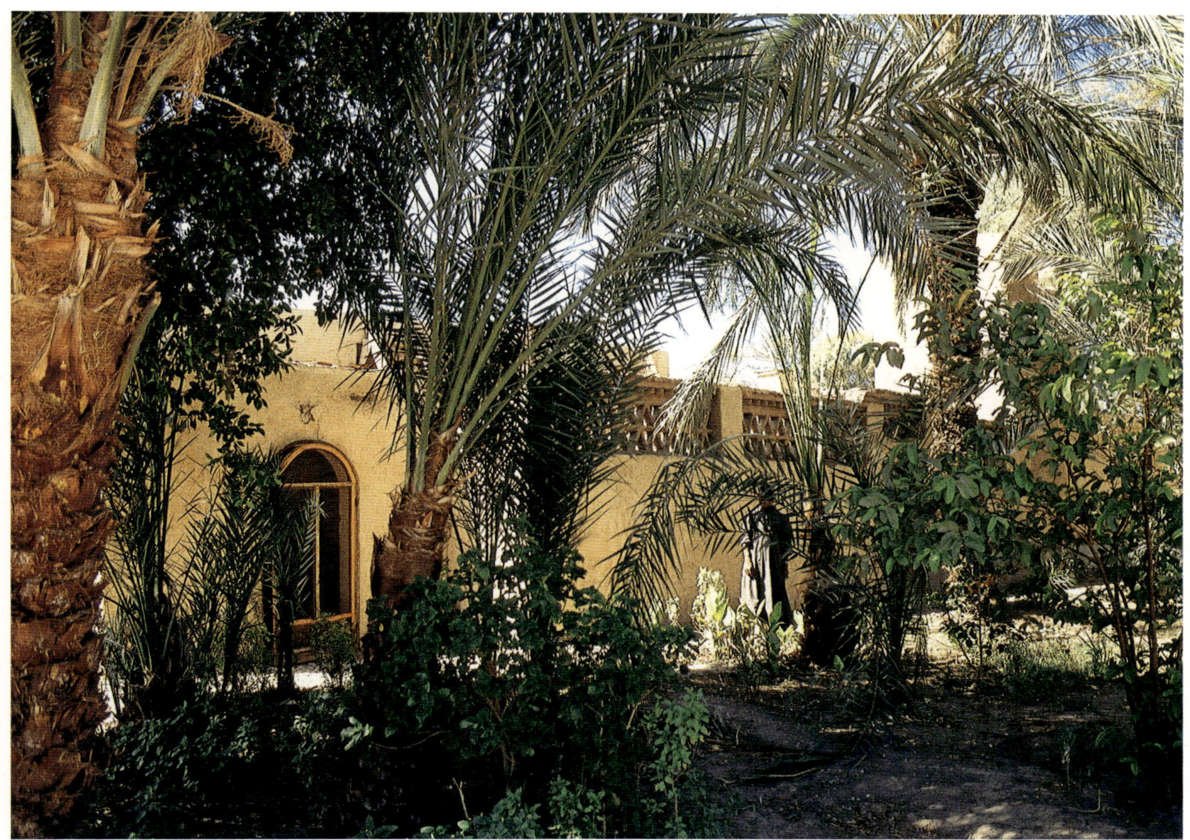

Above: Howard Carter's house seen from its former lush garden. Conveniently situated on the way to the Valley of the Kings, this is where Carter was living when in the late afternoon of 4 November 1922 he discovered the unrobbed tomb of Tutankhamun, the most spectacular discovery in the whole history of Egyptology. Another house, sitting atop an arid hill, is often pointed out to tourists as Carter's; but Carter's house stands on lower ground, closer to the Nile.

The three most complete and spectacular memorial temples on the west bank are those of Hatshepsut at Deir al-Bahari, Rameses III at Medinet Habu, and the Ramesseum of Rameses II. The famous Colossi of Memnon were also part of a memorial temple, that of Amenhotep III, but along with his palace it has almost entirely disappeared, and for a long time only the gigantic statues that once flanked its entrance were visible. However, ongoing excavations have revealed the statues that guarded the temple's inner gateways, and also the foundations of parts of the main body of the temple, where further statues have been re-erected.

The plain is backed by the Theban hills and behind them lies the desert plateau. Important people, including the nobility and various high office holders, including the priesthood, had themselves buried in tomb-chapels in the plain and the hills beyond. These usually combined the offering place and the burial place in a single unit, although a handful of the most privileged had their burial chambers in the Valley of the Kings, alongside the pharaohs and some members of the royal family. Others of the latter were interred in the Valley of the Queens or more remote locations. Not far from them was the town of the tomb workers at Deir al-Medina. All these sites (open daily; admission charge to most) are covered in the following pages.

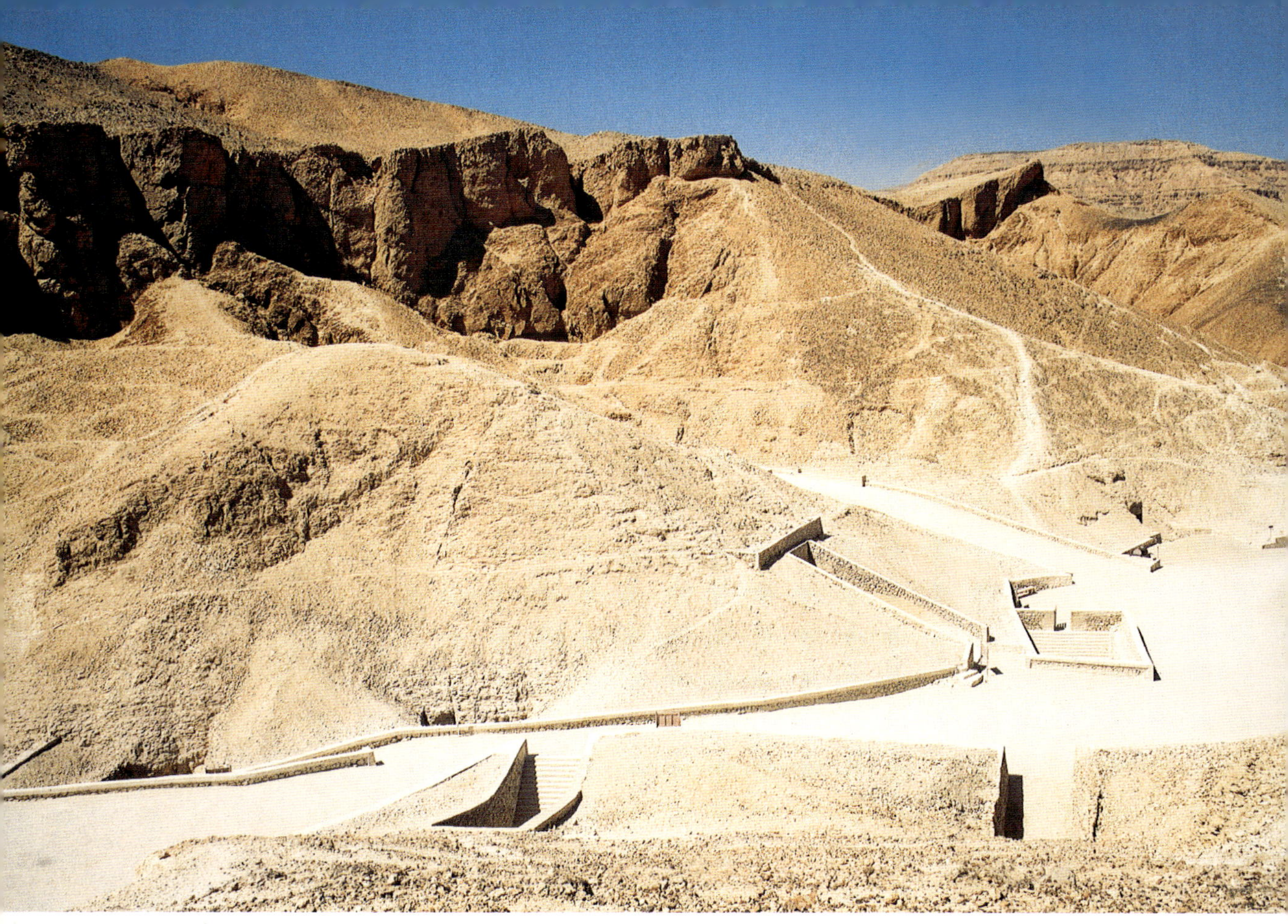

Above: The entrance to the tomb of Tutankhamun is within the square enclosure to the right. The tomb owed its survival to flash floods which deeply buried the tomb under waterborne debris, as well as the fact that workmen responsible for the adjacent tomb of Rameses VI built their huts on top of these layers.

The Valley of the Kings

The road climbs toward the oven of white sand and sun that is Biban al-Muluk—the "Gates of the Kings"—where unblinking tomb entrances stare vacantly from the narrow valley walls. Each tomb is numbered in order of discovery, sixty-four in all, though only a few are open to the public, and only a selection of these are open at any one time.

Burials at the Valley of the Kings date from the Eighteenth through Twentieth Dynasties. The tombs were cut into the soft limestone by two teams of twenty-five men working alternating ten-day shifts. They normally lived at Deir al-Medina, but when on shift stayed in huts within the valley, or on the ridge between the two. Construction of a tomb began at the beginning of a reign, but many tombs were still incomplete at the king's death. Most shared the same basic design concept, with the first corridors leading to a deep shaft, probably a security feature, but perhaps with some symbolic role as well. Beyond this would be a pillared hall, and then more corridors down to an antechamber and the pillared burial chamber. During the Eighteenth Dynasty, tombs had a bent axis; later on, they became straight.

Decoration concentrated exclusively on the transferring of the deceased from death to rebirth. The dead pharaoh, absorbed in the sun god, sailed through the underworld from sunset ("death") through the night in a boat, with enemies and dangers to be avoided along the way, culminating in sunrise ("rebirth"). This was first set out in the Book of *Amduat* ("What Is in the Underworld"), found in the earliest tombs in the Valley, and later supplemented by such works as the Book of the Gates and images of the king with the gods. The *Amduat* and Gates are divided into twelve sections for the twelve hours of the night. These are shown contiguously in some tombs, but in later ones they may be spread though the whole tomb.

Tomb robbing was a problem from the beginning. Under the powerful pharaohs of the Eighteenth and Nineteenth Dynasties local officials were closely supervised and tomb looting kept in check. But under the weaker rulers of the Twentieth Dynasty tombs were robbed. By the Twenty-first Dynasty, around 1000 BC, the priests decided that rather than leave looting to the anarchy of the grave robbers they would systematically empty the tombs themselves—and recycle what remained to replenish state coffers. The tombs and indeed the mummies of some of the greatest kings of the Eighteenth to Twentieth Dynasties were stripped bare by the priests, their ornaments sold, their gold melted down, and their coffins reused. When archaeologists came to the Valley of the Kings it looked as though not a single tomb had escaped being looted in antiquity: however, there would prove to be just one.

Below: The Valley of the Kings, a remote and inaccessible spot hidden within the crags and folds of the Theban hills.

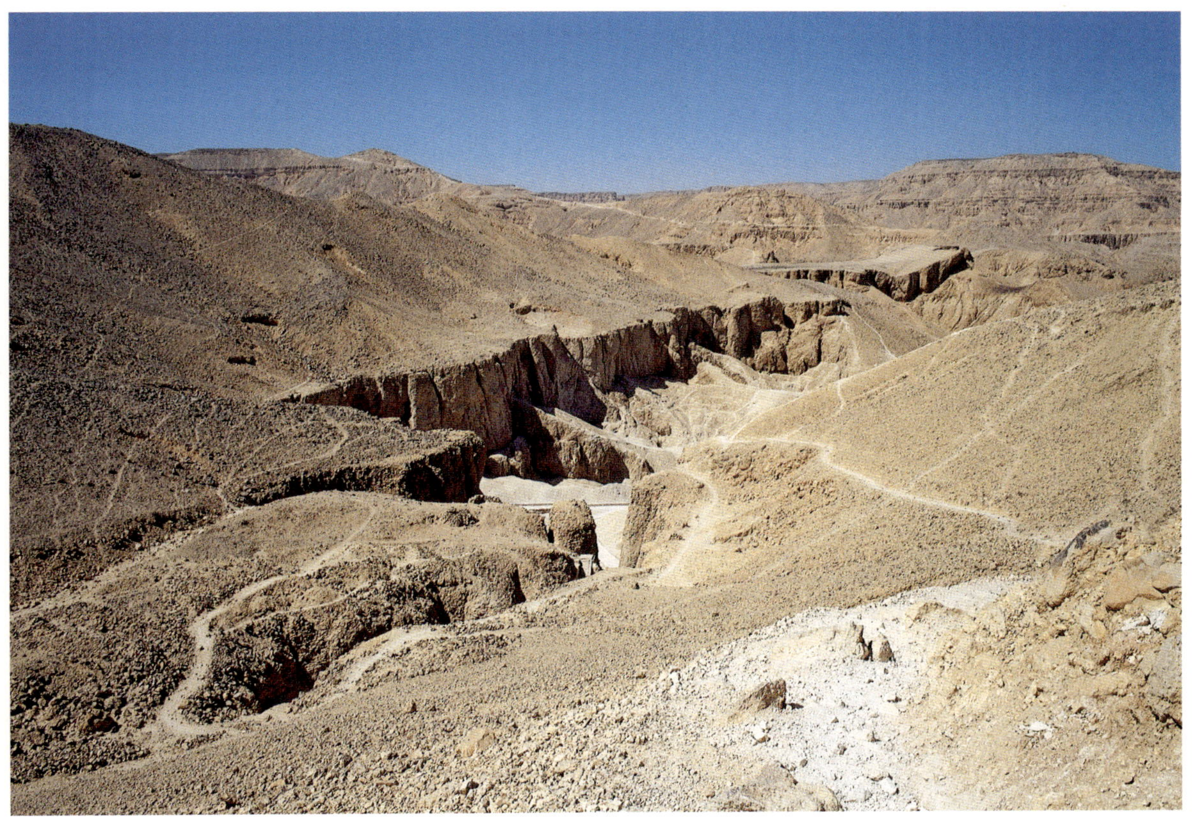

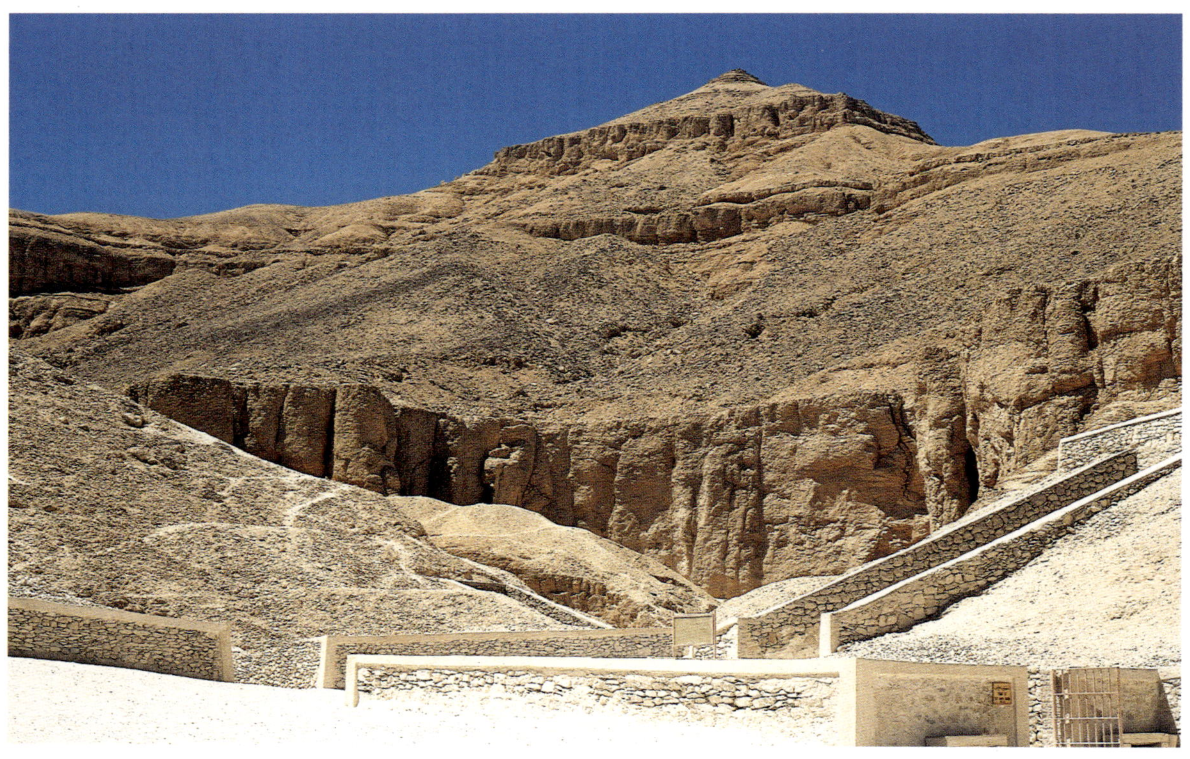

Above: Rising behind Tutankhamun's tomb is al-Qurn, known to the ancient Egyptians as *ta dehent*, "The Peak," and which may have reminded them of the pyramids of Old Kingdom royal burials.

Top right: The steps leading down into Tutankhamun's tomb.

Right: There are four chambers in the tomb, but only the burial chamber is decorated. On the left wall Tutankhamun is greeted by the goddess Nut, while the scene to the right of that depicts the ceremony in which Tutankhamun's successor, Ay, symbolically opens the dead king's mouth to ensure he can partake of nourishment during the afterlife. On the right wall, the principal officers of state are drawing Tutankhamun's coffin to the tomb on a sledge. Tutankhamun himself was interred within his beautifully carved sarcophagus. At its corners stand the four protective goddesses, Isis (left), Nephthys (foreground), Neith, and Selket.

The Tomb of Tutankhamun

Tutankhamun's tomb was discovered on 4 November 1922 by Howard Carter and opened three weeks later on 26 November after his patron Lord Carnarvon arrived from the United Kingdom. Carter was the first to look inside and was silent for a long while. Overlooked by grave robbers for more than 3,000 years, the long-lost tomb in the Valley of the Kings yielded a treasure of unimaginable magnificence. Carnarvon, unable to stand the suspense any longer, enquired anxiously, "Can you see anything?" "Wonderful things," Carter exclaimed as his eyes adjusted to the light from his flickering candle, "strange animals, statues and gold—everywhere the glint of gold." Those wonderful things were removed to the museum in Cairo, and are now in the new Grand Egyptian Museum at Giza. But Tutankhamun himself remains for the time being in his tomb, inside a sealed glass case.

Tutankhamun was probably the son of the heretic pharaoh Akhenaten, but it remains unclear which of the king's two wives—Nefertiti or Kiya—was his mother. Tutankhamun died young, at about the age of nineteen, and was buried in a tomb originally prepared for someone other than a king, his own tomb being presumably insufficiently complete to be used. A moving discovery that Carter made when he revealed the outermost coffin within the sarcophagus has led to speculation that one of the last people to leave the tomb 3,300 years earlier was Tutankhamun's young widow, Ankhesenamun. "Upon the forehead of this recumbent figure of the young boy king," wrote Carter, "were two emblems delicately worked in brilliant inlay—the cobra and the vulture—symbols of Upper and Lower Egypt, but perhaps the most touching by its human simplicity was the tiny wreath of flowers around these symbols, as it pleases us to think, the last farewell offering of the widowed girl queen to her husband. among all that regal splendor, that royal magnificence—everywhere the glint of gold—there was nothing so beautiful as those few withered flowers, still retaining their tinge of color. They told us what a short period three thousand three hundred years really was—but Yesterday and the Morrow."

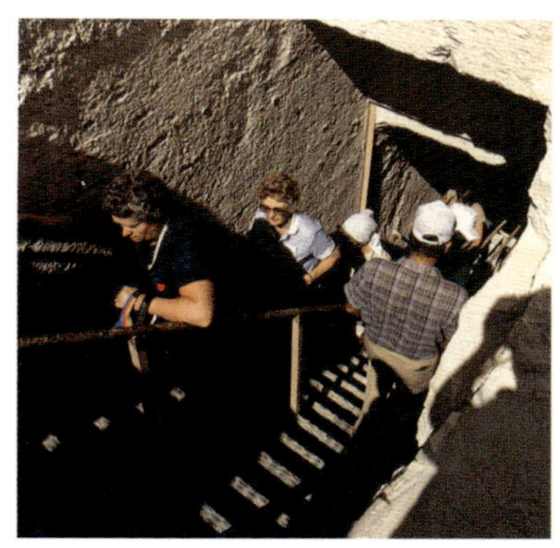

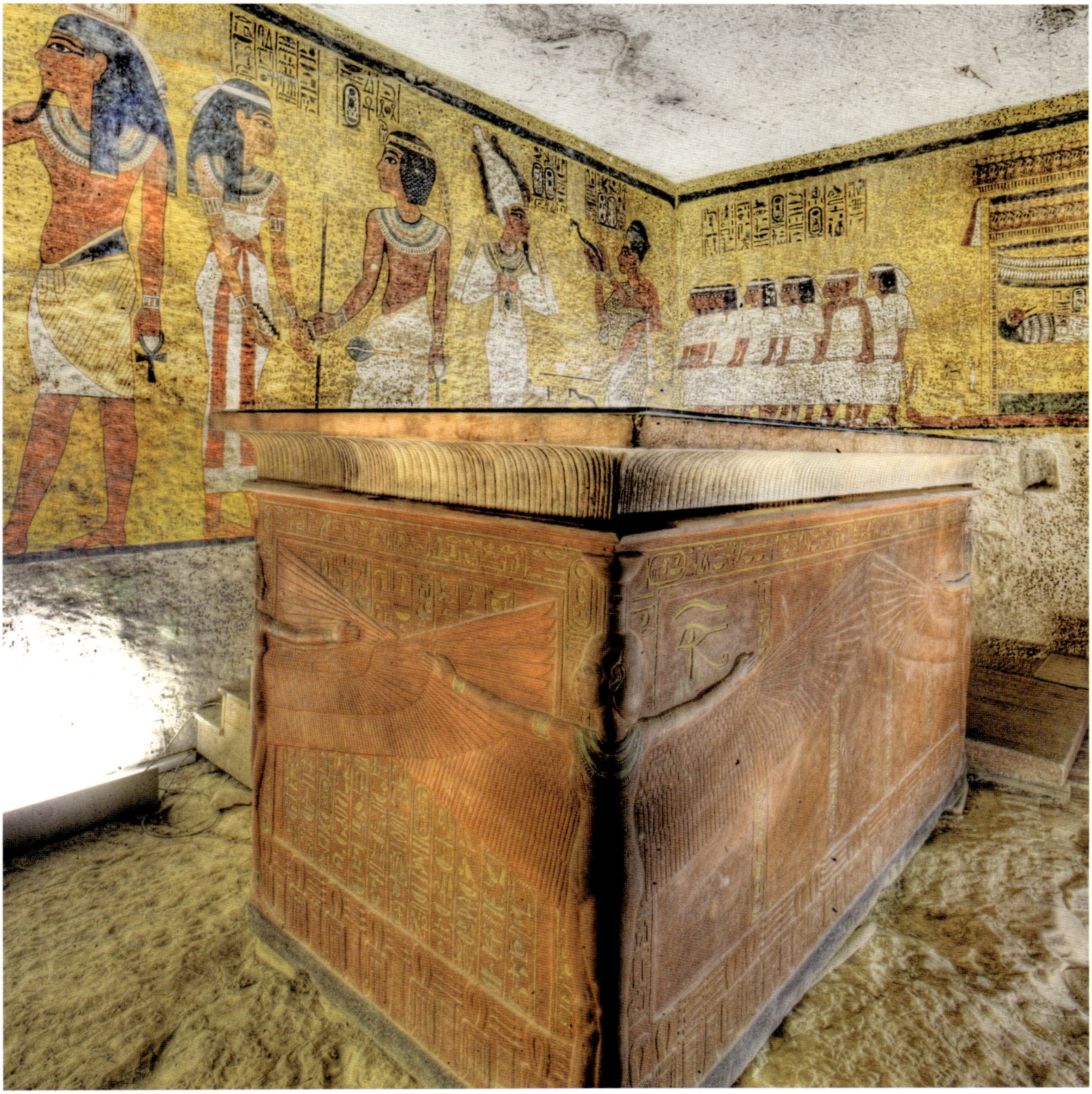

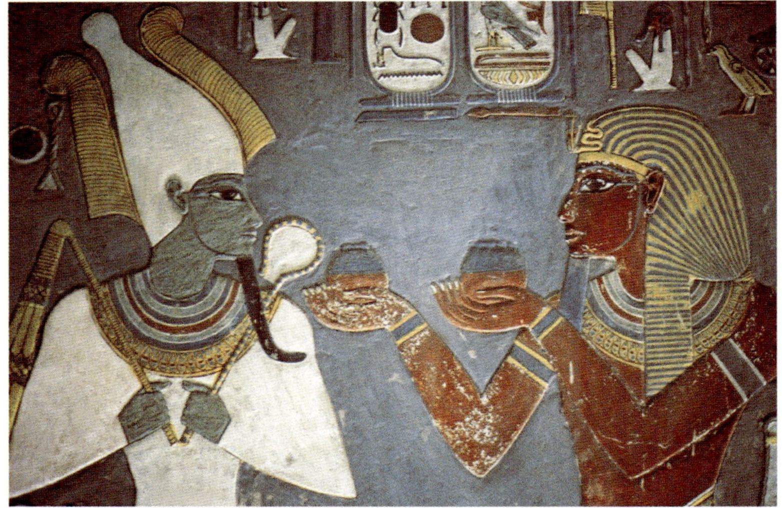

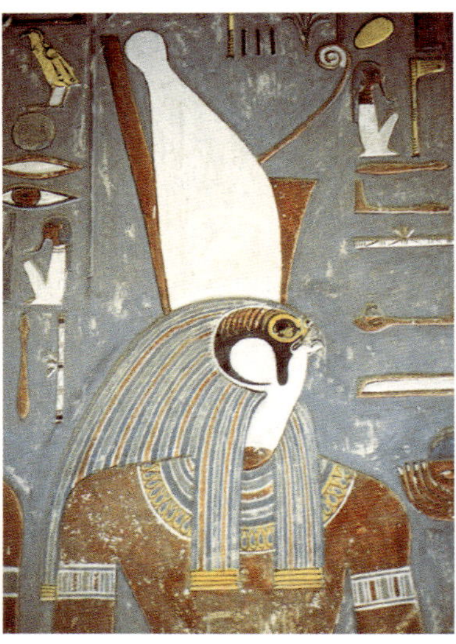

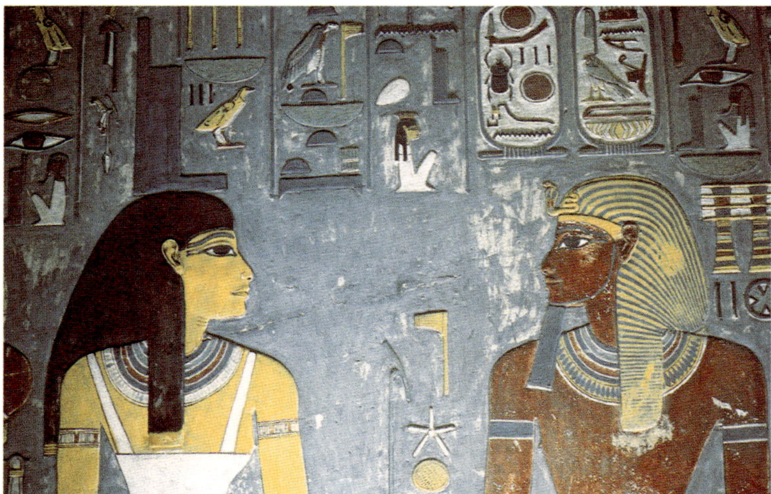

Above left: The decoration in Horemheb's tomb is the first in the Valley of the Kings to be made in painted relief, rather than simply painted on plaster. One chamber is adorned with multiple images of the king paired with a protective deity. In this case Horemheb, on the right, is making offerings to Osiris, the lord of the underworld.

Above: Horus, the son of Isis and Osiris, in Horemheb's tomb.

Left: Horemheb faces Isis. Pharaohs identified with her son Horus in life, and her husband Osiris in death. Here the goddess wears her regular headdress in the form of a throne.

The Tombs of Tutankhamun's Successors

Tutankhamun was raised in the court of his probable father Akhenaten, the pharaoh who had overthrown the worship of Amun and the many gods of Egypt in favor of one god, the Aten. But following Akhenaten's death, when Tutankhamun was only eight, the old religion was restored by those ruling in the young king's name. Key figures among them were Ay and Horemheb, both generals in Akhenaten's army. When Tutankhamun died around 1312 BC, Ay became pharaoh and was in turn succeeded by Horemheb, who was childless. With his death the Eighteenth Dynasty was succeeded by the Nineteenth, founded by yet another general, Rameses I. His son was Sethy I, whose son in turn was the great Rameses II. The illustrious name of Rameses was also adopted by most of the kings of the Twentieth Dynasty, but when the last of them died in about 1078 BC the New Kingdom came to an end and Egypt became weak and divided.

Right: The vaulted ceiling in the burial chamber of the tomb of Rameses VI is splendidly painted with the Egyptian conception of the sky, with its goddess Nut appearing twice, back to back, framing the Book of the Day on one side, the Book of the Night on the other. Here she swallows the setting sun, which passes through her body to be reborn at morning.

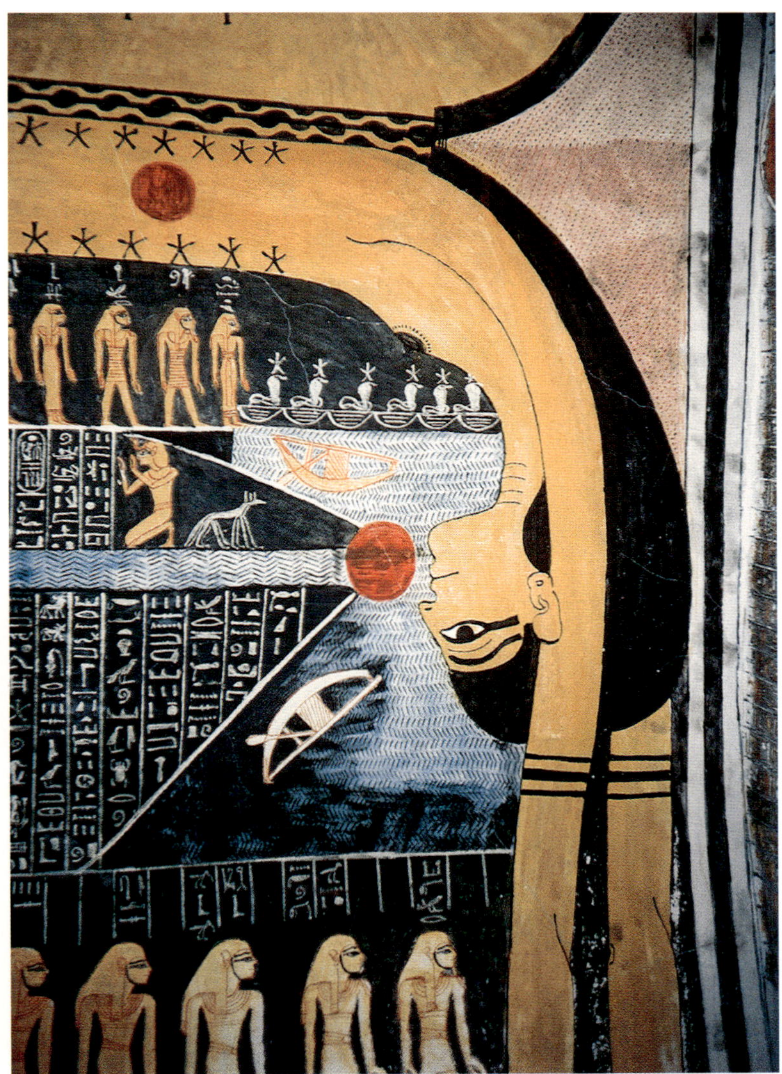

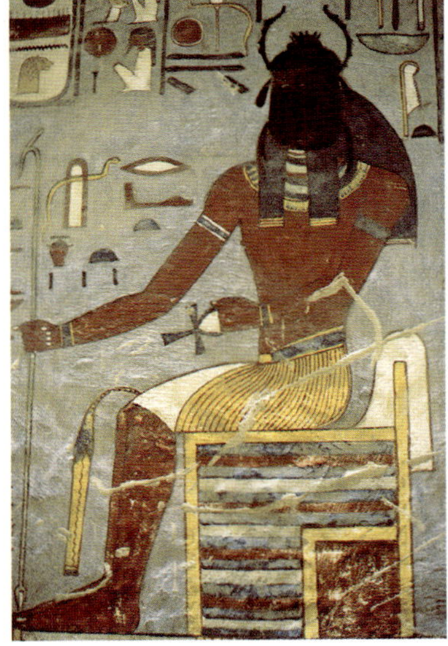

Above: Khepri was the aspect of the sun god at dawn. Observing how scarab beetles busily roll balls of dung across the ground, the ancient Egyptians saw the scarab as the motive force that made the sun rise through the sky each morning. The scarab was thus associated with creation and rebirth. Khepri is shown here in the tomb of Rameses I; he is depicted in an anthropomorphic form, with a beetle for a head.

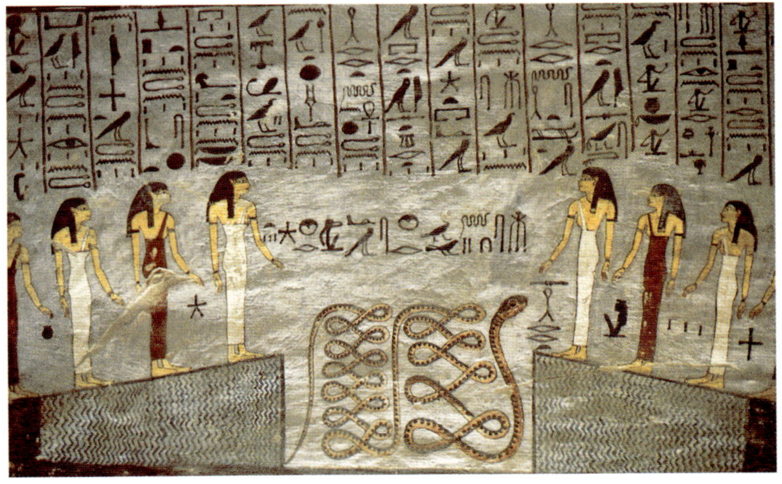

Right: The goddesses of the hours of the night as shown in the *Amduat*, here in the version in the tomb of Rameses I.

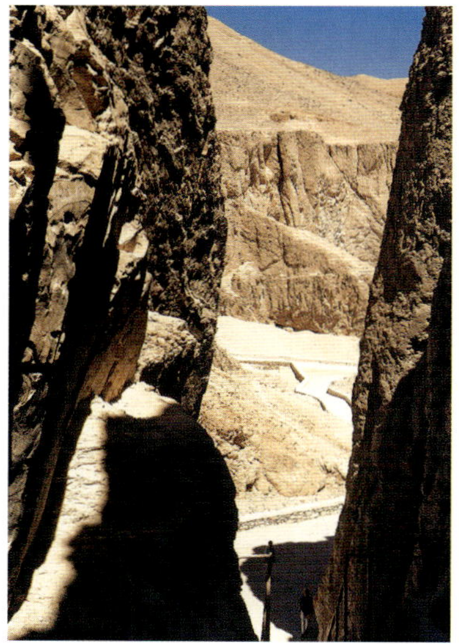

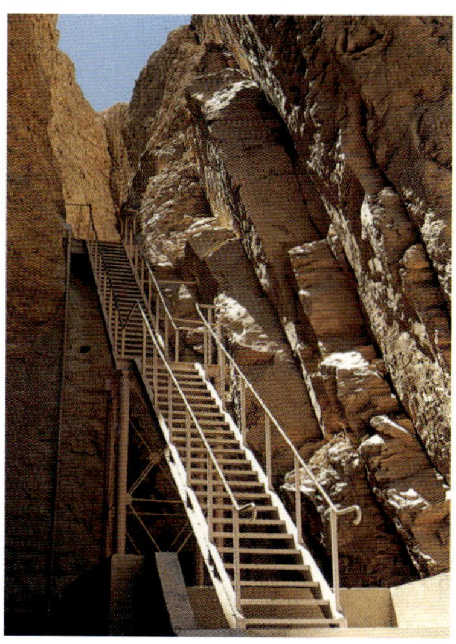

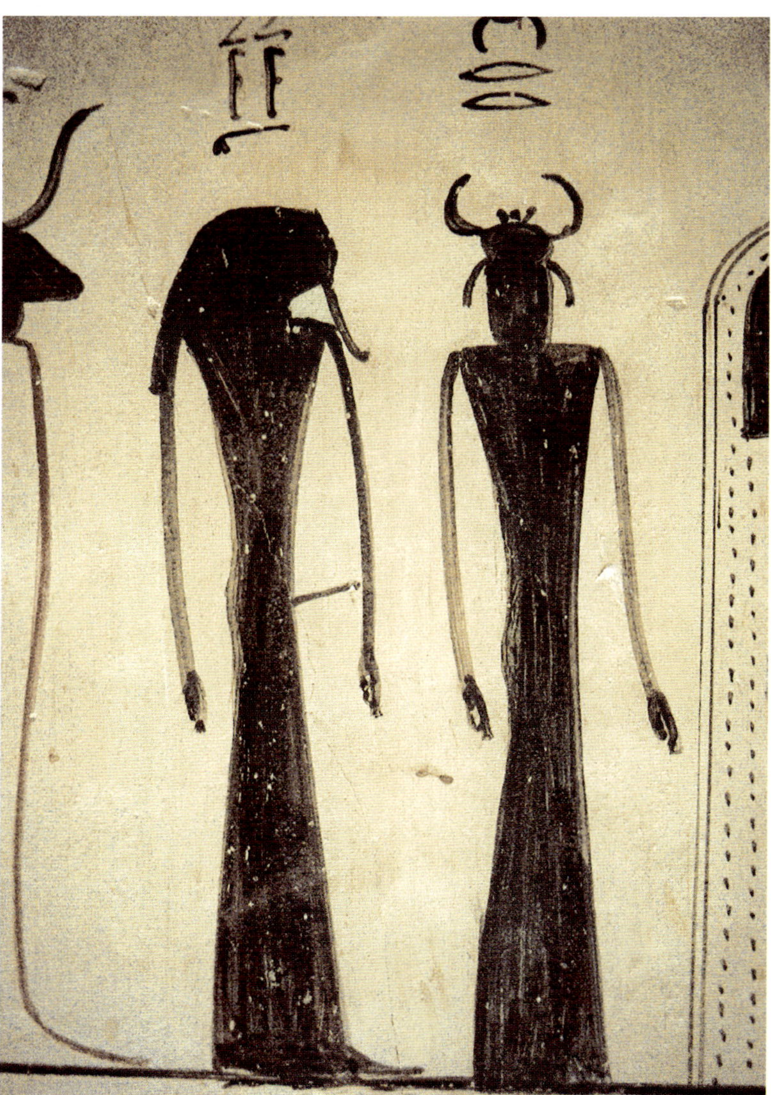

Top left: View down into the Valley of the Kings, from the ascent toward the entrance of Thutmose III's tomb.

Above: The modern metal steps climbing up to Thutmose III's tomb.

Above right: With a brilliant and powerful simplicity, beings from the Litany of Ra are drawn in black on one of the pillars in the burial chamber.

The Tomb of Thutmose III

Both architecturally and in decoration, the tomb of Thutmose III is one of the most original and sophisticated in the Valley of the Kings. Hidden deep within a cleft at the far end of the valley, it would require the agility of a mountain goat to reach its entrance, but the installation of metal steps makes the steep climb easier, though you must then twirl down through equally steep corridors to reach the oval burial chamber deep beneath the rock. The spareness of the decorations is striking, and also their style; the walls are painted in red and black only, and are covered with cursive figures, hardly more than brush strokes, that for all the world look like art deco illustrations in a 1930s magazine. In fact the walls in the tomb chamber are covered with the *Amduat*, rendered as though written on a gigantic papyrus, and its pillars are painted on all sides with the Litany of Ra.

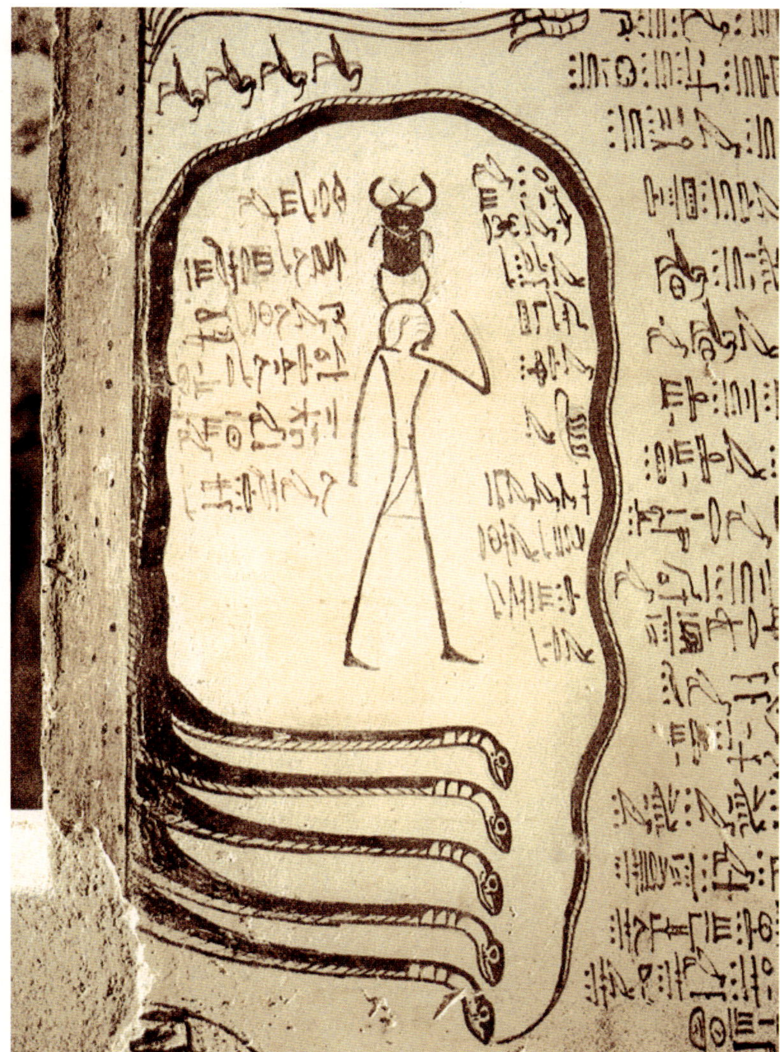

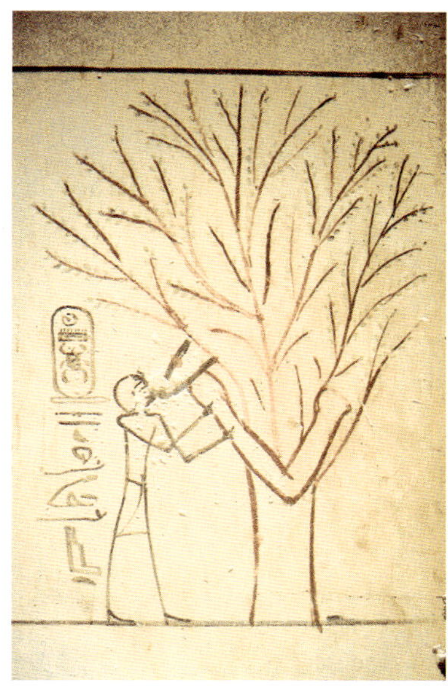

Left: The Sixth Hour of the *Amduat*, which is wrapped like a scroll around the curved walls of the tomb chamber in three registers.

Above: In this unique scene, Thutmose is being nursed by Isis in the form of a tree goddess. There is a pun involved, for Thutmose's actual mother was named after the goddess.

Below left: Part of the First Hour of the *Amduat* on the burial chamber wall, showing the sun god in the form of a scarab.

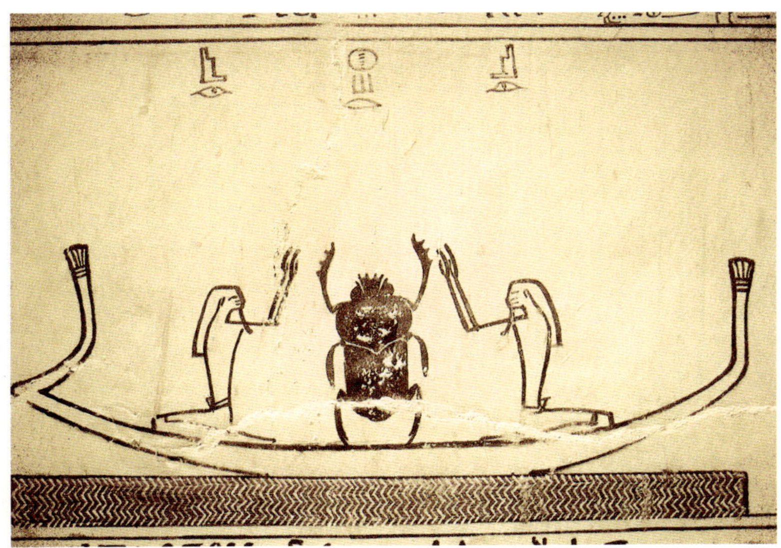

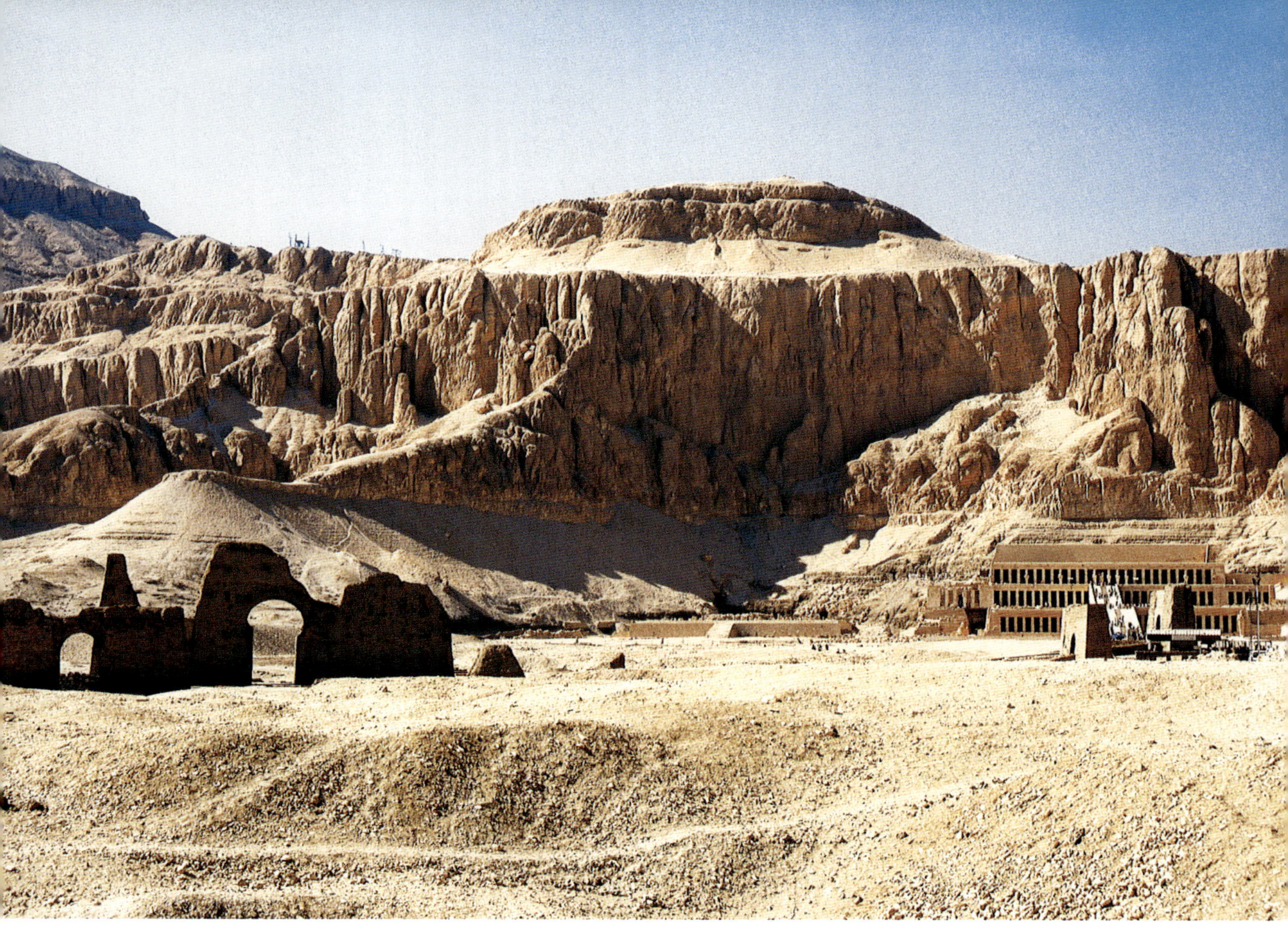

Above: View toward the memorial temple of Hatshepsut, with a group of large Twenty-fifth/Twenty-sixth Dynasty tombs in the foreground. An early Christian monastery once occupied the ruins of Hatshepsut's temple, causing the place to be dubbed in the early nineteenth century "the Northern Monastery," in Arabic Deir al-Bahari.

Top right: Hatshepsut incorporated the looming cliff face at Deir al-Bahari into her architectural conception, as though taming the wild mountainside with the elegance of her gleaming white limestone terraces.

Bottom right: Hatshepsut's funerary temple at Deir al-Bahari is set within a magnificent amphitheater cut by nature into the rugged flank of the Theban hills.

Deir al-Bahari

Here at Deir al-Bahari, Hatshepsut, who had made herself king of Egypt, as co-ruler of Thutmose III, constructed one of the finest buildings of all time. An inspired interworking of architecture and landscape, the terraces emphasize the stratification of the cliff behind and the line between rock and sky. At the same time, the bold rhythm of the pillared colonnades, their vertical shafts of light-reflecting stone framing and contrasting with the shadowed ambulatories, reflects the dark gashes of gullies and fissures in the cliff face itself. The temple mediates between the wildness of the mountain and the cultivation of the valley. The power of the landscape is gripped and subdued with a confidence that is breathtaking, and then played throughout the structure so that as you walk around the temple you feel an atmosphere of majestic calm.

The daughter of Thutmose I, Hatshepsut married her half-brother, Thutmose II, who had a different mother. She did not have a son, and when Thutmose II died he was succeeded by the offspring of a junior wife, Iset. For six years Hatshepsut ruled as regent, but then declared herself pharaoh and for the remainder of her life entirely overshadowed

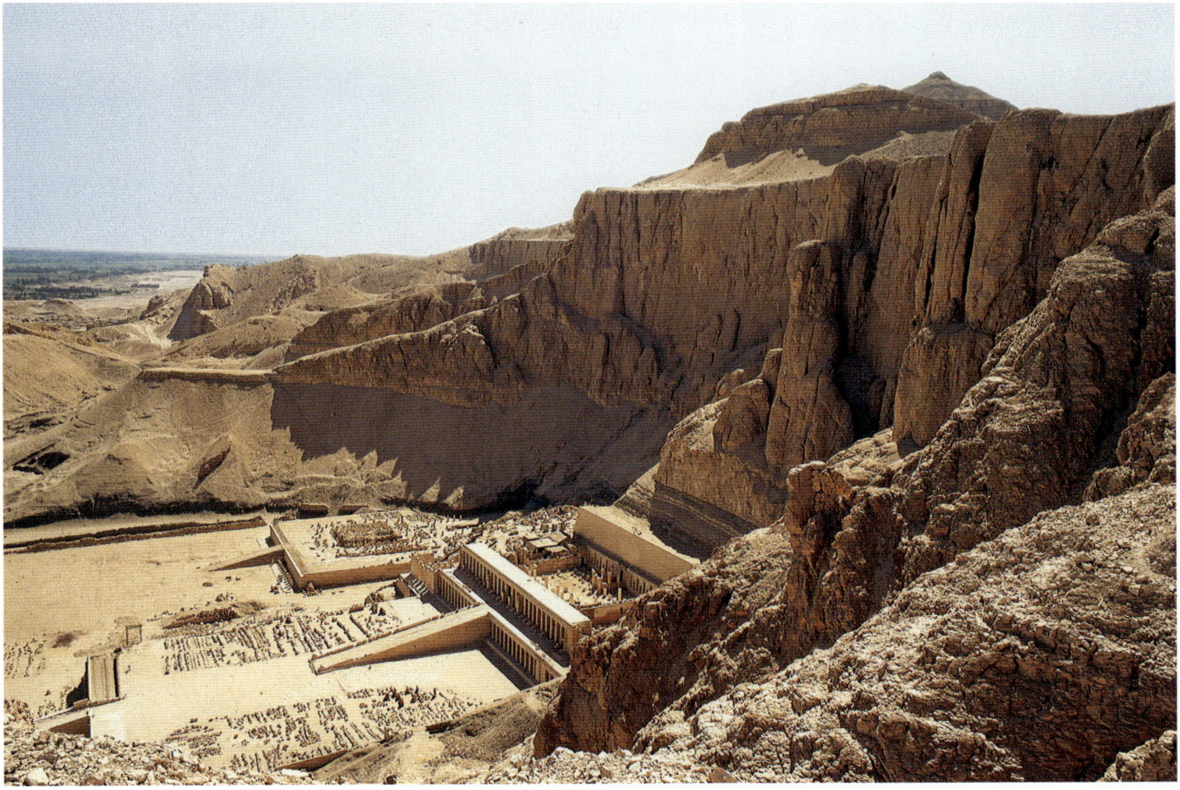

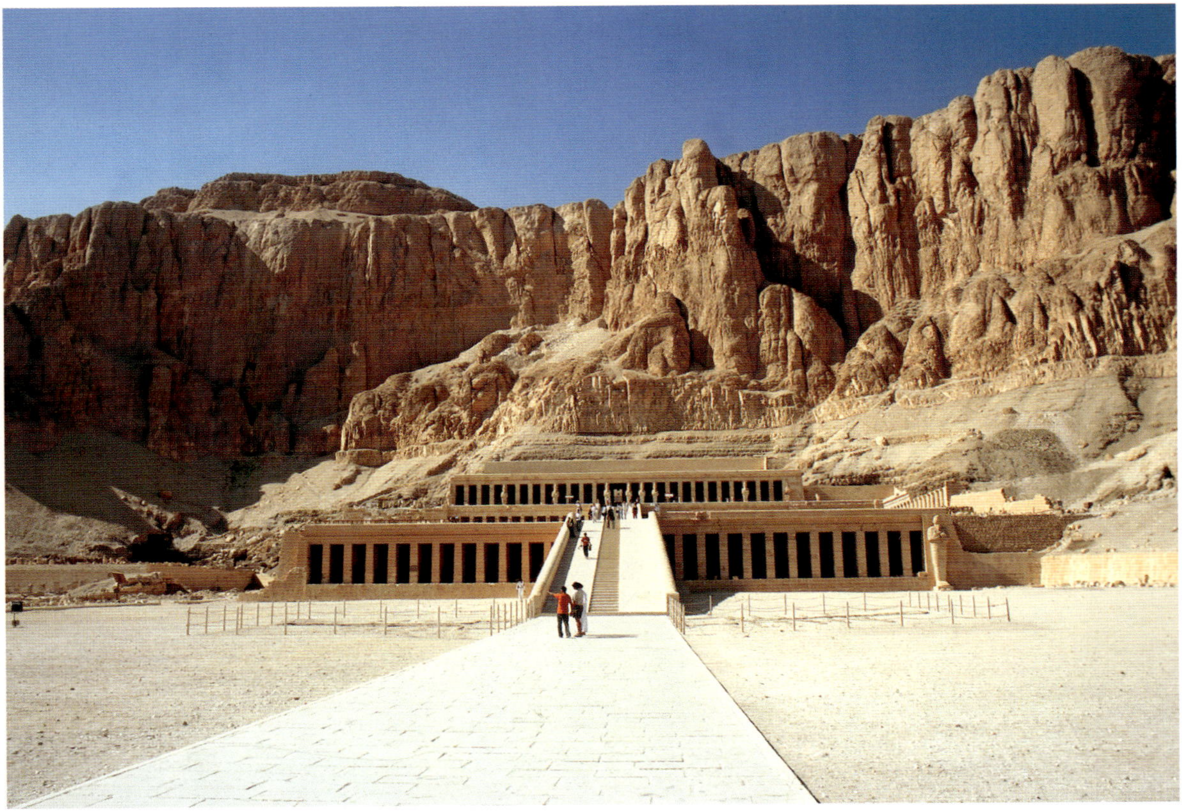

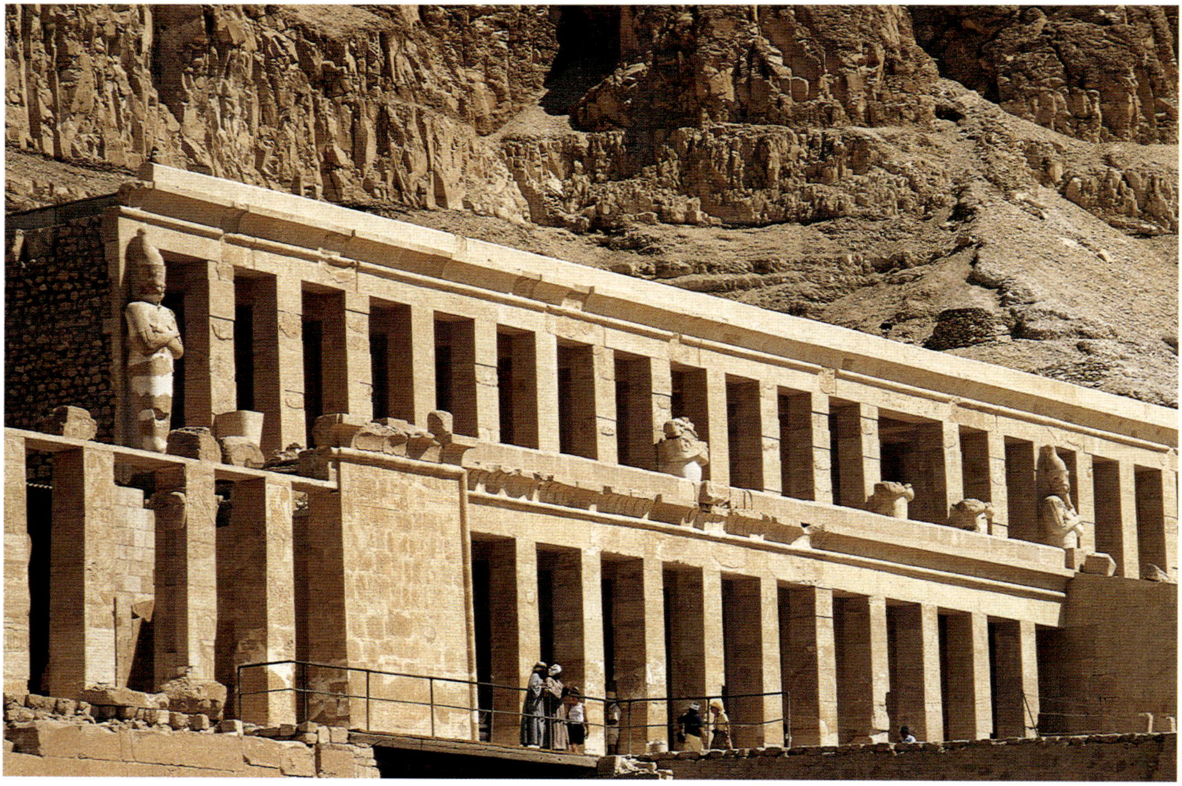

Above: The upper terraces of Hatshepsut's memorial temple.

Right: The chapel of Anubis, part of Hatshepsut's memorial temple. The fluted columns here anticipate by at least seven hundred years the Doric columns of ancient Greece.

Below: A head from one of Hatshepsut's statues, now displayed on a terrace of her temple.

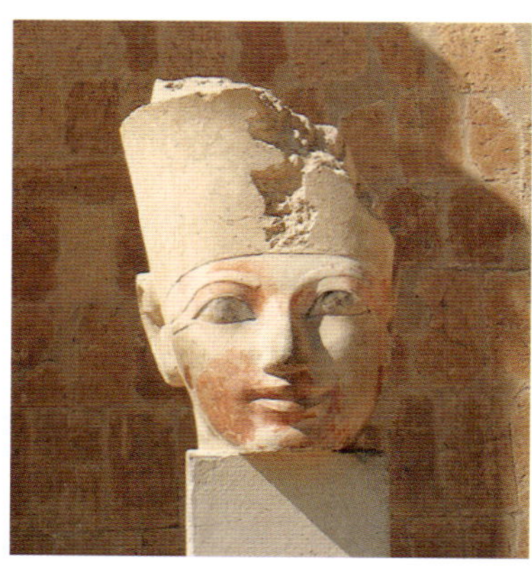

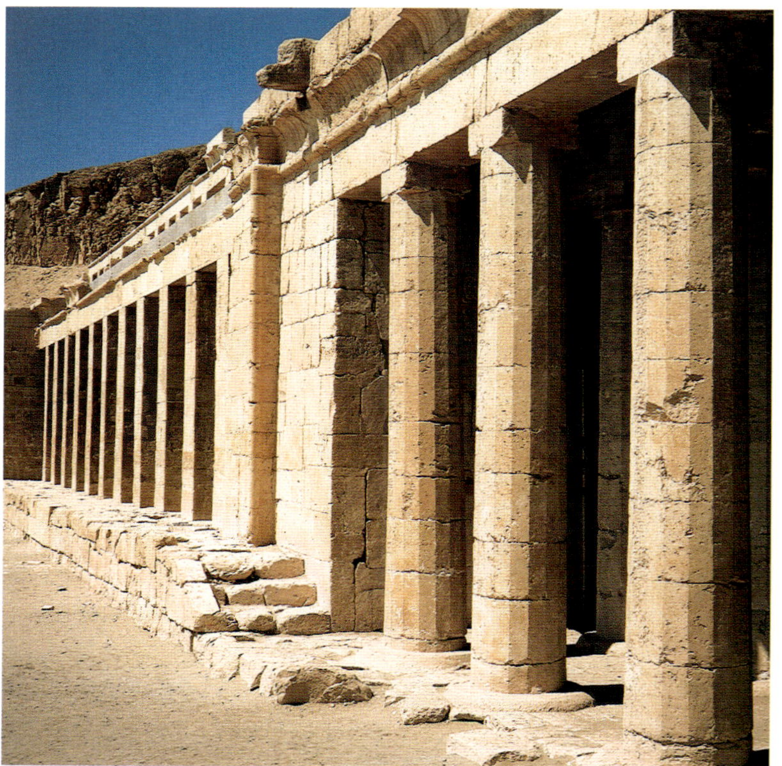

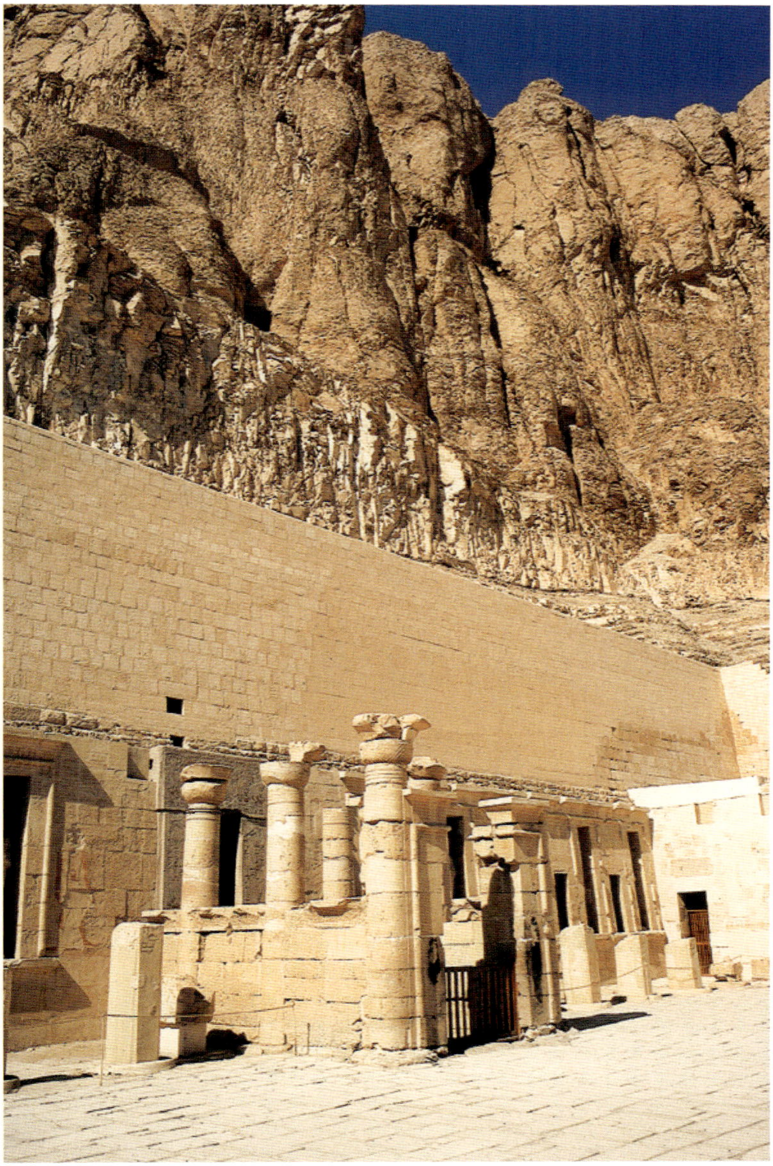

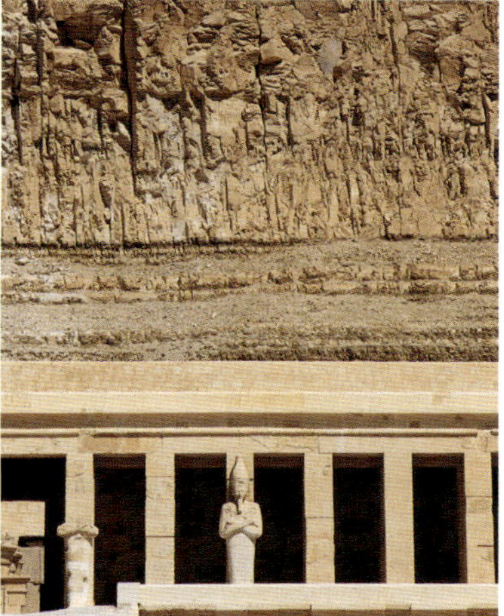

Above: The dramatic and exciting interplay between the rugged cliffside and the elegant temple façade.

Left: The sanctuary of Amun on the top terrace of the temple; it runs deep into the rock. The structure in front dates from the Ptolemaic Period, when the sanctuary was adapted as a shrine of the deified ancient architects Imhotep and Amenhotep-son-of-Hapu.

Below: A Hathor-headed column in the goddess's chapel in Hatshepsut's Deir al-Bahari temple.

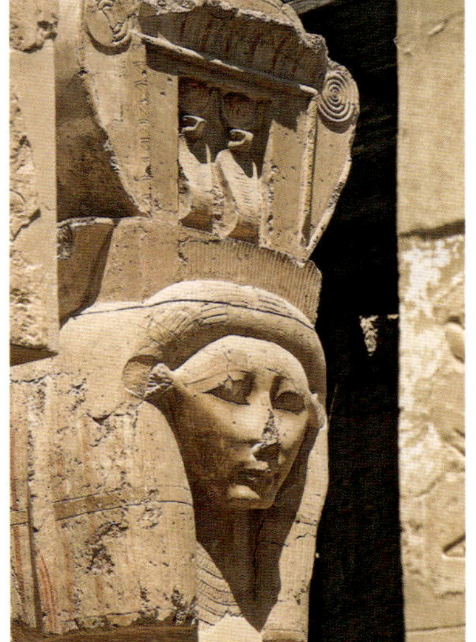

Thutmose III, her nominal co-ruler. Although it has often been claimed that her reign was peaceful, she certainly undertook military activity in Nubia, apparently leading the army in person. She also sponsored trade, especially an expedition to Punt on the Red Sea coast, which returned with myrrh trees which she planted on her temple terraces.

Hatshepsut and Thutmose III are often depicted acting together on the walls of the temple, but over twenty years after her death, the images of Hatshepsut were erased and/or reworked to depict Thutmose I or II, both here and at Karnak and other temples. In addition, the many statues placed in the Deir al-Bahari temple were smashed. The reasons for this belated attack on Hatshepsut's memory are obscure.

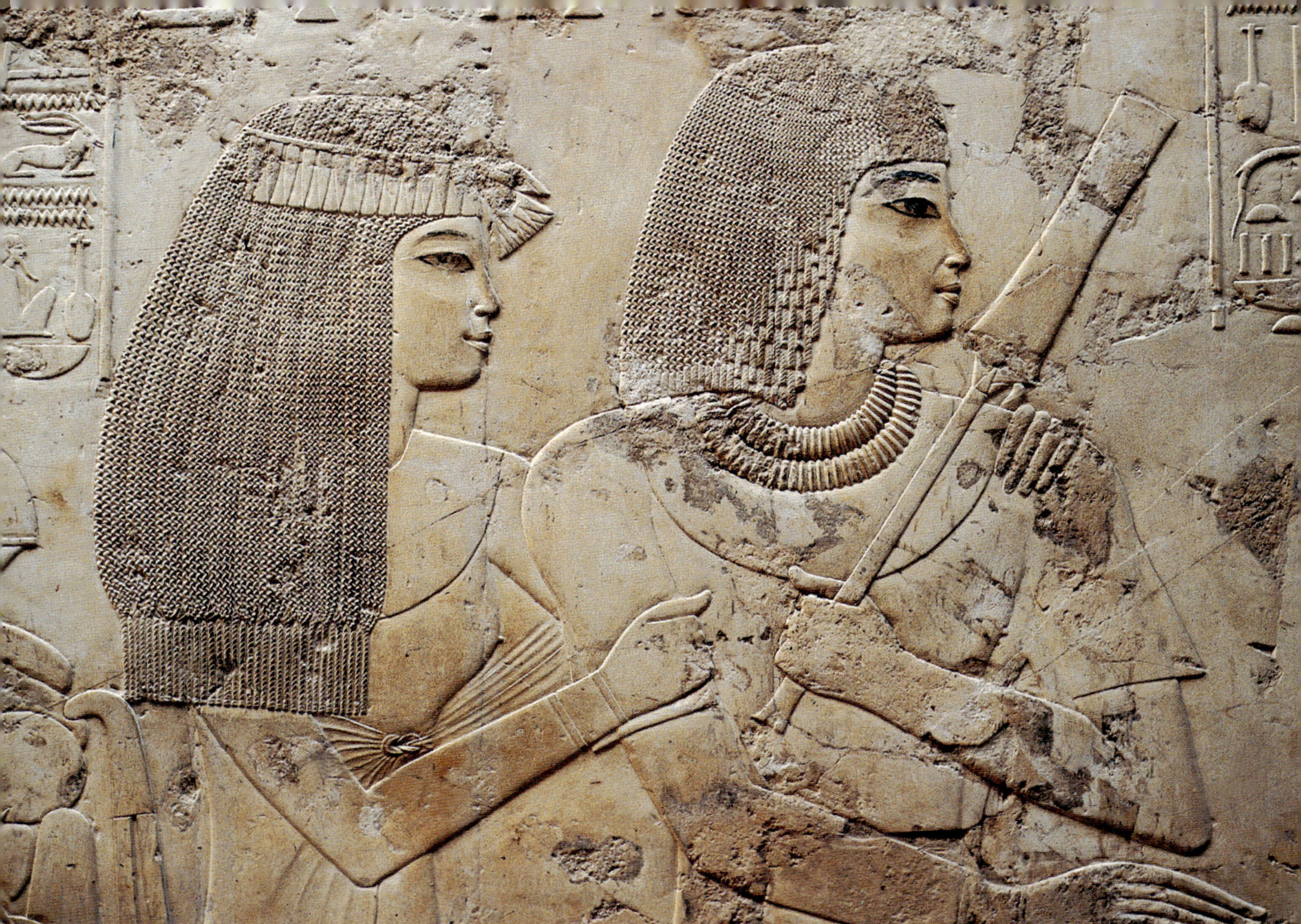

Above: A couple attending the funeral banquet in Ramose's tomb-chapel.

The Tombs of the Nobles

The noble tomb-chapels, which include those of priests and high officials, are in the plain and on the low hills of the west bank, between the road to the Valley of the Kings and Medinet Habu. They combine two distinct elements: at their upper level were funerary chapels where priests and visitors left offerings and performed various rites; below this was the sealed burial chamber where the deceased was laid to rest. Decoration was usually painted on plaster, owing to poor-quality stone, but in a few places the rock was good enough to be adorned in carved and painted relief.

Until the end of the Eighteenth Dynasty, the chapels were decorated with scenes relating to what has been called "daily life," including the production of food, feasting, sporting activities, and the career of the deceased. Later on, however, the scenes change to ones focusing on the funeral and elements from the Book of the Dead. The latter is the basis for the adornment of the tiny handful of burial chambers that bear decoration. This parallels the situation in royal funerary monuments, where the memorial temple has scenes of a king's career and such activities as hunting, while his tomb in the Valley of the Kings has decoration entirely devoted to the next world.

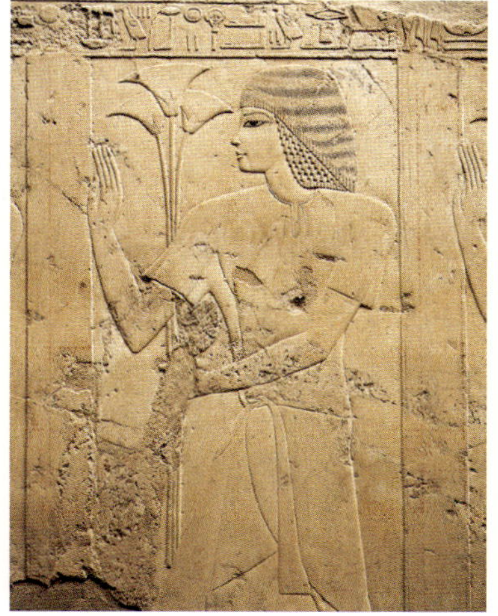

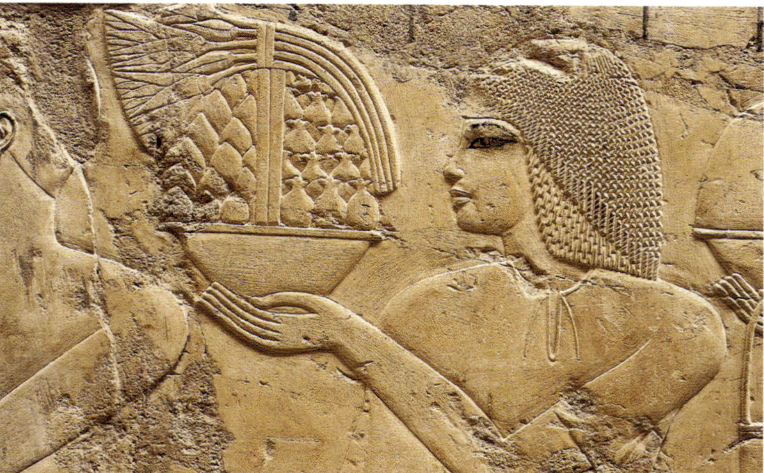

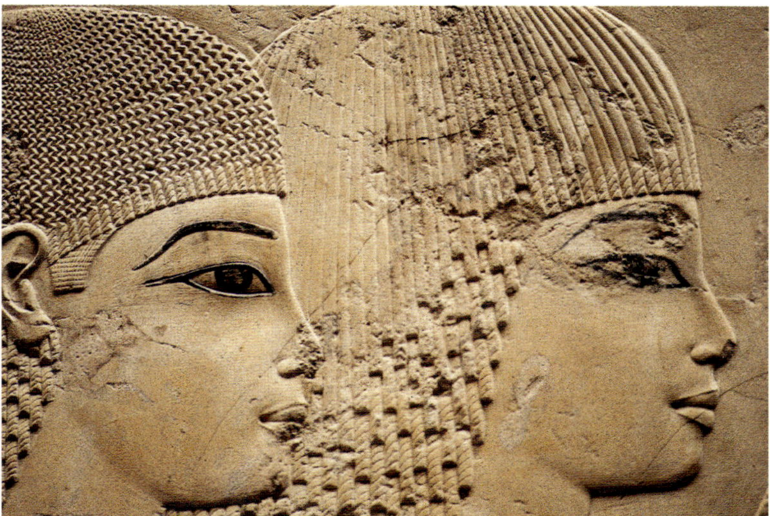

Above left: A figure bringing offerings to Ramose's tomb.

Above: Serving fruit at the funeral banquet.

Left: Closeup of another couple in the funeral banquet scene. The convention was to portray people in the prime of life, whatever their actual age.

A number of noble tombs are open to the public; all are interesting and most contain delightfully painted decorations. But the finest is the tomb of Ramose, who had the good fortune of constructing his tomb in better quality rock, and who was able to afford costly carved decorations. Ramose was governor of Thebes and vizier during the early years of the reign of Amenhotep IV (later Akhenaten), and he provided the upper level of his tomb with two pillared halls, although only the first had been partly decorated before Ramose's death. Exquisite reliefs behind show Ramose with his wife, as well as friends and relatives, making offerings, performing purification rituals, or, as on these pages, attending Ramose's own funeral banquet. These reliefs are all the more delicate for being unpainted, except to give coloring to the eyes. As well as these scenes in the classical Egyptian style, one area has them in the revolutionary style that accompanied the introduction of the Aten cult, and another has a painted depiction of the funeral procession.

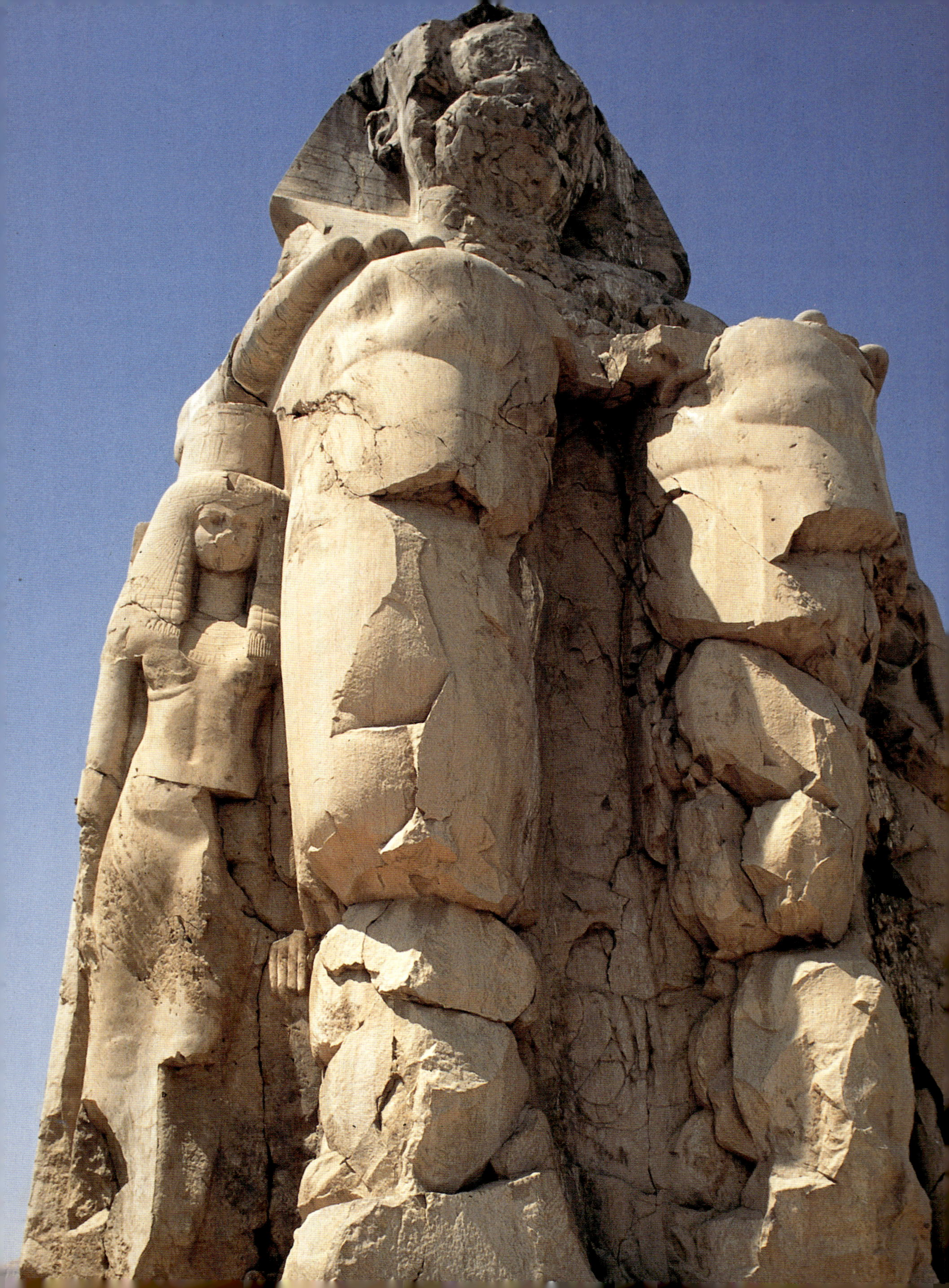

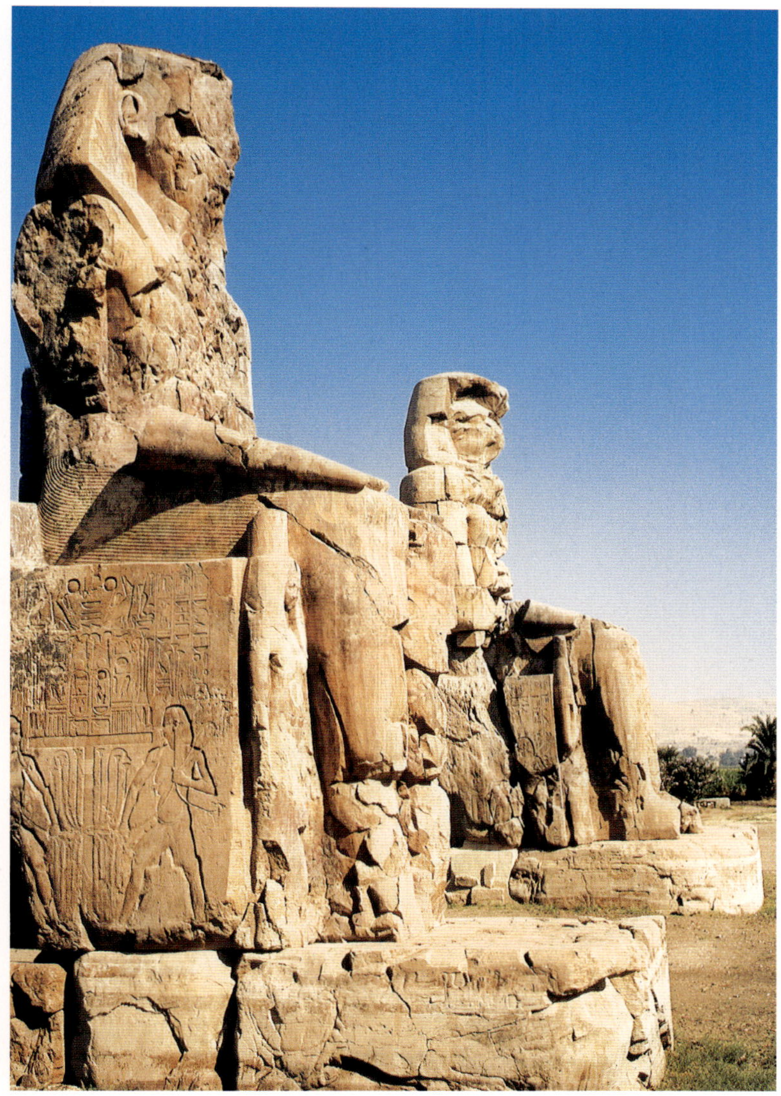

Far left: The left-hand or southern colossus. The power and divinity of a pharaoh was represented literally by his superior size; Queen Tiye, the beloved wife of Amenhotep III, stands on the left, not quite knee high.

Left: Greek and Roman tourists were especially attracted to the colossus on the right, for after it was shattered by earthquakes it would sometimes emit a musical note as the sun rose over Thebes. Visitors, including eight Roman governors, cut graffiti into the legs of the colossus, the inscriptions reaching as high as a man could stretch. The Roman emperor Hadrian came in AD 130 with his wife and a large retinue, and they camped out for several nights at the feet of the colossus and regarded themselves favored by the gods when they were finally rewarded by three performances in a single morning. A legend was invented to account for the phenomenon: Memnon was said to have fallen at Troy and now greeted his mother Eos with a sweet and plaintive sound when she appeared at dawn. Nowadays it is thought that the rapid change in temperature as the sun rose caused quartzite particles to split off, which resonated within the fractures. Once the colossus was repaired in AD 199, it cried out no more.

The Colossi of Memnon

Like other New Kingdom pharaohs, Amenhotep III built himself a funerary temple, but it was destroyed almost entirely within the next two centuries by his successors who used it as a quarry for building their own works. The most prominent remains are the two famous Colossi of Memnon that once guarded its outer gates. The colossi are in fact gigantic statues of the enthroned and divinized Amenhotep himself and were the largest free-standing statues surviving from ancient Egypt. At one time they wore the royal crown and were even higher. Over the centuries all memory of Amenhotep was forgotten and the Greeks decided the statues were of Memnon, son of Tuthonus, a legendary king of Egypt, and of Eos, the Dawn. Both statues have been damaged by earthquakes and are lacking their faces, and the torso of the colossus on the right was heavily restored by the Romans.

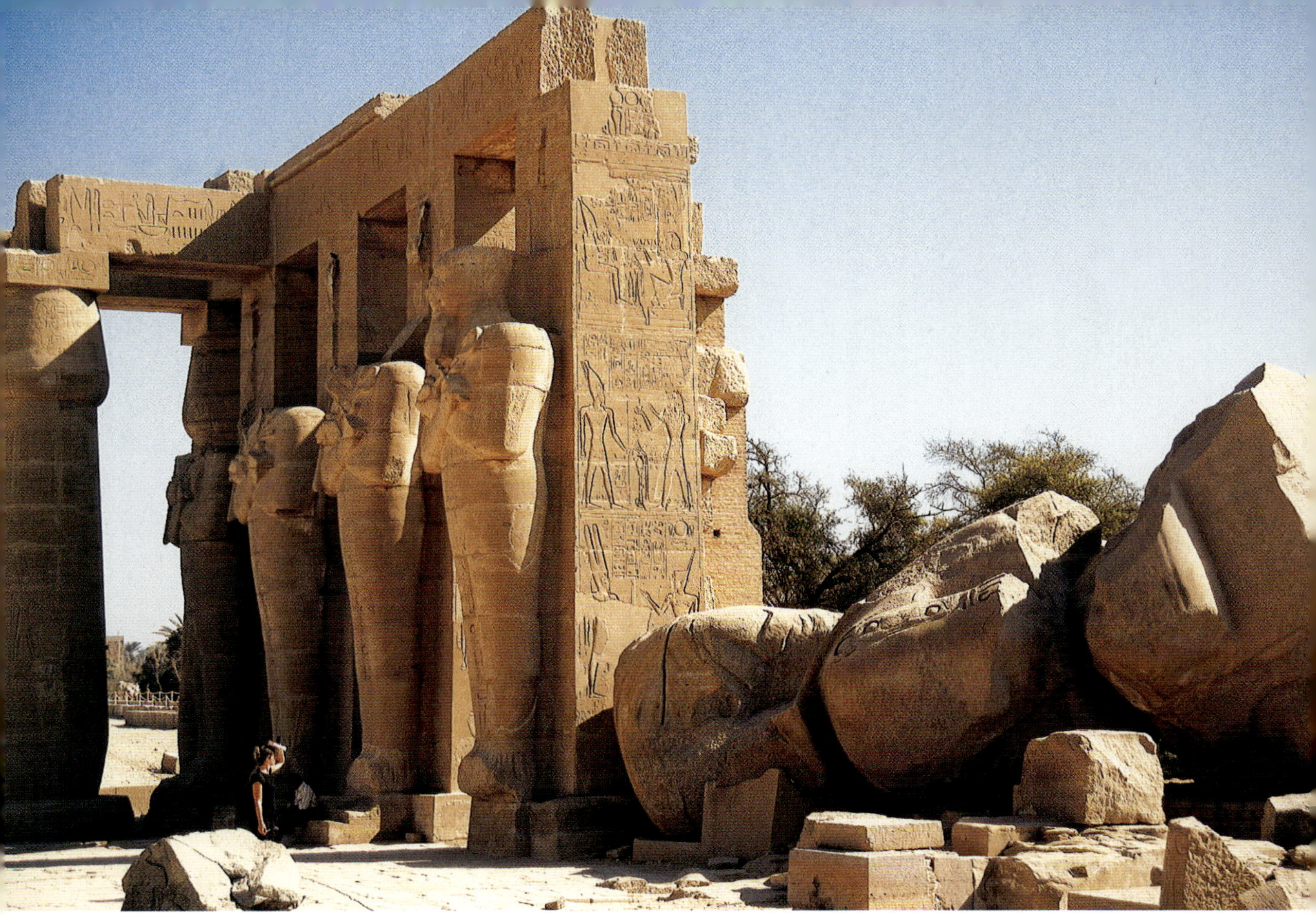

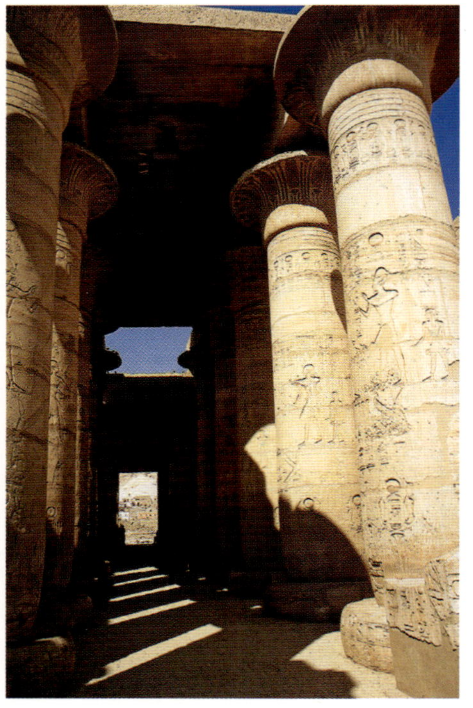

The Ramesseum

The Ramesseum, the memorial temple of Rameses II, is largely ruinous. But it is famous for its fallen colossal statue of the king. The first century BC Greek historian Diodorus was impressed. Coming upon the granite colossus of Rameses he fancifully interpreted its inscription, corrupting the pharaoh's prenomen, Usermaatre, as he went: "I am Ozymandias, king of kings. If any would know how great I am, and where I lie, let him excel me in any of my works." These were the words that inspired the English poet Percy Bysshe Shelley to write his poem "Ozymandias," the crushing reply to pretentious claims of power.

> I met a traveller from an antique land who said: Two vast and trunkless legs of stone Stand in the desert . . . Near them, on the sand, Half sunk, a shattered visage lies, whose frown, and wrinkled lip, and sneer of cold command, Tell that its sculptor well those passions read which yet survive, stamped on these lifeless things, The hand that mocked them, and the heart that fed. And on the pedestal these words appear: 'My name is Ozymandias, king of kings: Look on my works, ye Mighty, and despair!' Nothing beside remains. Round the decay of that colossal wreck, boundless and bare The lone and level sands stretch far away.

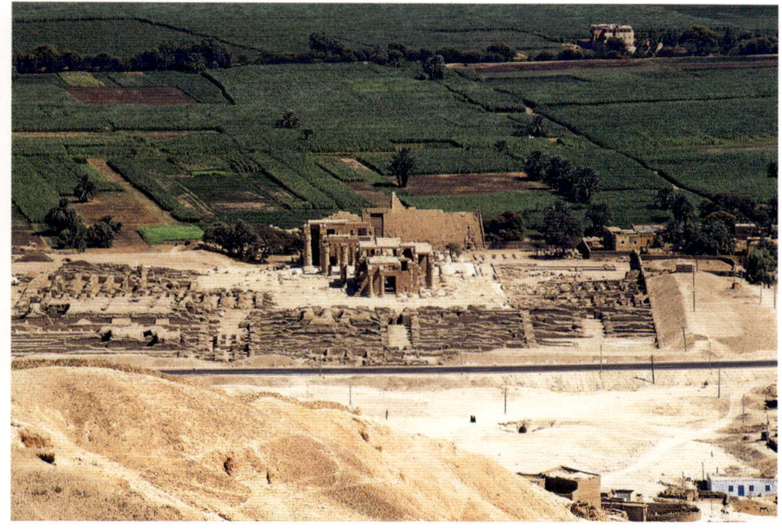

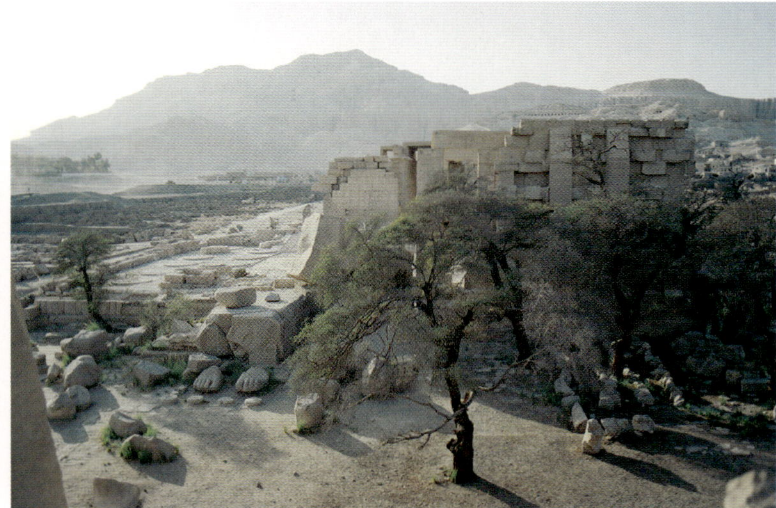

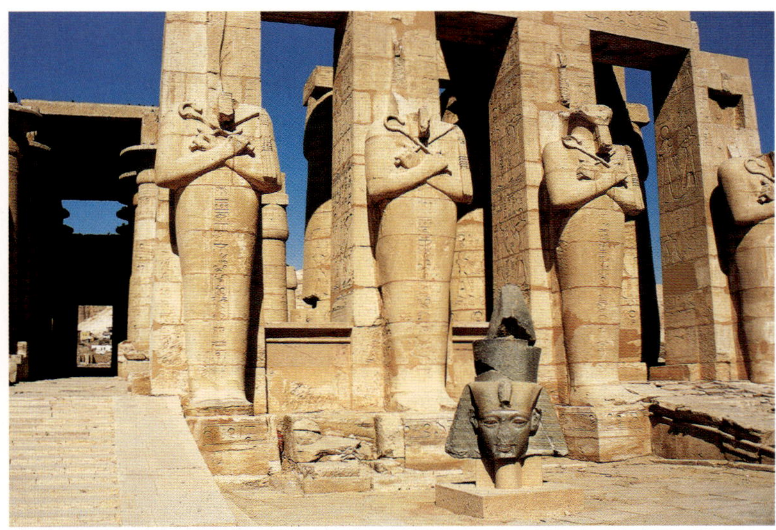

Far left: The fallen colossus of Rameses II, the Ozymandias of Shelley's poem, at the back of the first court of the Ramesseum.

Bottom far left: The great hypostyle hall leading from the second court. Only twenty-nine of its original forty-eight columns remain. Such halls were a typical feature of New Kingdom temples, with a higher ceiling over the central aisle allowing illumination through windows set upon the architraves of the adjoining rows of shorter columns.

Above left: The Ramesseum, the memorial temple of Rameses II, is part of a still larger rectangular complex enclosed by its original mud brick wall. The area was filled with vaulted mud brick storehouses, now largely ruinous, which held the vast resources needed to service the staff and maintain such a great temple.

Left center: The view westward over the first court of the Ramesseum from the top of the first pylon. The giant feet on the left belong to the fallen Ozymandias, which lies behind the doorway at the center. Weighing more than 900,000 kilos and once standing 17.5 meters high, this was one of the largest free-standing statues in Egypt. It is surpassed among extant Egyptian statues only by the Colossi of Memnon, and then only because of the extra height given to Amenhotep's statues by their pedestals. Just the index finger of Rameses's fallen colossus is one meter long.

Left: The front and back of the second court is lined with pillars bearing sheathed images of Rameses II. Where three stairways rise to the west portico of the great hypostyle hall, the head of another fallen granite colossus, not so large as the first, has been propped up. It is in good condition with only its nose smashed. Within a few centuries of its completion, the Ramesseum's stones were being recycled, its walls and pillars torn down by Egyptians, Greeks, Romans, and Christians to serve as building blocks in their own constructions.

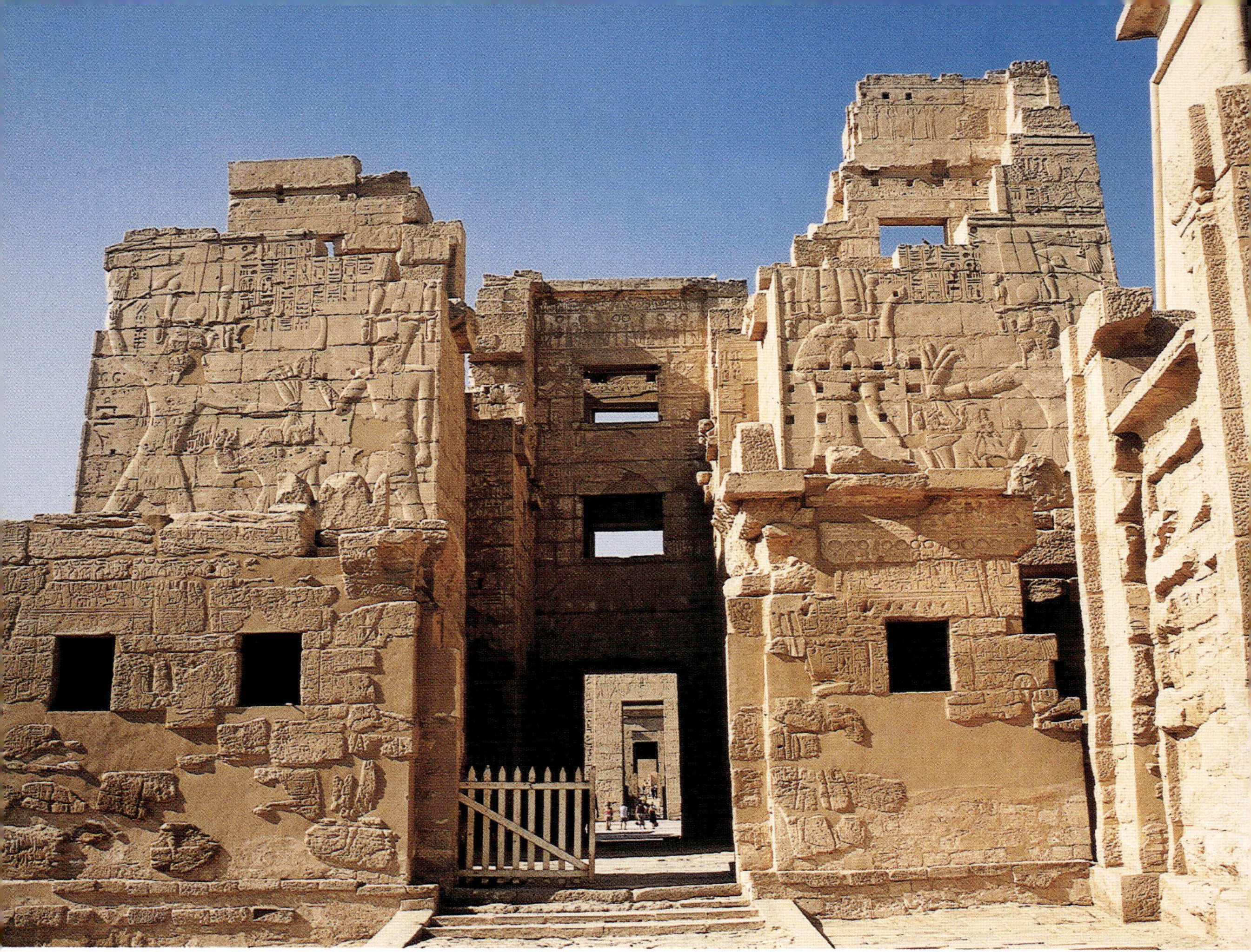

Above: The entrance gatehouse at Medinet Habu was modeled after Syrian fortresses familiar to Egyptian armies from their campaigns into Syria-Palestine. But here the purpose was not military: instead paintings in the upper stories show that it served as a rest house where Rameses III could amuse himself with members of his harem.

Top right: A winged solar disc representing Ra carved over the doorway leading from the west side of the second court.

Medinet Habu

The Twentieth Dynasty king Rameses III modeled himself in name and actions on his hero Rameses II of the preceding dynasty. Almost from the moment of his accession, he began work on his memorial temple at Medinet Habu, a close copy of the nearby Ramesseum and much better preserved today. He depicted his victories on its walls, and indeed he proved to be the last great warrior king of Egypt, though his battles were mostly defensive. He boasted of the security and tranquility that Egypt enjoyed under his rule: "I caused the woman of Egypt to walk freely wheresoever she would, unmolested by others upon the road," reads this fragment from his palace archives. Not long after his reign, the power of the pharaohs declined and Egypt became divided once more. His Medinet Habu temple was the last major architectural work of the New Kingdom. The temple incorporated a small palace on the south side of its first court. From here, the king could make appearances at a window that overlooked the court where ceremonies and entertainments took place in his lifetime.

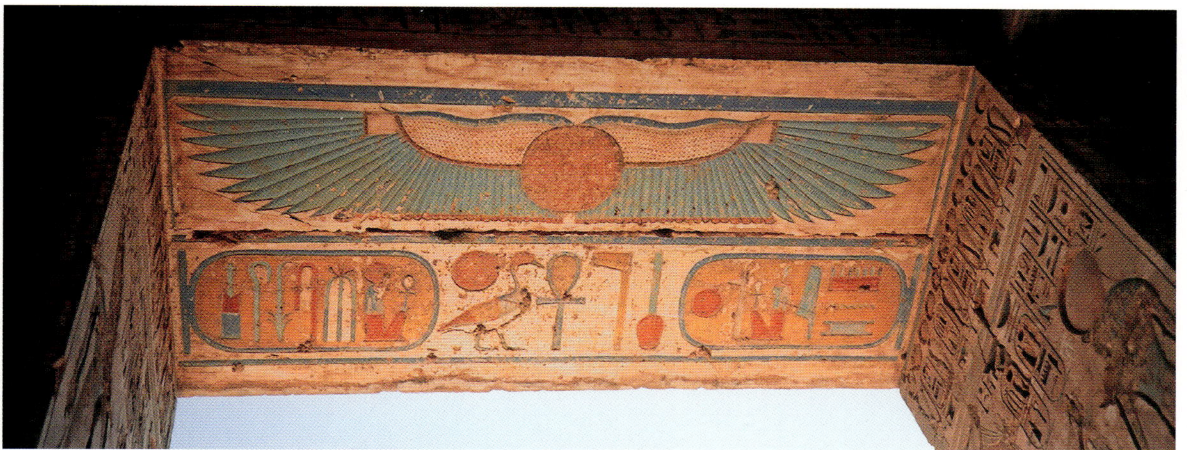

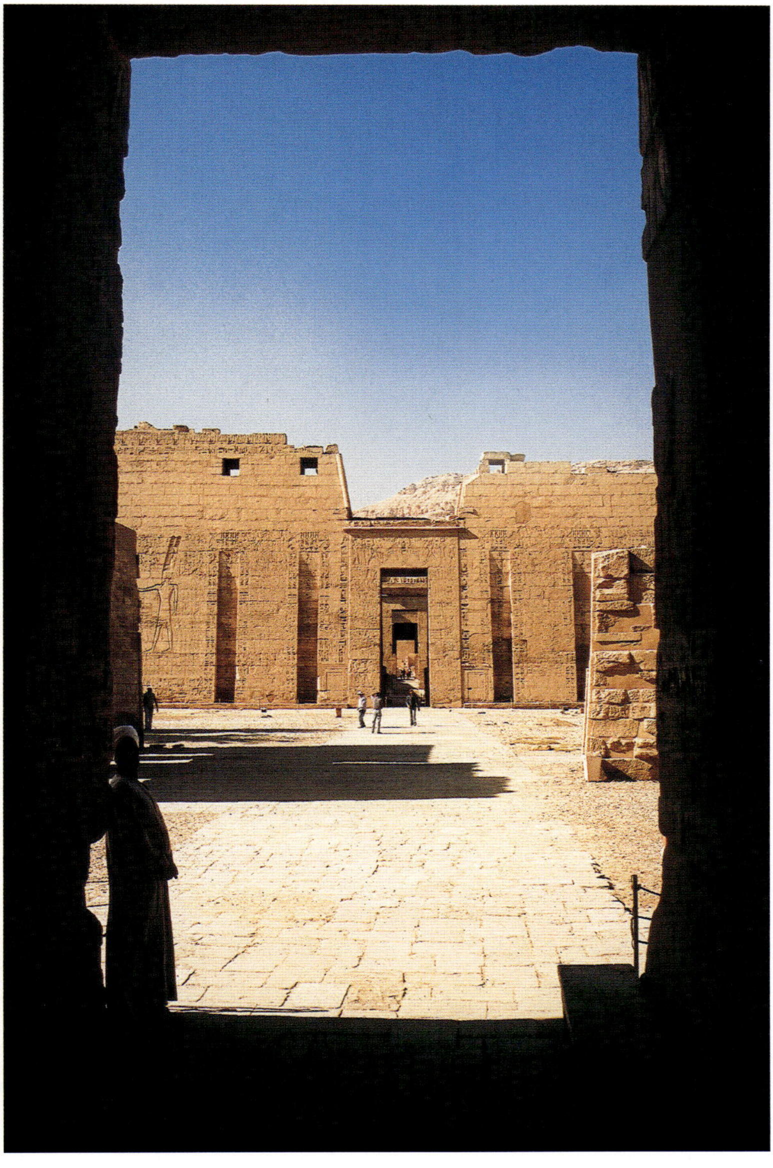

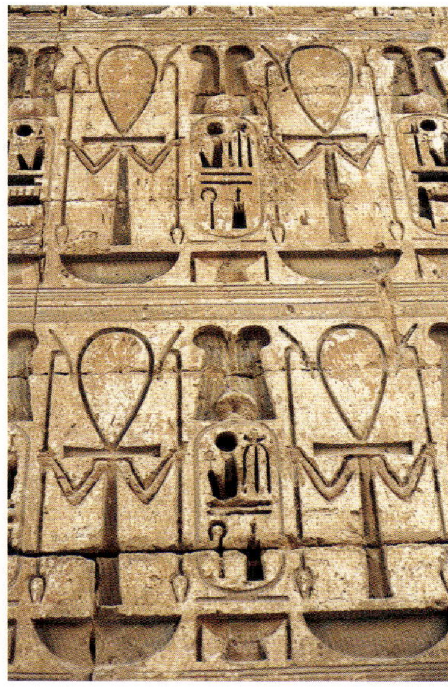

Above: The *ankh*, the sign of life, is usually depicted as a simple sandal strap. But at the funerary temple of Rameses III these *ankhs* have been given anthropomorphic form. Egypt's early Christians were inspired by the *ankh*; they prayed with their arms raised, and the halos hovering over the heads of Christian saints and martyrs in statues and reliefs were taken straight from the central loop of the hieroglyph.

Left: The first pylon seen through the entrance gate to the temple complex. Pylons, columns, and chambers become smaller as you go deeper into the temple, a characteristic of Egyptian temples generally.

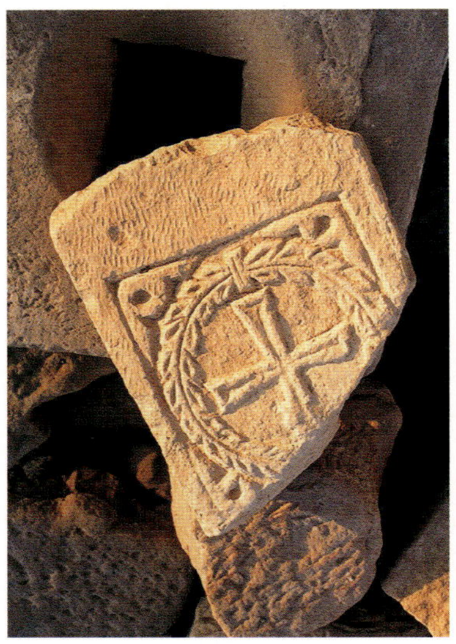

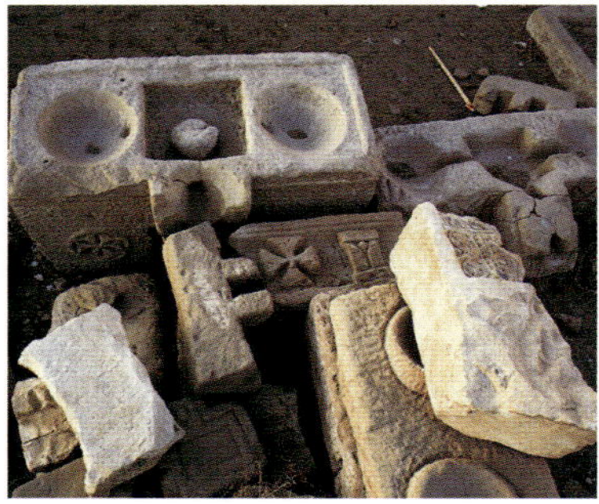

Top left and above: Fragments from the Christian church and monastery that once stood in the first and second courts at Medinet Habu.

Right and far right: The columns around the second court are in excellent condition and retain their bright colors.

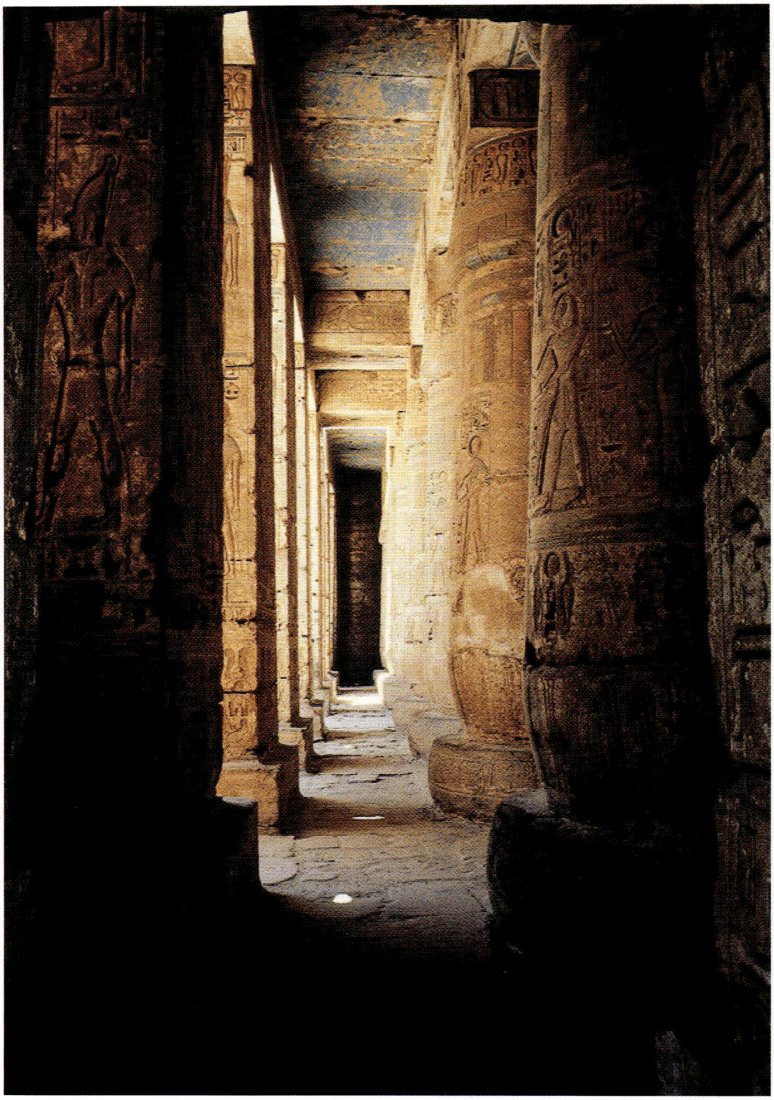

By late Roman times, the first court was filled with houses and a monastery, while the second court held the principal church of what was now a town of some size. Beyond the second court is the first hypostyle hall, roofless now but once with a raised ceiling over the central aisle as at the Ramesseum and Karnak. The halls and chambers farther west are largely destroyed. At the west end of the third hypostyle hall it is possible to trace the outlines of three sanctuaries, of Mut, Khonsu, and between them Amun. This central sanctuary was once finished with electrum, which is a mixture of gold and silver; its doorway was made of gold; and the doors themselves were made of copper inlaid with precious stones. Nothing remains but the granite pedestal at the center, which once supported Amun's sacred boat. To the south of this complex lie the chambers of the king's own funerary chapel, and to the north that of Ra-Horakhty.

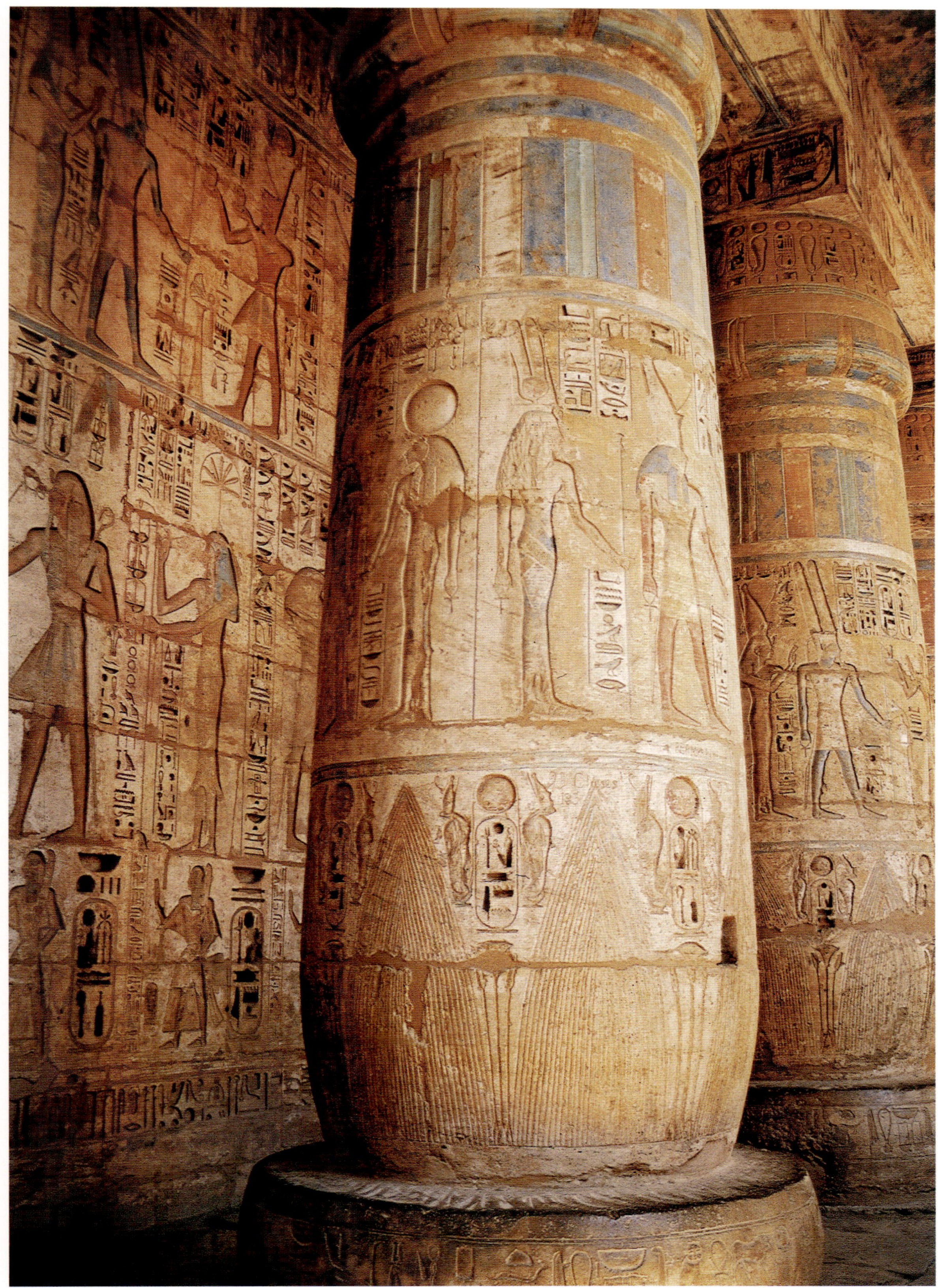

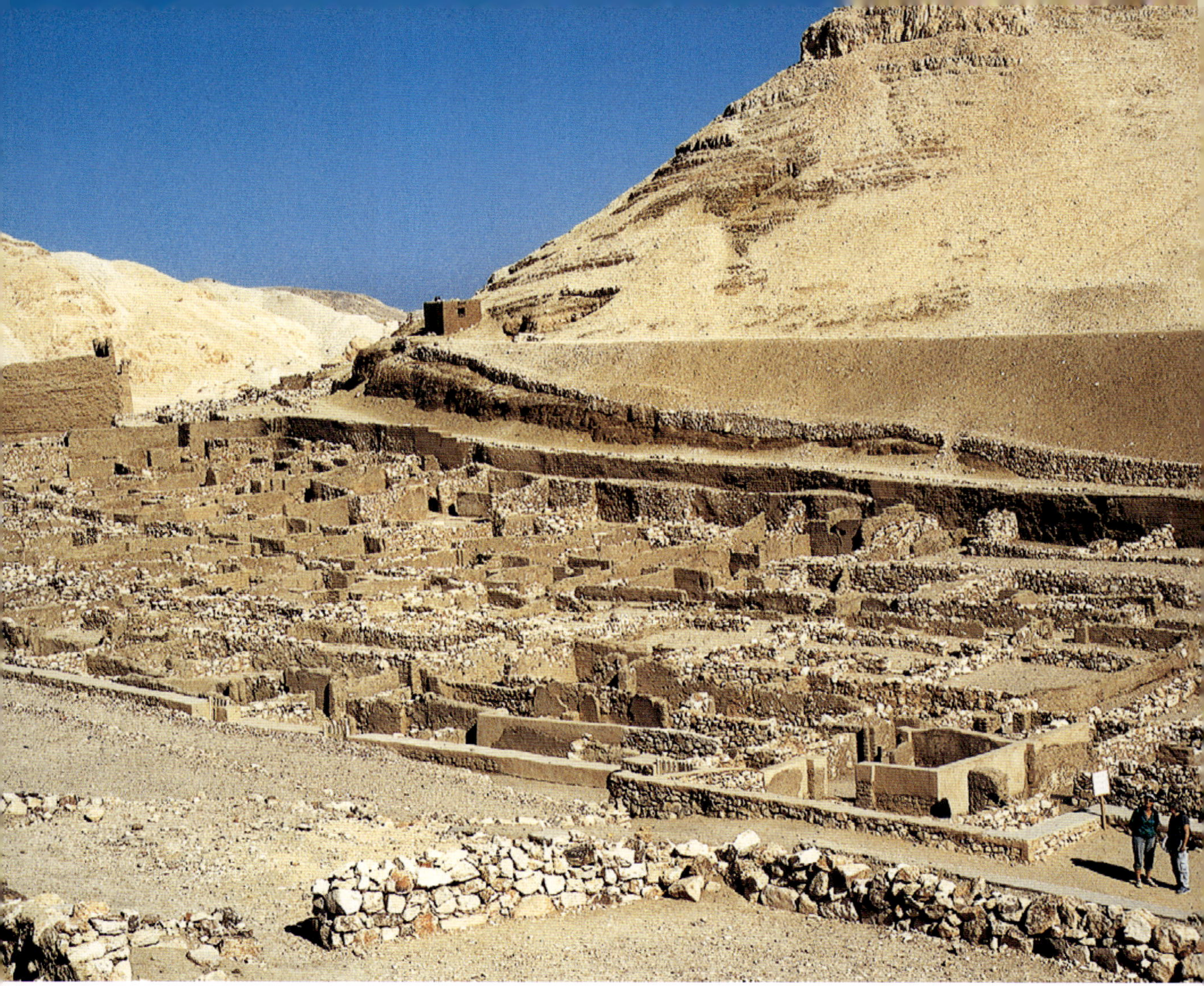

Above: The remains of the workmen's village lie in the foreground; beyond it to the left are the mud brick walls of the Ptolemaic temple of Hathor.

Deir al-Medina

Deir al-Medina was the village of the ancient tomb workers. The mud brick walls of their houses rise on stone foundations along straight and narrow alleys. The houses also had a second story or at least a living area on the roof, reached by stairs. These men, who were directly employed by the pharaoh and worked at the Valley of the Kings, were highly skilled and pampered artisans and freemen whose food was delivered to the village by serfs, and whose houses were swept by slaves. They made their own tombs and decorated them with scenes of the afterlife, borrowing from their experience of the royal tombs, and over their tomb entrance they would build a small pyramid. The tombs, like the village itself, date from the Eighteenth to Twentieth Dynasties. Deir al-Medina means the "monastery of the town," for the workmen's village and a small Ptolemaic temple to its north were occupied by monks during the early years of Christianity.

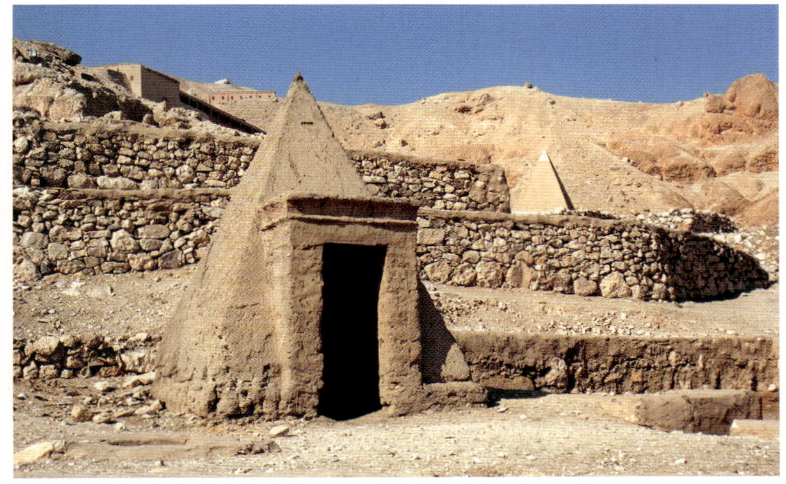

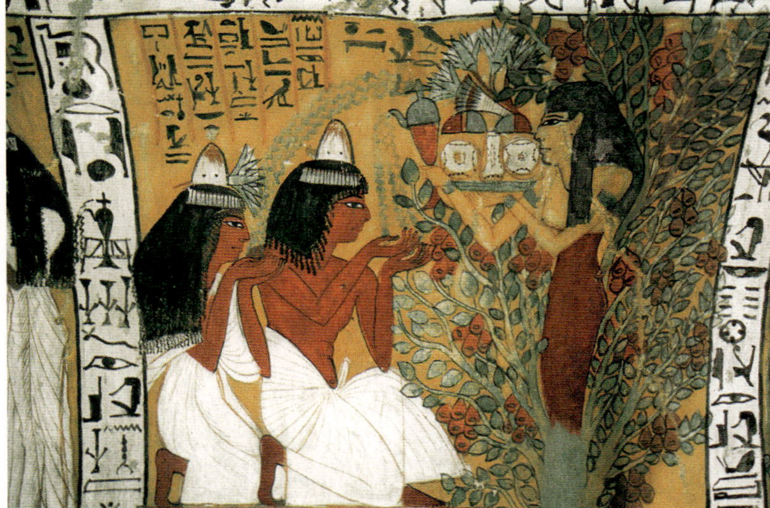

Above left: Deir al-Medina was founded for tomb workers by Thutmose I, the first pharaoh to be buried in the Valley of the Kings. The necropolis workers built tombs for themselves overlooking the village, often surmounted by pyramids.

Left center: Sennedjem and his wife make offerings to a tree goddess.

Below left: This scene in the tomb of Inherkhau shows a knife-wielding demon at a gate of the underworld.

Below: Osiris in the tomb of Sennedjem.

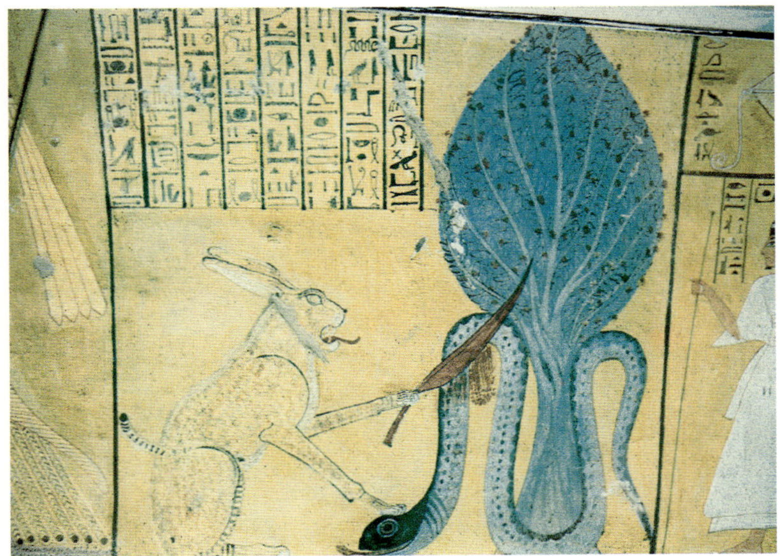

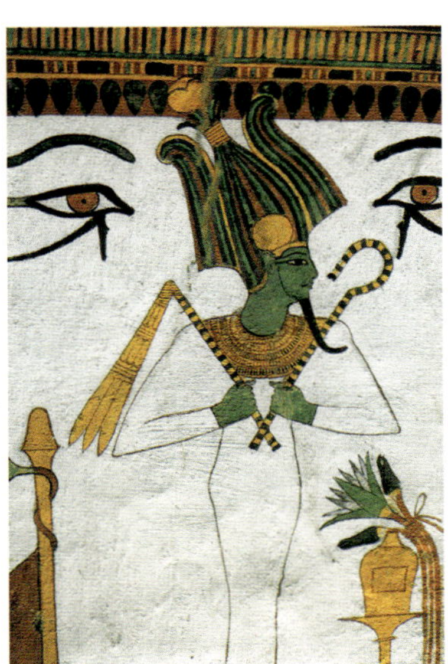

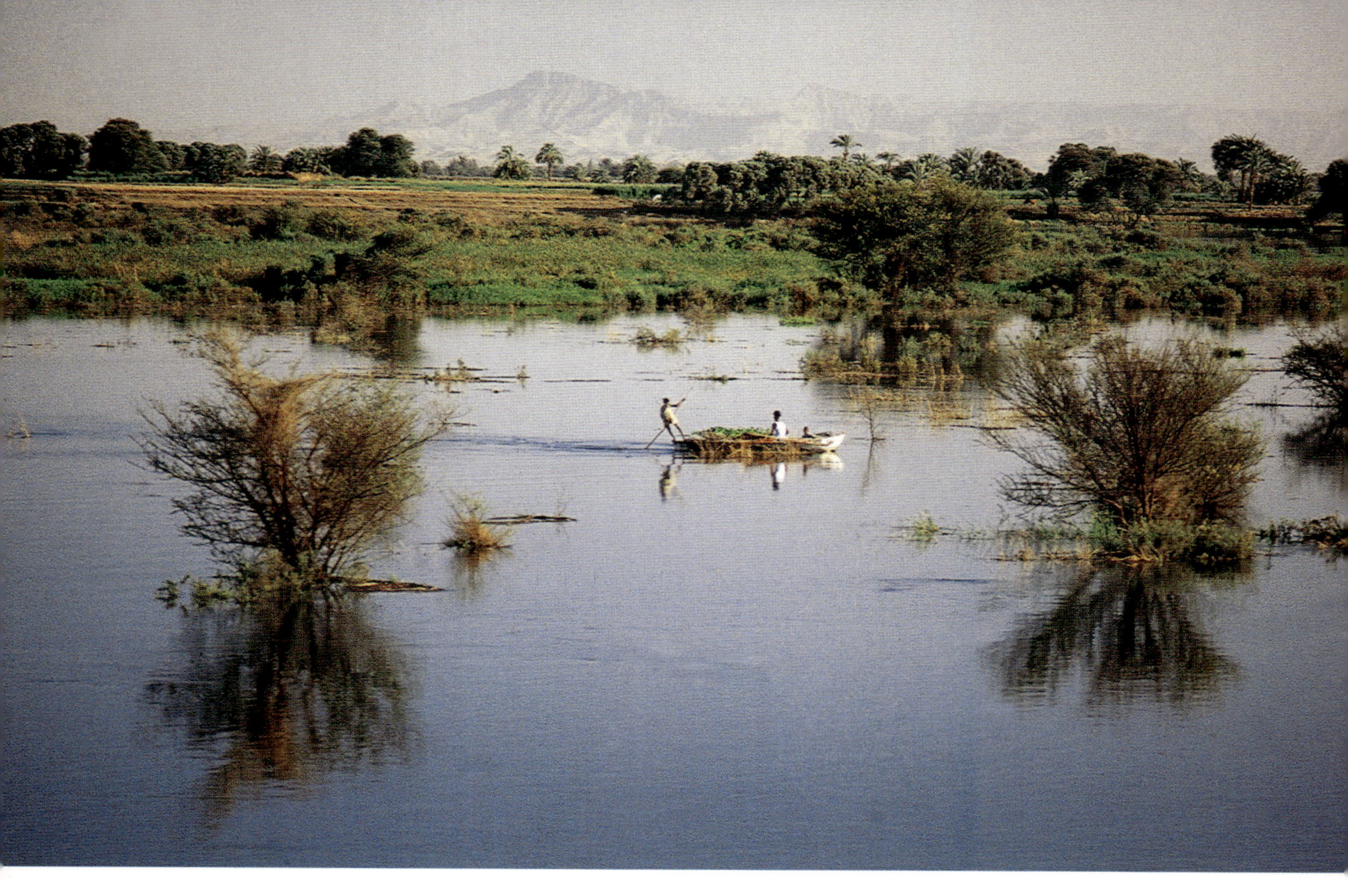

Above: The Theban hills seen from a hot air balloon. A paved road leads to the Valley of the Queens at the center. Deir al-Medina, the village of the tomb workers, is visible on the right. The tomb workers followed a path over the mountain to reach their work in the Valley of the Kings.

Right: Nefertari as painted on a wall in her tomb. Restoration of the paintings has revealed a startling freshness of color, as brilliant as it was on the day Rameses laid his queen to rest.

The Valley of the Queens

South of Deir al-Medina is the Valley of the Queens, the burial place of over 70 queens, princes, and princesses of the Eighteenth, Nineteenth, and Twentieth Dynasties. The earliest tombs were very simple, but some of the later ones are in many ways miniature versions of contemporary kings' tombs, the most impressive being that of Nefertari, wife of Rameses II.

Hardly any other woman of ancient Egypt was so honored by monuments as Nefertari, the wife and chief queen of Rameses II. Yet nothing is known of her background. Nefertari shared the first twenty-four years of Rameses's sixty-six year reign, those daring, dangerous, and glorious years when he took to the field against the Libyans, the Nubians, and most famously the Hittites at Qadesh. The two appear to have been very close, and clearly he adored her. We see her in the third year of his reign in the first court of the temple of Luxor, her graceful high-breasted figure standing beside Rameses's striding legs; she is also at Abydos, Karnak, and the Ramesseum, but she is most celebrated at Abu Simbel. There at the Temple of Hathor, completed in the twenty-fourth year of Rameses's reign, Nefertari appears as often as her husband. But for once Nefertari was not there beside Rameses when he dedicated the temple to his queen, as it is the last we hear about her until she was brought to her tomb in the Valley of the Queens.

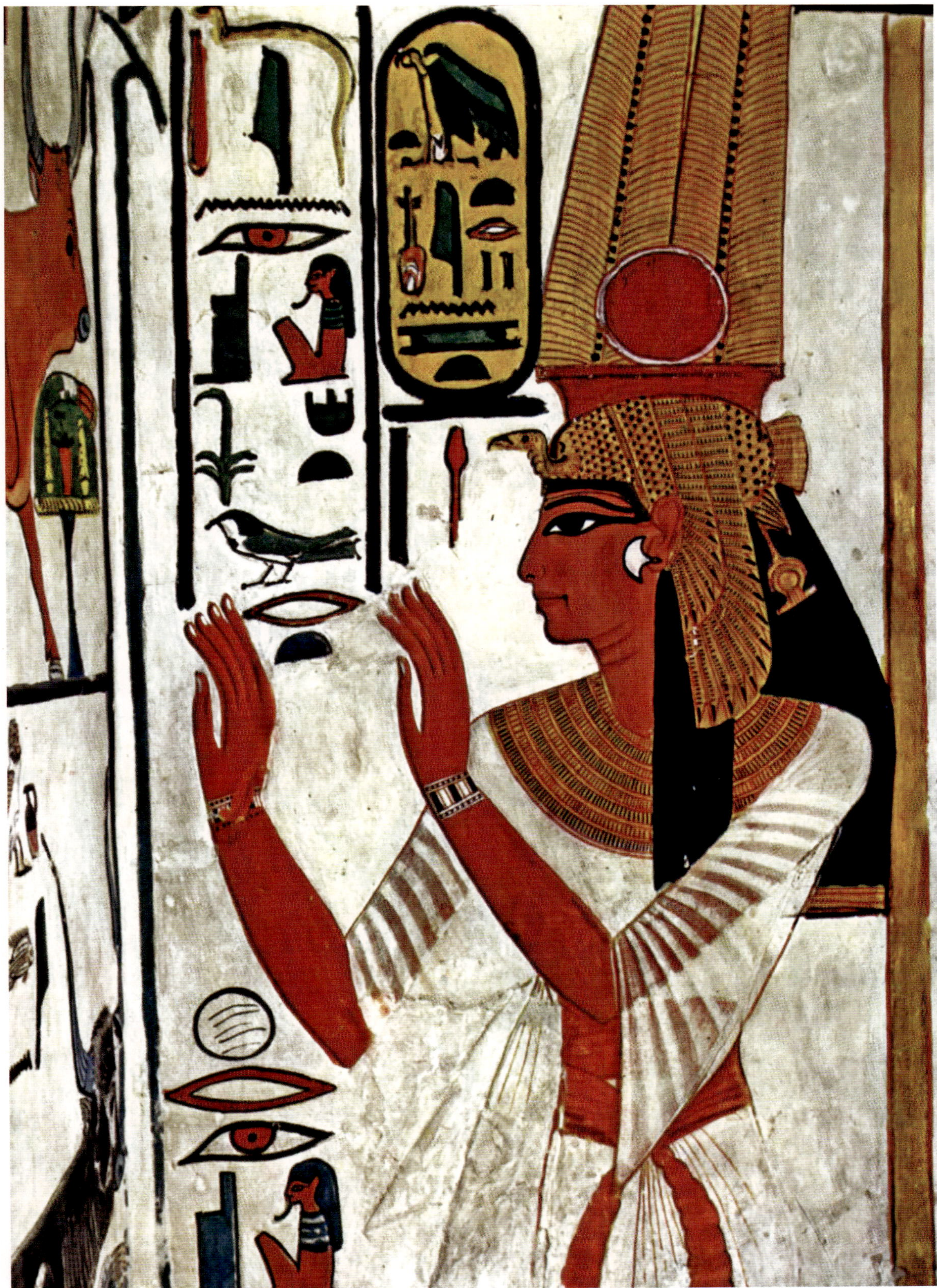

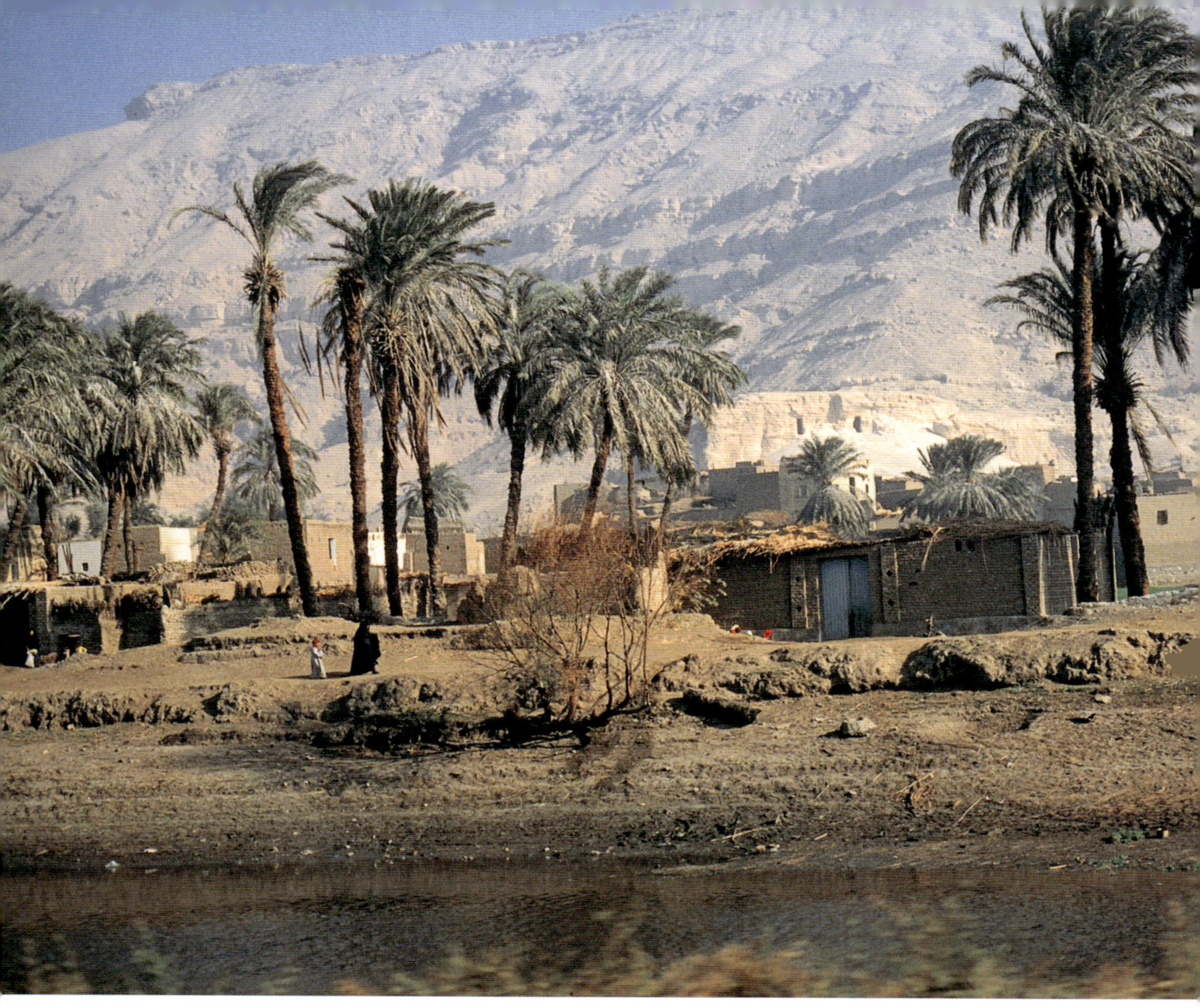

Above: A Nile landscape of village cliffs north of Luxor.

The Nile north of Luxor

As you follow the Nile toward the holy sites of Dendera and Abydos, the river meanders between the hills and cliffs that form the walls of the valley, a great groove worn through the sandstone and limestone of Egypt that has been filled with fertile mud from Africa. Sometimes the river swings against the rock and you notice the openings to tombs or the caves of early Christian hermits. When the Nile flows broadly, there are shallows and mudbanks and low-lying fields where land and river mingle. Hunters and fishermen pole their boats through knee-deep water, animals graze on half-sunken islands, and palm-roofed dwellings, like seasonal encampments, suggest the earliest settlements along the Nile. Egyptians have made their lives along this river since time immemorial, and before them this was the river of the gods, a magical sensation that lingers to this day.

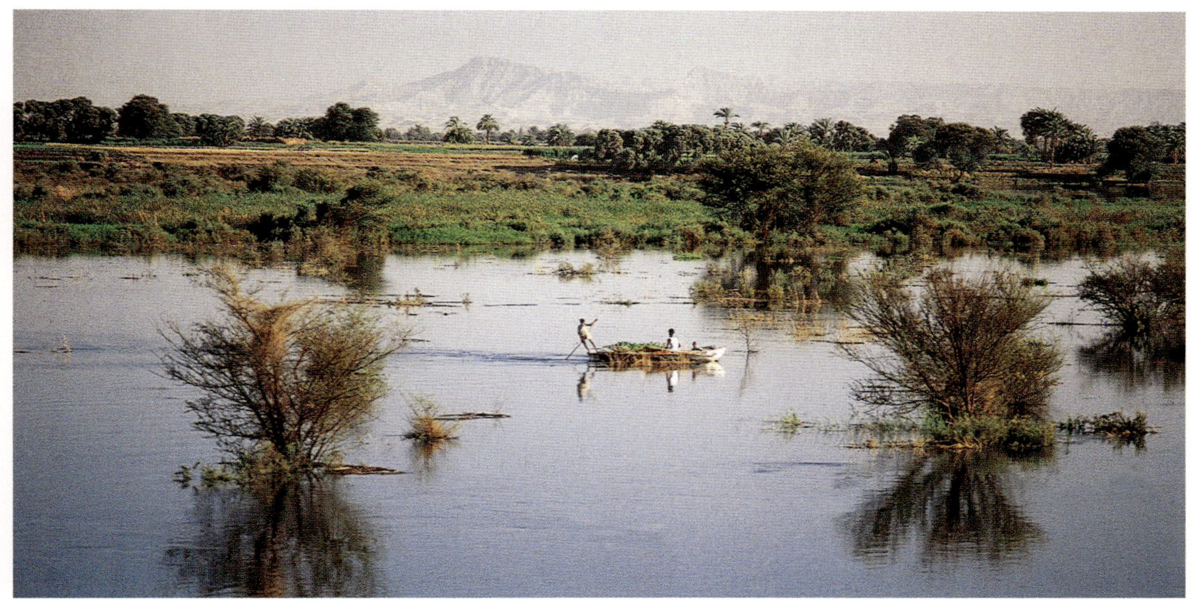

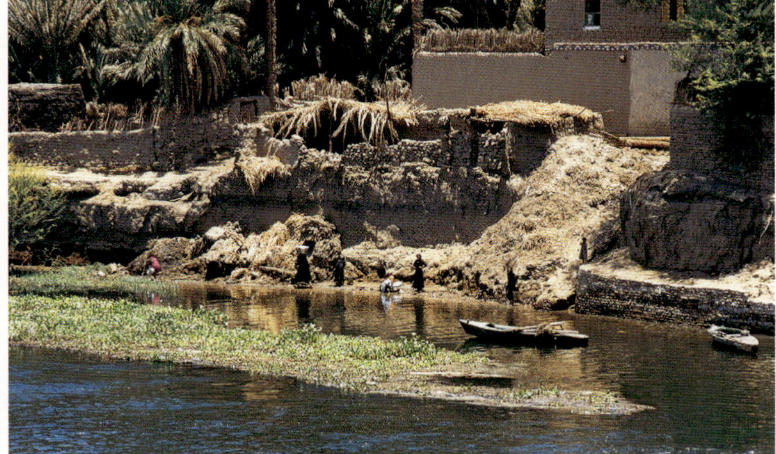

Above: Fishermen near Dendera pole their way amidst a watery landscape of reeds and river and low-lying fields.

Left: Women do their washing in the river.

Bottom left: Until the construction of the High Dam at Aswan, the Nile flooded the fields and left a fertile deposit of silt; now the river merely cuts away at the mudbank and farmers have to rely on artificial fertilizers instead.

Below: The entrance to an ancient rock-cut tomb close by the Nile.

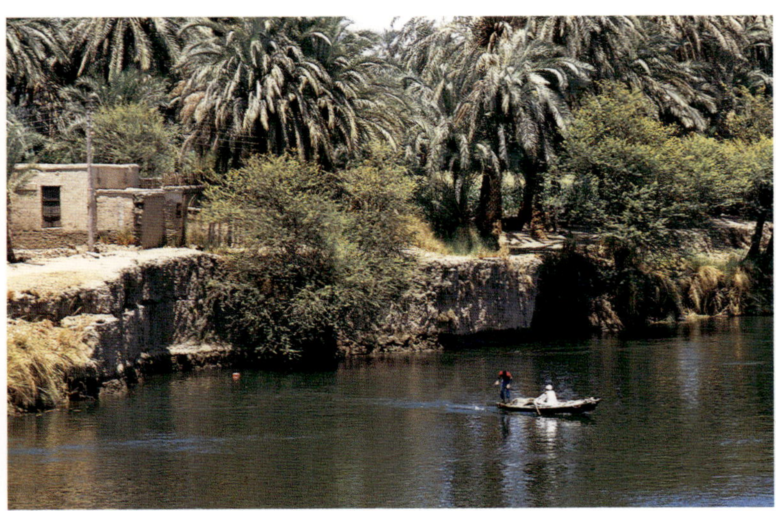

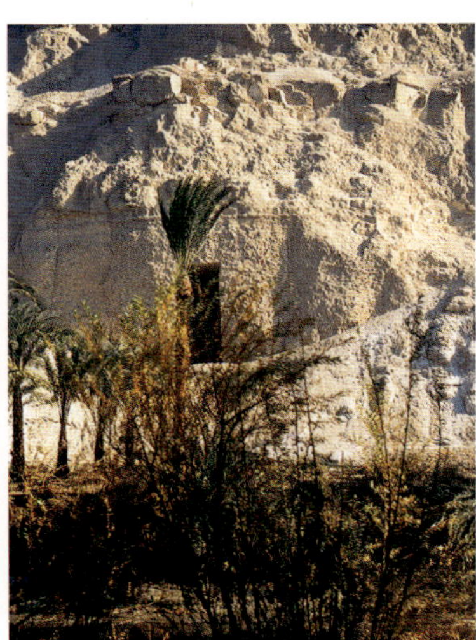

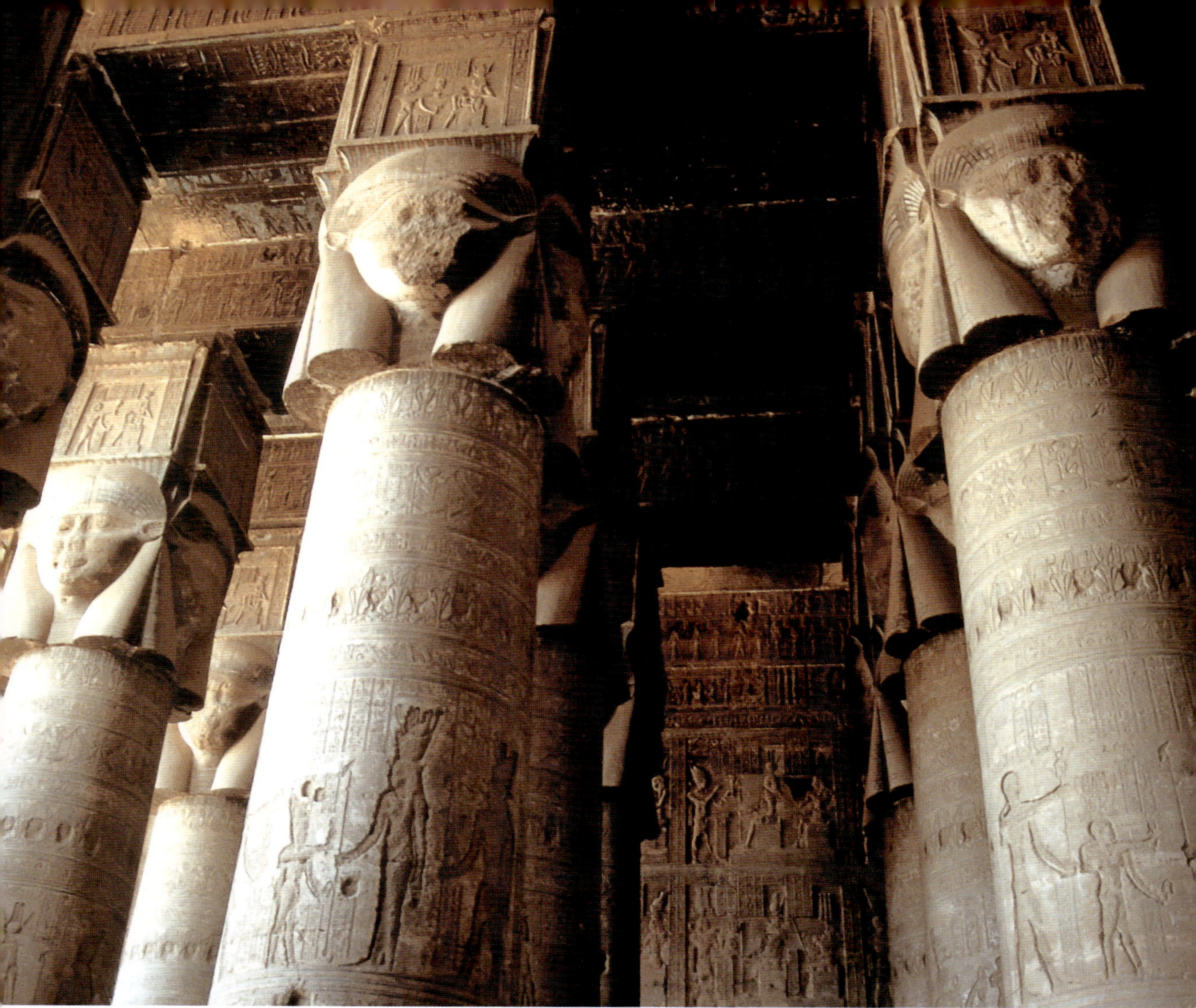

Above: Hathoric columns in the entrance hypostyle hall show the goddess with a human face but cow's ears. In her bovine form Hathor suckled and protected the king.

Dendera

The temple of Hathor at Dendera, across the Nile from modern Qena, was one of the holiest sites in ancient Egypt. Hathor was essentially the goddess of femininity; her various roles could include that of a patron of the dead and a goddess of fertility. She suckled the newborn god Horus, son of Isis and Osiris, and later she lay with him and became his wife. Their passion was re-enacted by a great annual pageant when Hathor emerged from her temple here at Dendera and went to join Horus in his temple at Edfu. As each pharaoh was Horus incarnate, numerous kings of the Old, Middle, and New Kingdoms built at Dendera, but the well-preserved temple that one sees today was built by the Greek Ptolemies, the last dynasty of all, and embellished by the Romans.

The entrance doorway of the temple opens on to a great hypostyle hall with Hathoric columns. Its ceiling decorations include the signs of

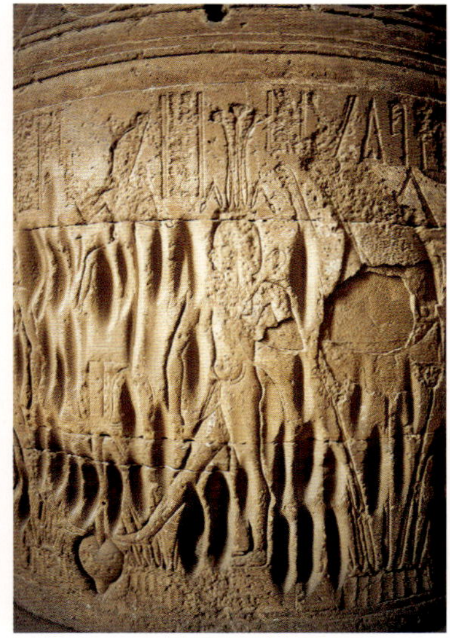

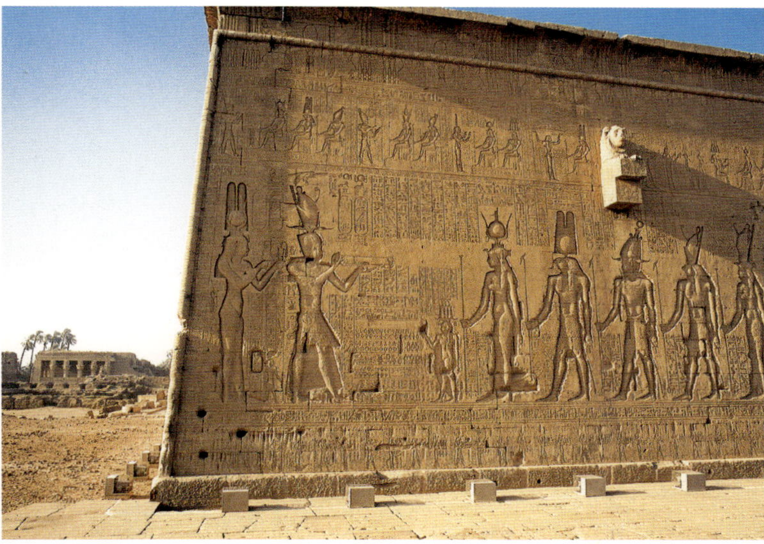

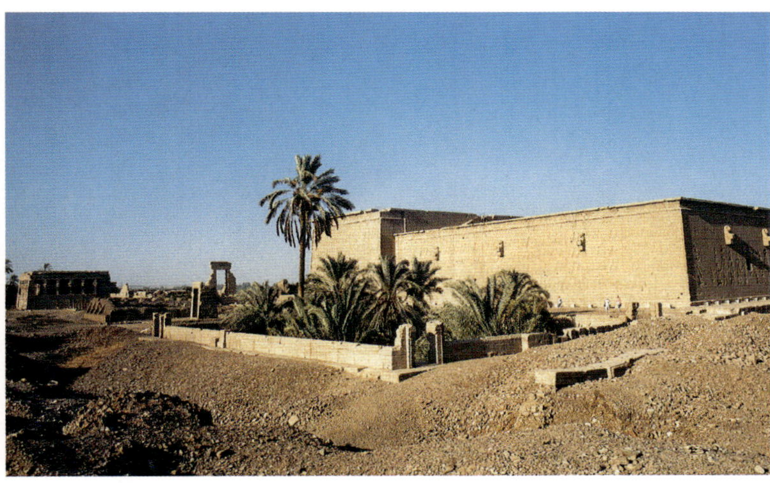

Above left: People who believed in the magical properties of the stone dust wore grooves into the columns.

Above: Colossal reliefs show Caesarion, son of Julius Caesar, with his mother Cleopatra VII, the last of the Ptolemies, behind him, making offerings to the gods.

Left: The priests cleansed themselves in the sacred lake in the foreground. Mysteries associated with the birth of Horus were performed in the birth house in the distance.

the Egyptian zodiac, with the various deities traversing the heavens in their sacred boats amid bursts of stars. The divinity reliefs on the columns were once covered with gold, and it is possible that even the floor bore a veneer of gold and silver.

The successive chambers become smaller, lower, darker. The sanctuary lies within, approached through the Hall of Offerings from where the divine images were carried in New Year processions up the staircases to the roof to a kiosk where they made contact with the rays of Ra—a spiritual emergence from darkness into light. The sanctuary was kept bolted and in complete darkness, but it was opened and illuminated by torchlight to permit the pharaoh to adore the goddess. These and other rituals are depicted on the inner walls. From a chapel behind the sanctuary the goddess embarked on her annual voyage to Edfu and congress with Horus.

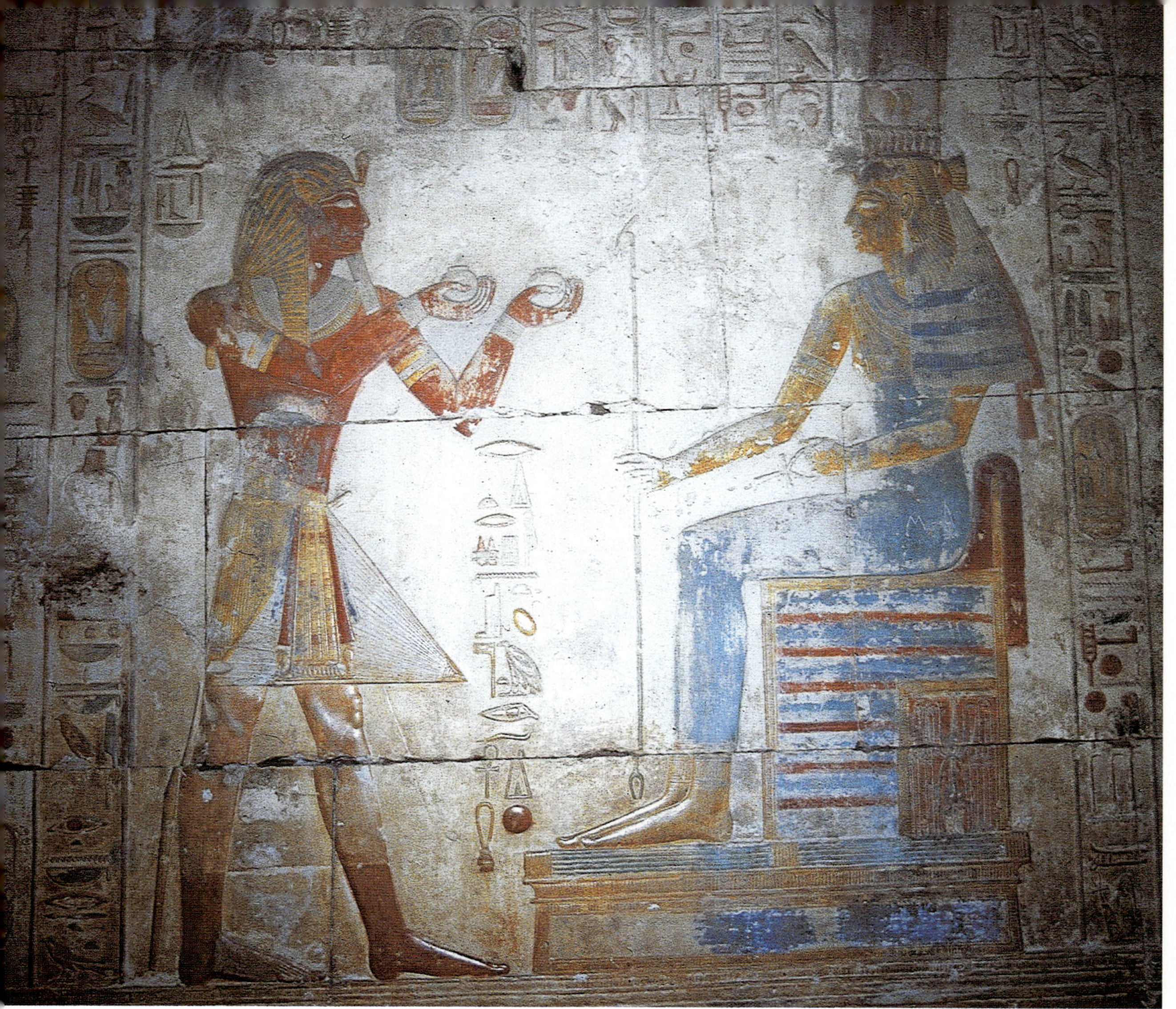

Above: Sethy I makes an offering to Isis.

Abydos

One of the most sacred spots to an ancient Egyptian was Abydos, on the west bank of the Nile between Dendera and Assiut. Abydos was the cult center of Osiris since earliest times, and the central role Osiris played in Egyptian ideas about the afterlife made Abydos a national shrine. The goal of all Egyptians was to visit Abydos during their lifetimes or, failing that, in death. For this was the very spot where the head of Osiris was buried after Seth dismembered him and scattered his remains. Isis, sister to Seth and wife to Osiris, put the pieces together again and miraculously restored Osiris to life as king of the underworld. Thus, for everyone the story of Osiris was the promise of life after death.

Abydos was the cemetery of the first kings of Egypt, and many later monarchs built shrines and temples at the site. The best preserved of these was built by Sethy I and is famous for its fine reliefs and its list of kings.

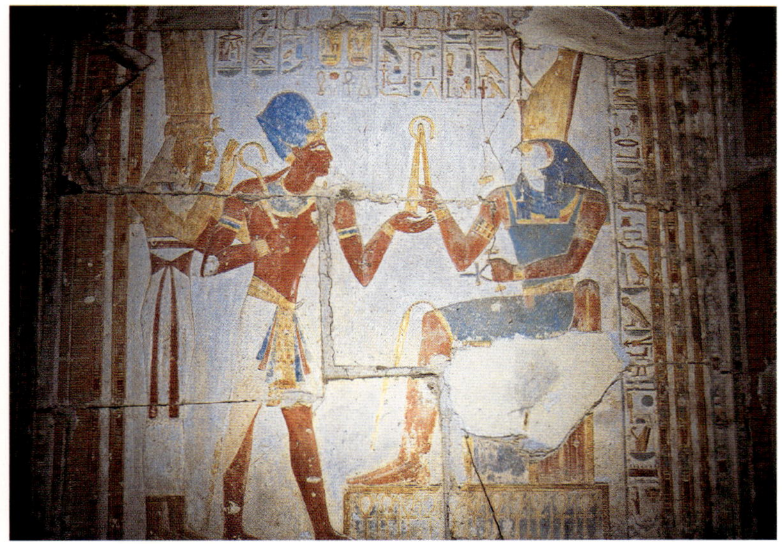

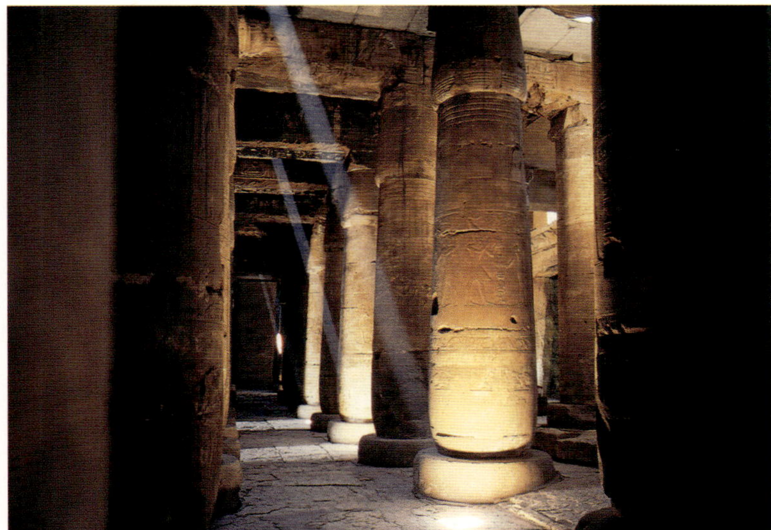

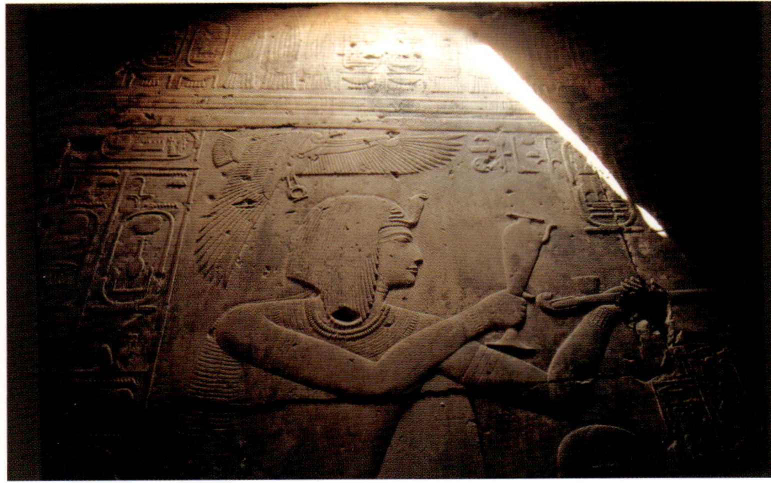

Left: With isis standing behind him, Sethy makes an offering to Horus, her son with Osiris.

Center: The second hypostyle hall contains Sethy's beautifully colored and exquisitely carved raised reliefs. In contrast to the technique of sunk relief employed by many other New Kingdom pharaohs, and which depended for its effectiveness and visibility on bright sunlight and strong shadows, Sethy favored the more difficult and time-consuming technique of raised relief.

Bottom: This delicately worked raised relief profile of Sethy I adorns the Gallery of Kings, which is carved with the cartouches of his predecessors. The list is incomplete, with the late Middle Kingdom and the whole Second Intermediate Period missing, probably for reasons of space. The list also jumps from Amenhotep III to Horemheb, with Akhenaten and his immediate successors omitted for political and theological reasons. Nevertheless the seventy-six cartouches have assisted Egyptologists in determining the correct order of pharaonic succession from the time of the first pharaohs onward.

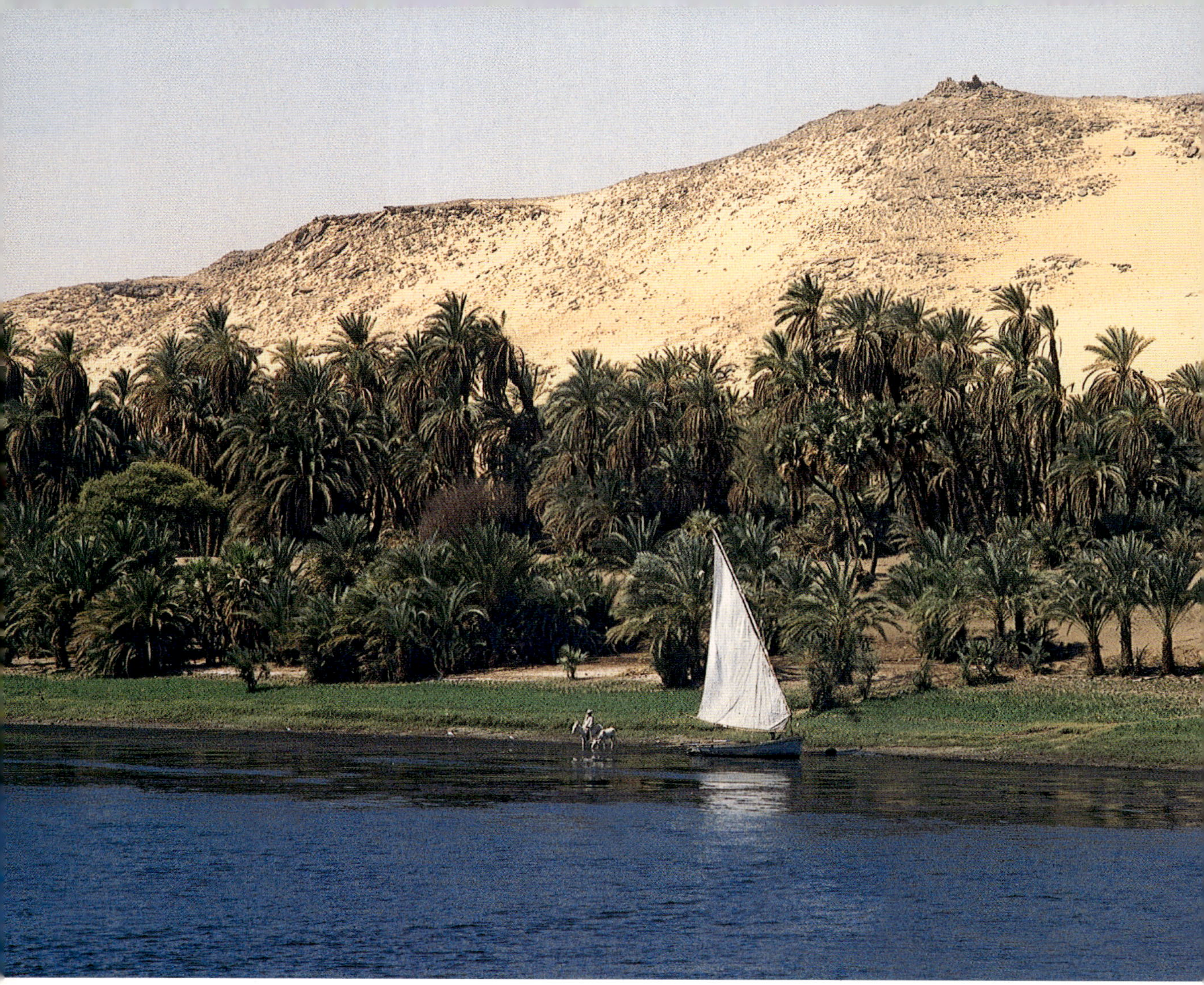

Above: The date palm is characteristic of Upper Egypt. Its dense sweet fruit is highly nutritious and requires little water. Cultivated in Egypt for six thousand years, the date palm has long been seen as a symbol of fertility, growing miraculously on the edge of the desert and nourished by the Nile.

The Nile south of Luxor

The landscape along the Nile changes as you head upstream toward Aswan. The limestone bed of Egypt gives way to the sandstone used in almost all ancient temple building from the New Kingdom onward. The width of the cultivation begins to narrow and the forbidding desert encroaches on either side. Though Egyptian skies are virtually rainless, the Nile is a pulsing artery of life, its banks vibrant with the rhythm of bright green fields. The very existence of the Egyptian people depends on the Nile, which throughout their history has been both their provider and taskmaster.

Farming developed in the Nile Valley around 5500 BC, and even the narrowest patches brought superabundant harvests which allowed for the development of an increasingly sophisticated civilization. The Ptolemies in particular left their mark along this stretch of the Nile, building temples at Esna, Edfu, and Kom Ombo.

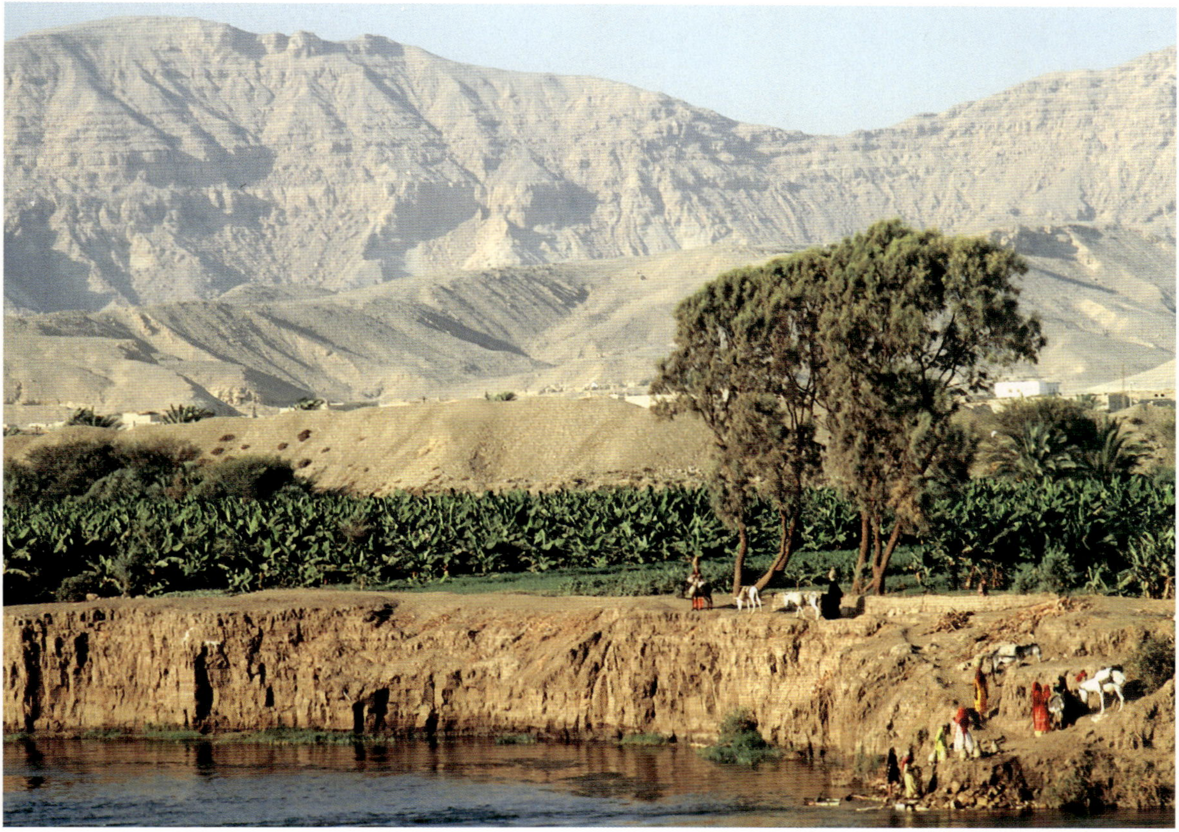

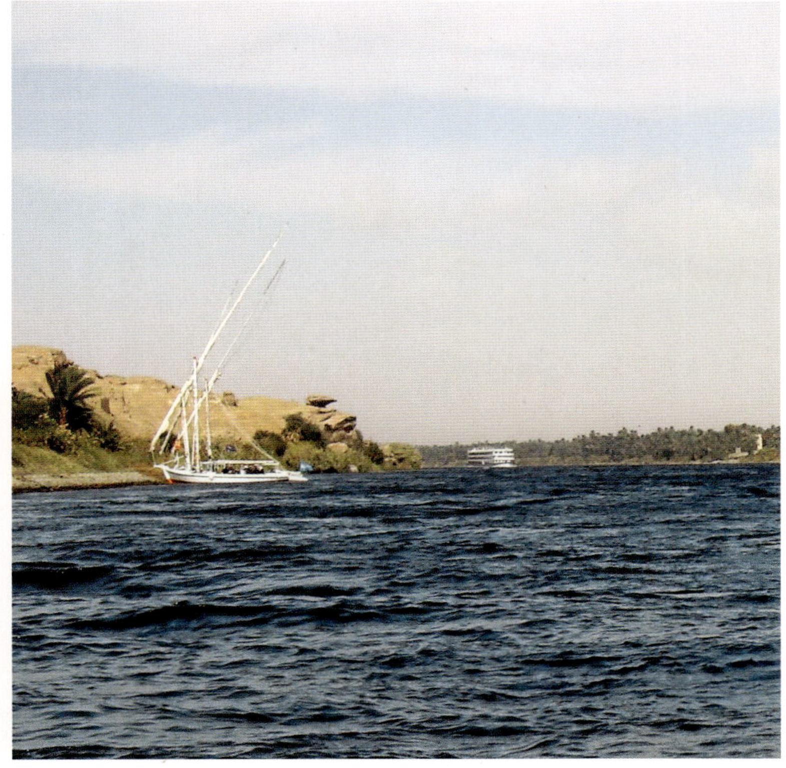

Above: Egypt is an almost entirely rainless country of dry and barren desert. The Nile is the only perennial source of water and nearly all the nation's inhabitants are confined to the three percent of the country taken up by the Nile valley and the Delta.

Left: At Silsileh, the Nile passes through a defile, with the desert hills coming right down to the river, and once thought to mark a cataract. It was from here that the sandstone used in building temples of Upper Egypt was extracted, the underlying rock of Egypt changing from limestone to sandstone just south of Edfu, some 30 kilometers to the north of Silsileh.

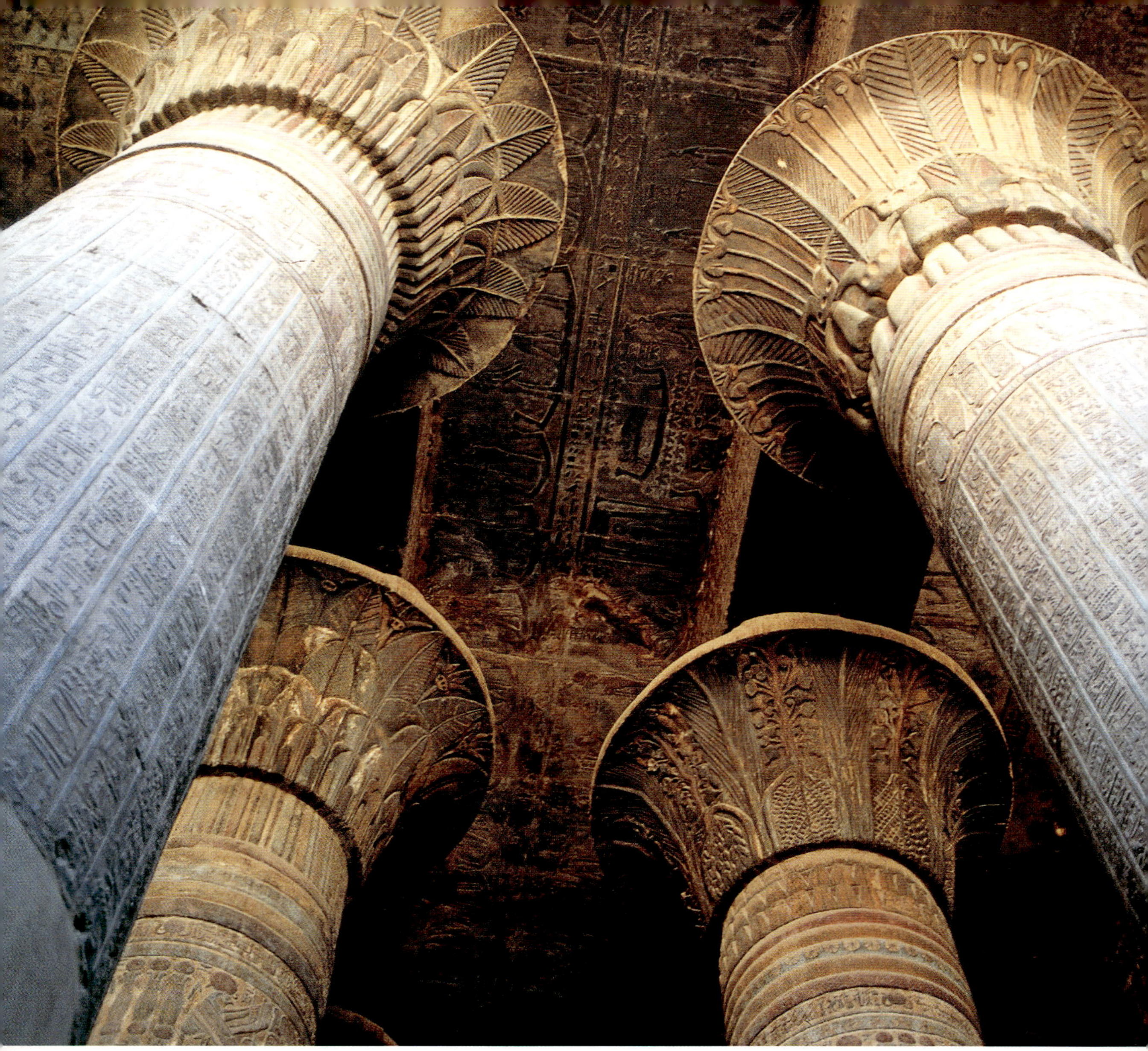

Above: The twenty-four columns of the hypostyle hall of the Temple of Khnum at Esna are covered with reliefs and inscriptions and have elaborate floral capitals. The texts on the columns give a full and rich picture chronicle of the sacred year. The ceiling is carved with astronomical representations.

Esna

The god Khnum was associated with annual Nile flood, which renewed the fertility of the land, and his ram's head likewise suggested procreative powers. At the Temple of Khnum at Esna he was also worshiped as the god who fashioned man on his potter's wheel. Ptolemy VI built the temple in the early second century BC over the ruins of earlier structures. The Roman emperor Claudius added a hypostyle hall in the mid-first century AD. The ground level subsequently rose and the entire temple was once covered over with houses. The site, which is in the middle of town and adjoins a flourishing awning-covered market, has never been completely excavated, but the hypostyle hall was cleared in the

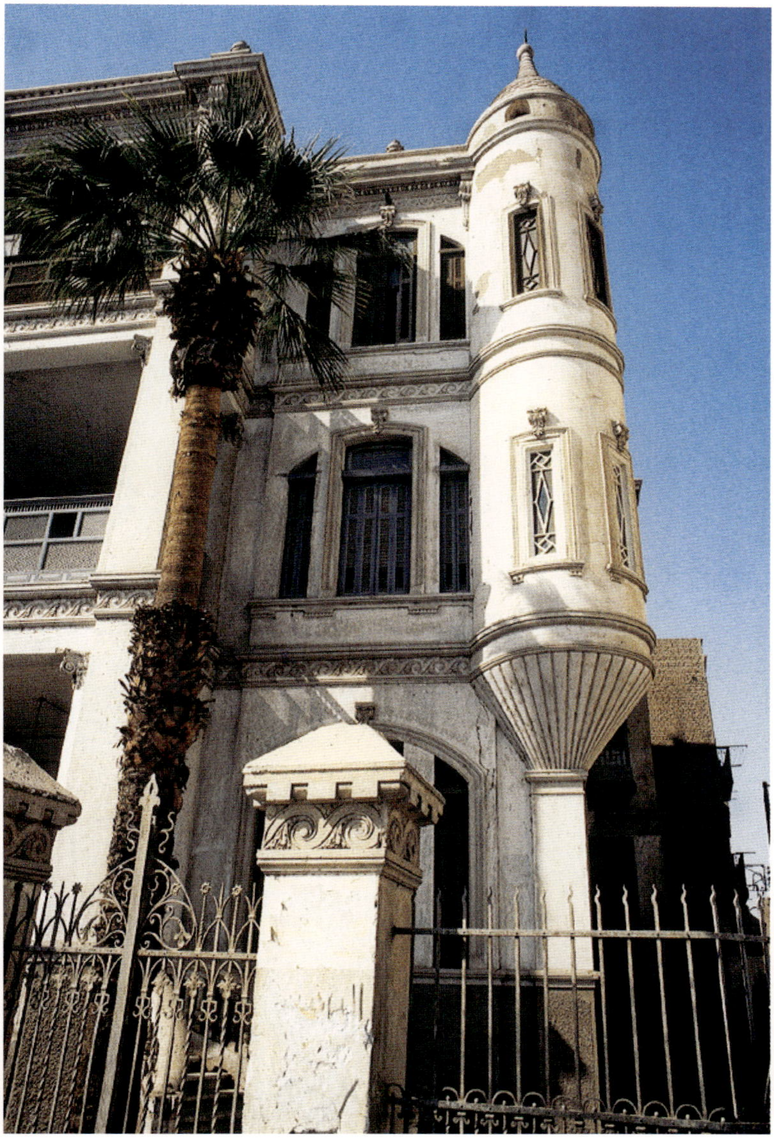

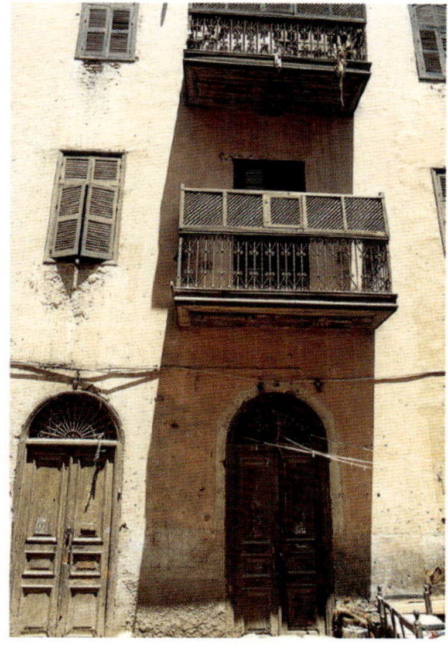

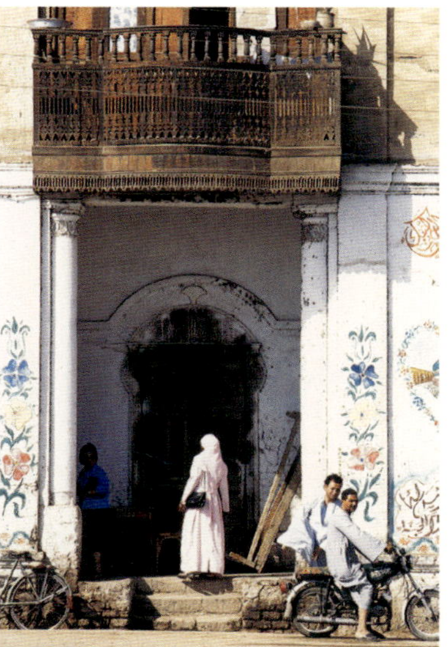

Above left, top, and bottom: Esna was once a terminus for caravans that picked their way from oasis to oasis across the desert from Sudan and places beyond, but this trade virtually expired with the passing of the nineteenth century. It remains, though, a merchant town and weaving center, and after exploring the colorful covered market to the south of the temple, you can walk north into a quarter of handsome old merchant houses with fine brickwork and *mashrabiya* screens. There are more fine houses along the Nile Corniche.

nineteenth century, and was cleaned in the 2020s. A staircase descends to the ancient ground level.

The roof of the hypostyle hall is supported by twenty-four columns with sixteen different capitals, still displaying their original colors, and they are marvelous to see. The best way to experience their effect is to stand and slowly revolve while looking upward at the myriad palm and composite plant capitals, arranged without symmetry or order, but pleasing all the same, as though you were standing among trees, admiring the subtle and powerful architecture of a forest. Afterward it is enjoyable to wander around the market and explore the town, which has several interesting churches and mosques and many beautiful houses.

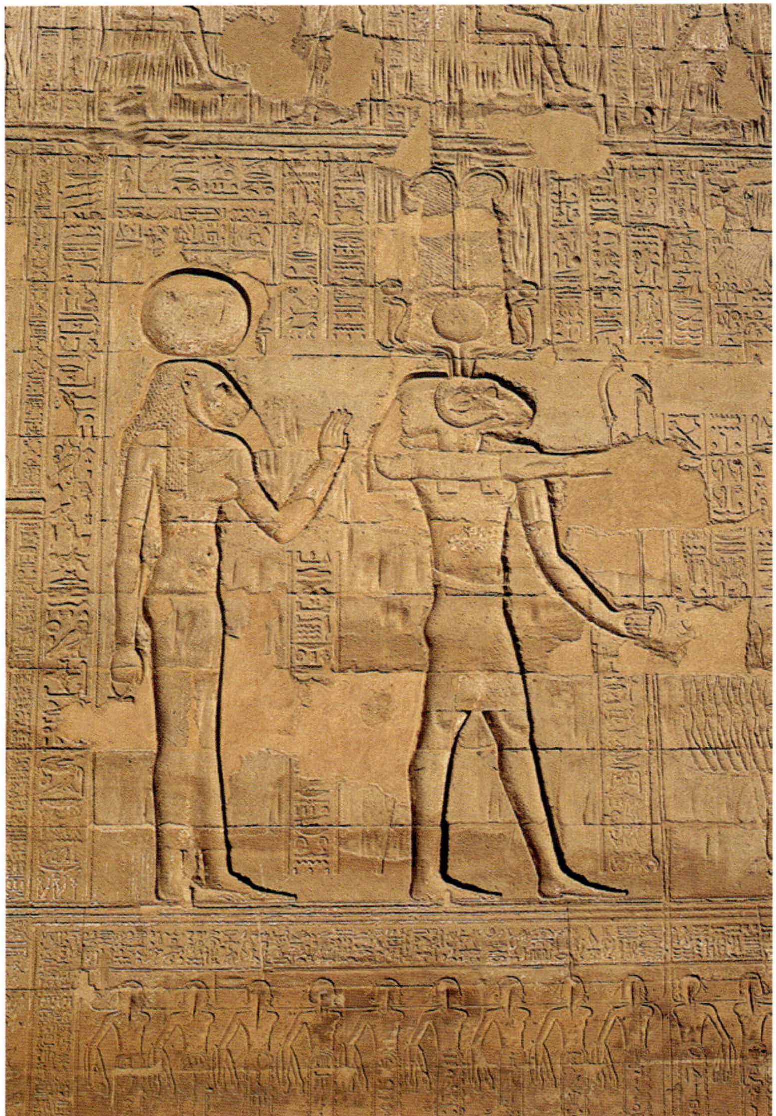

Left: The principal shrine of the ram-headed god Khnum was on Elephantine Island at Aswan, where the Nile's annual flood entered Egypt. His association with the river's fertile silt perhaps gave rise to Khnum being presented as the potter who created man on his wheel. Khnum was also worshiped at Esna where his consort was the town's local lion-headed goddess Menhyt, seen here standing behind him. The annual festival of Menhyt celebrated the Nile's flood; women played tambourines in her honor and urged her to bring fertility to the land and make it grow green again.

Right: The hypostyle hall at Esna was one of the last major temple structures built in the ancient Egyptian style. A Roman addition to the earlier Ptolemaic temple, it was begun by Claudius in the first century AD, but its decoration was not completed until two centuries later under the emperor Decius around AD 250.

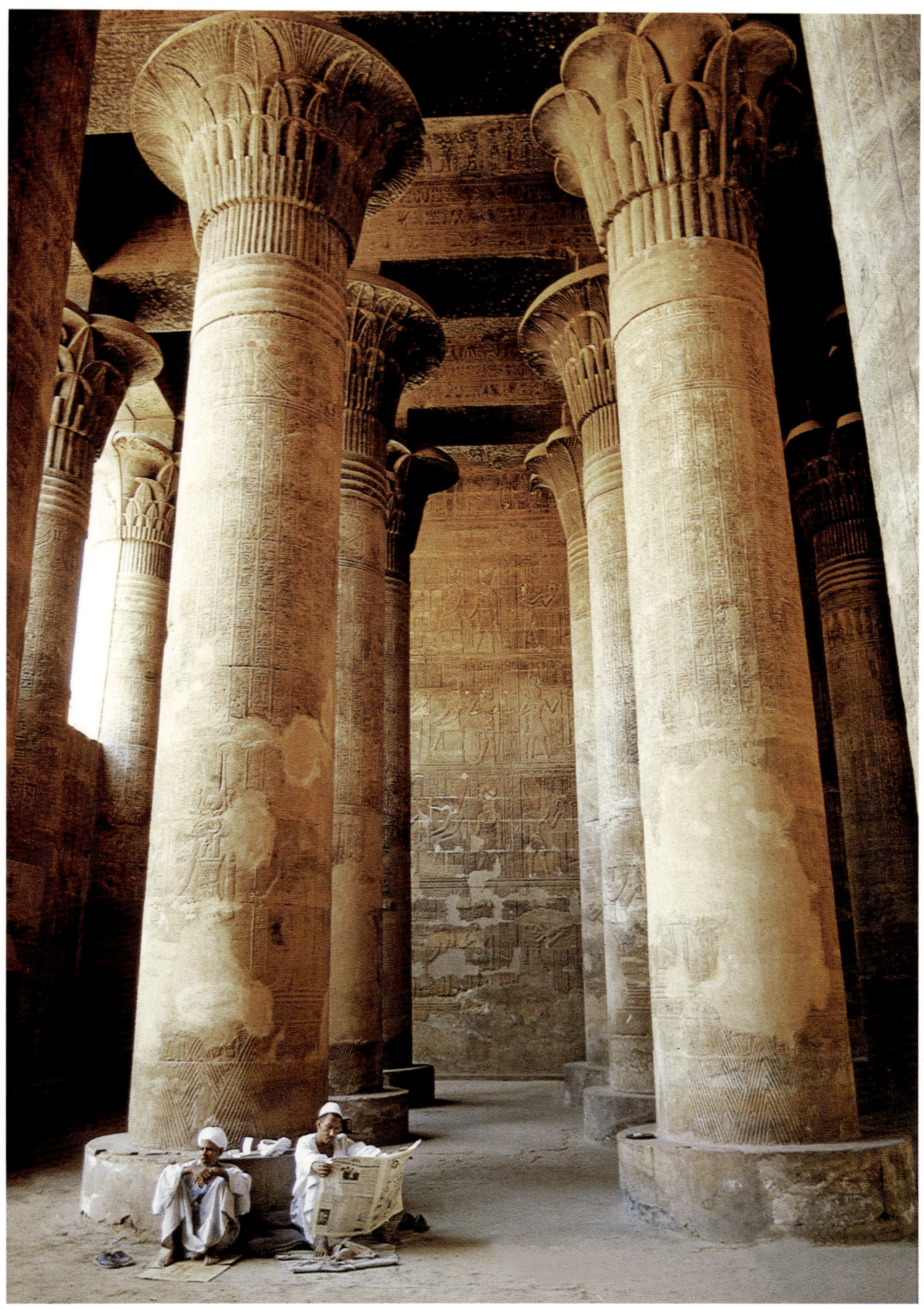

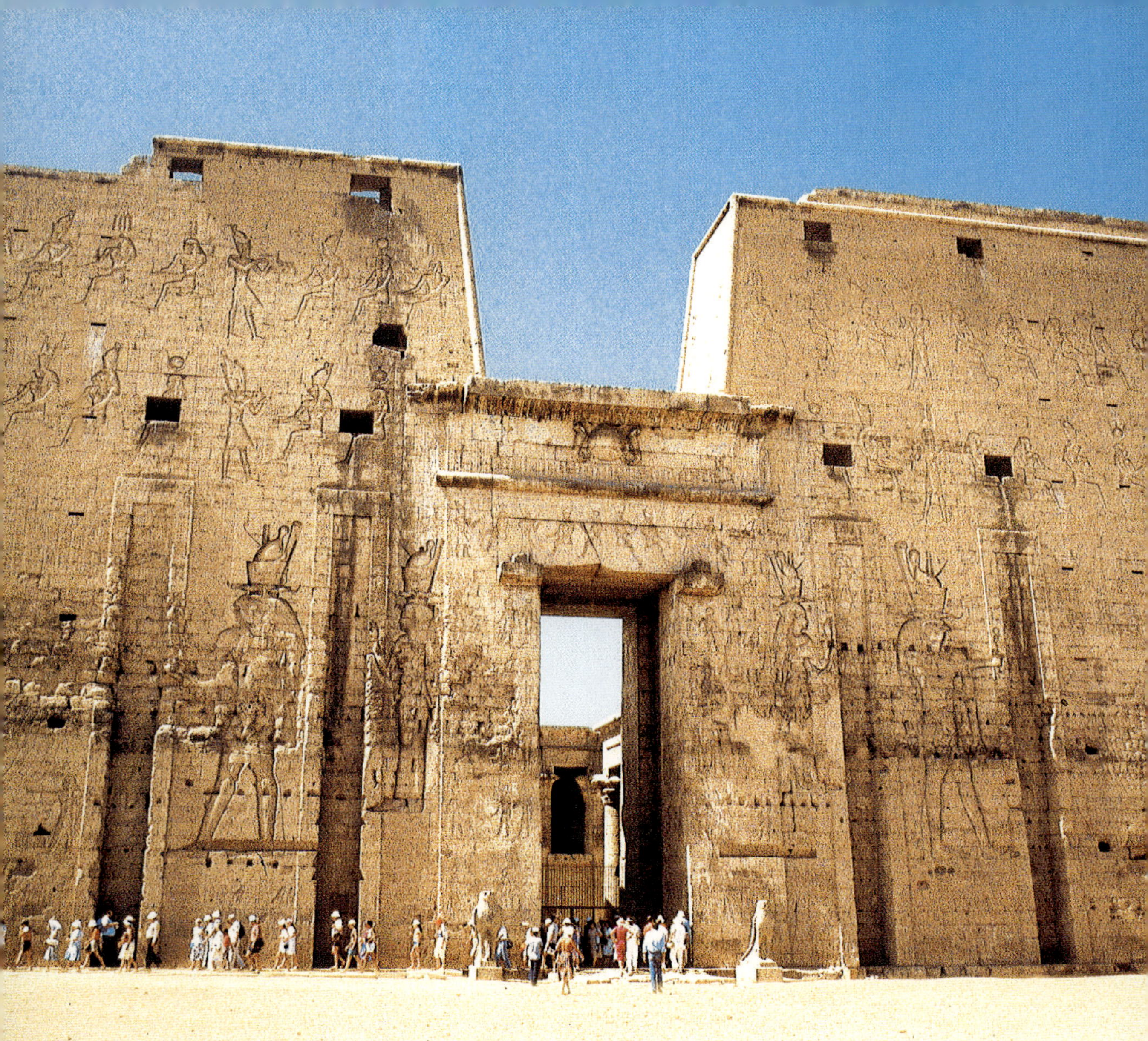

Above: The Greek Ptolemies maintained ancient Egyptian traditions, as here on the pylon at Edfu where, facing the god Horus, Ptolemy XII Neos Dionysos smites his enemies in exactly the same way as pharaohs had done since unification of Egypt, some three thousand years before. He was the father of the famous Cleopatra VII.

Edfu

Edfu is on the west bank of the Nile halfway between Luxor and Aswan. On the western outskirts of the town, part of which is built on the mound of the ancient city, is the Temple of Horus, the best preserved in Egypt. Original coloring is to be seen everywhere both inside and out. Construction began under Ptolemy III Eeuergetes in 237 BC and it was completed on 5 December 57 BC, after 180 years. Rites celebrated annually here at Edfu were the triumph of Horus over Seth, the conjugal visit of Hathor from Dendera, the re-enactment of the divine birth of Horus, and the coronation in the main court of a live falcon as the living symbol of Horus on earth.

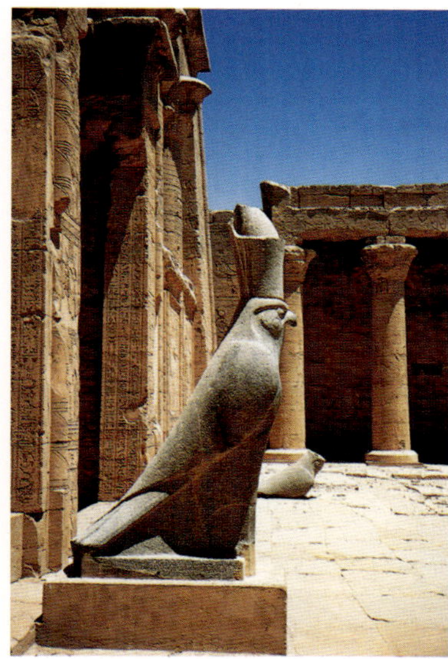

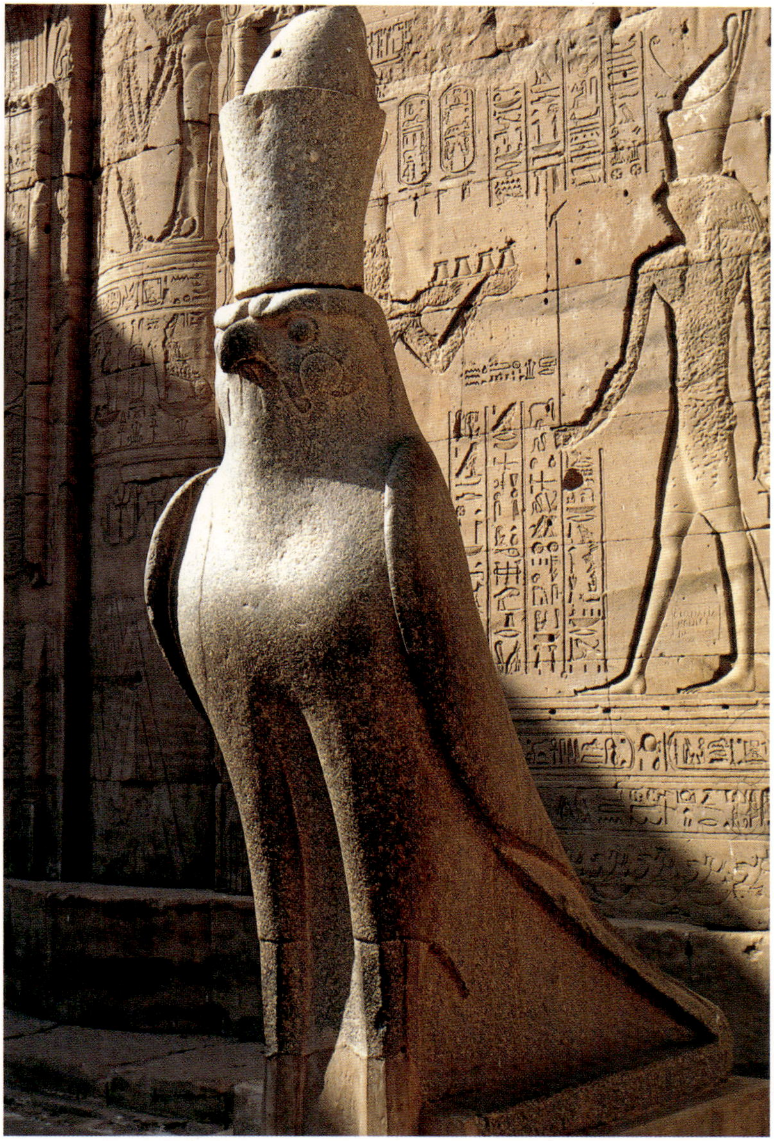

Above: The falcon god Horus flanked by the columns of the temple courtyard.

Top right: When Osiris was murdered by Seth, his body was hacked into pieces, but the parts were collected by Isis and reassembled. His penis had been eaten by a fish, but a magical substitute was created to allow Isis to have intercourse with her husband. She gave birth to the falcon god Horus who then did battle with Seth to avenge his father's death. Pharaohs identified with Horus in life just as they identified with Osiris in the afterlife, and so the Ptolemies were eager to link themselves with the Osiris–Horus–Isis story, which they celebrated in many temples throughout Egypt.

Bottom right: The walls of the passageway surrounding the inner temple are decorated with various sacred scenes and inscriptions, including Horus in a boat spearing Seth, who is being speared here in the form of a hippopotamus or a crocodile. The king is on the shore to the left, also with a spear, while on the right, behind Horus, is his mother, Isis.

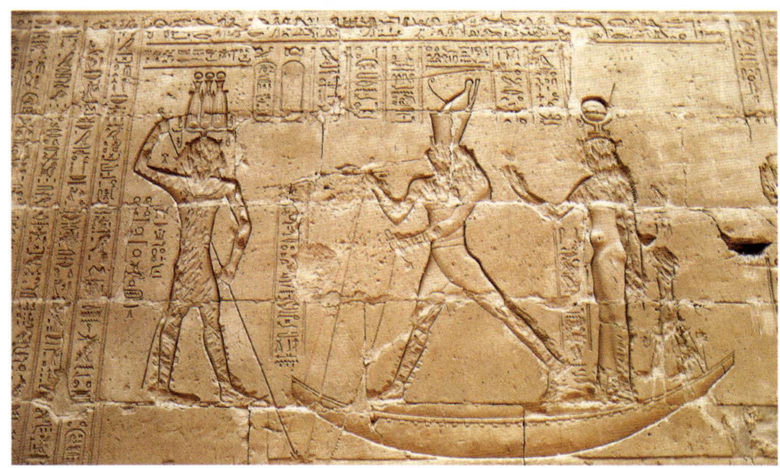

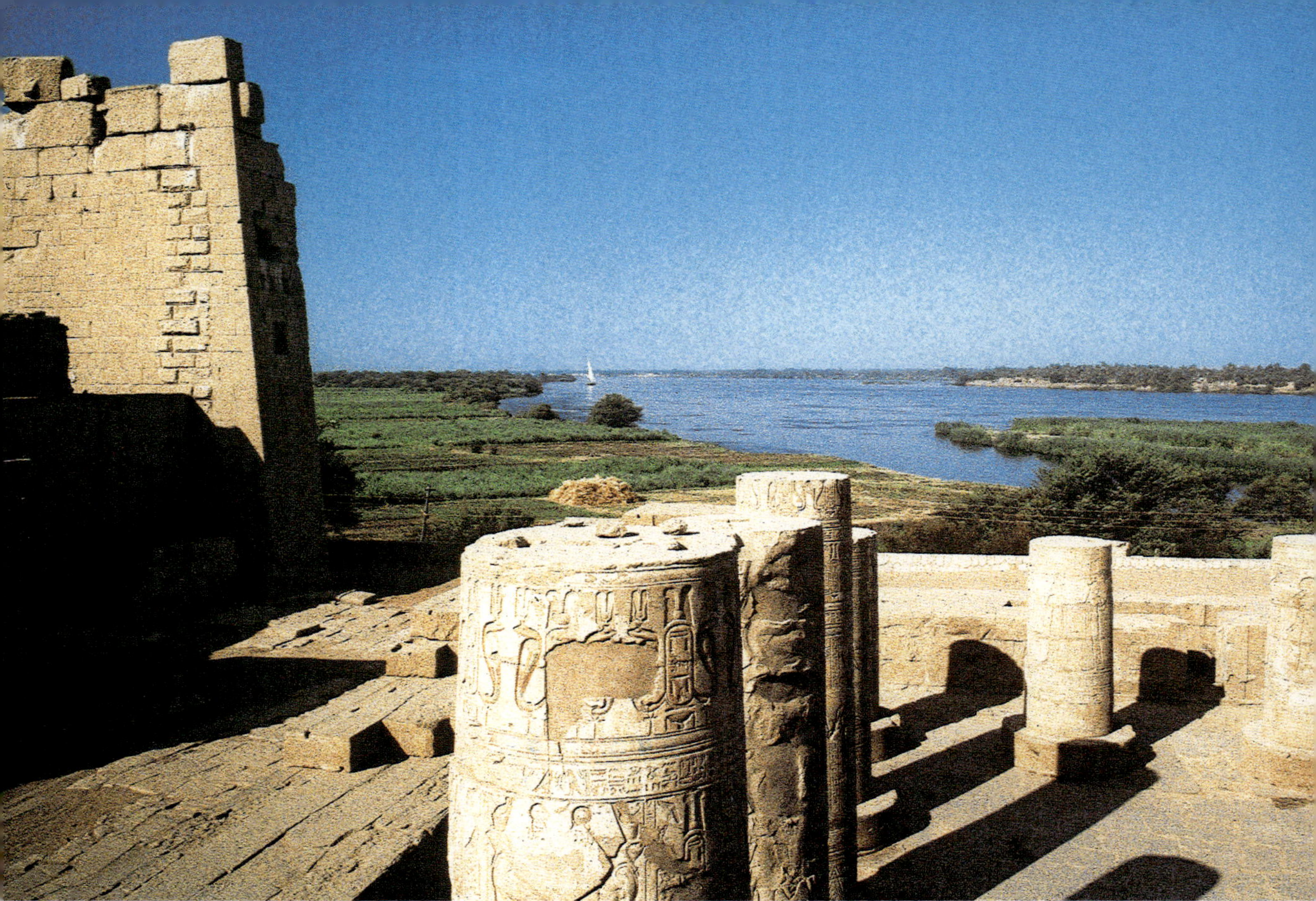

Above: The Nile has eroded away much of the pylon and the forecourt of the temple at Kom Ombo, where only the stumps of its sixteen columns remain. But thanks to its elevation, its seclusion, and the combination of sun and flowing water, the temple is one of the most beautiful in Egypt. The area of cultivation is unusually broad for this upper stretch of the Nile. With the construction of the High Dam at Aswan and the creation of Lake Nasser, many Nubians were settled here.

Kom Ombo

The Temple of Sobek and Haroeris at Kom Ombo stands on a promontory overlooking a great bend in the Nile. Its position by the water makes it one of the most beautifully situated temples in Egypt. A very unusual symmetrically-twin temple, the left side is dedicated to Haroeris, "the Elder Horus," also known as the Healer; the right to Sobek, the local crocodile god. The temple enjoyed renown as a healing center; pilgrims came from far and wide seeking treatment for their infirmities. Begun by Ptolemy VI in the mid-third century BC, it was completed over two hundred years later by Augustus, although decoration continued to be added by Roman emperors into the second century AD.

The Nile has eroded away part of the outer court and almost all the pylon, and though much of the upper courses of the structure has fallen, much of interest remains and the pattern of the temple is clear, as a smaller version of those other Ptolemaic temples at Dendera and Edfu. Little is left of the sanctuaries, but they are all the more revealing for that. Between them, at a lower level, is a crypt which communicates with a chapel. The crypt is now exposed but was once covered with a sliding slab. You can imagine the priests creeping down there from the chapel to eavesdrop on prayerful pleas or to utter prophesies.

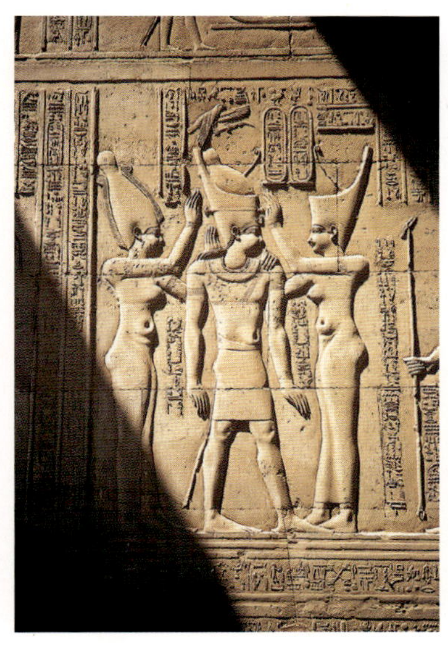

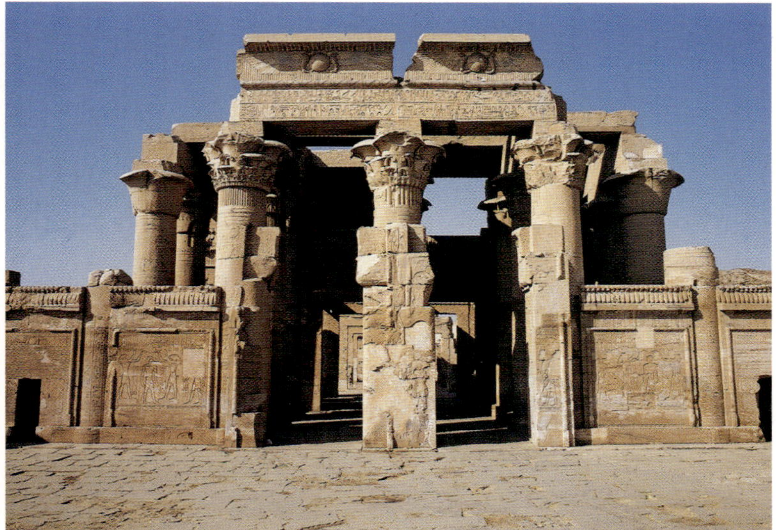

Above: A relief within the first hypostyle hall showing Ptolemy VIII Euergetes II being crowned with the double crown of Egypt. Reliefs of bare-breasted women and goddesses are nearly always Ptolemaic; earlier pharaonic reliefs show the breasts covered, if only transparently so.

Top right: Except for the three center columns framing the dual passageways leading to the twin sanctuaries, the façade of the first hypostyle hall has lost the upper parts of its columns where they rise above the screen wall. The surviving columns burst into floral capitals, and above them, across the remaining section of the cavetto cornice, are two winged discs emphasizing the duality of the divine presence here.

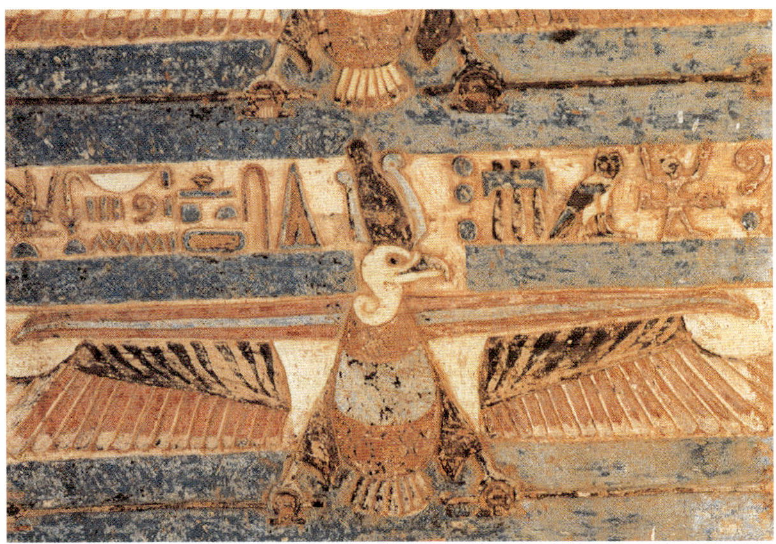

Right center: The ceiling of the first hypostyle hall is decorated with flying vultures, the protectors of royalty.

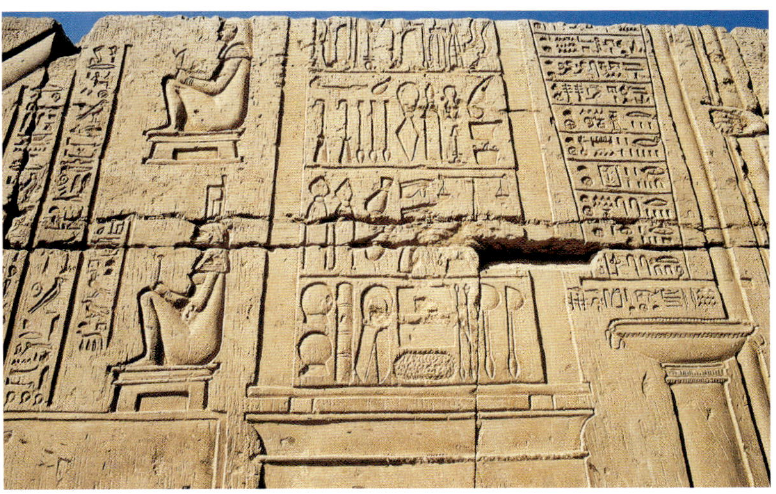

Bottom right: Beyond the sanctuaries is an outer corridor decorated with Roman Period reliefs. Among them is an illustration of medical instruments, including suction cups, scalpels, retractors, scales, lances, bone saws, dental tools, and chisels for surgery within the skull, a testimony to the advanced degree of medical learning in Egypt 2,000 years ago.

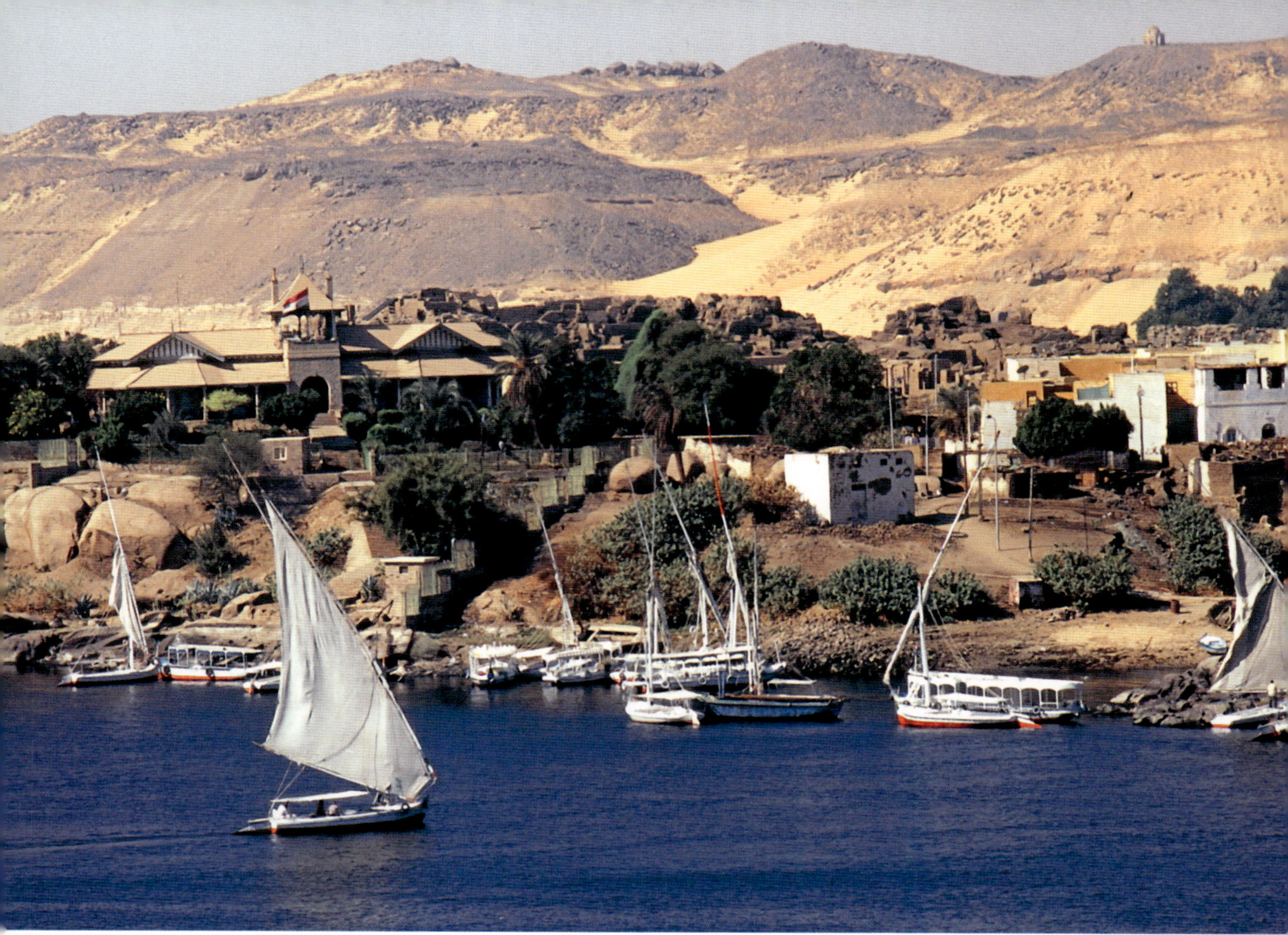

Above: A felucca sails across from Aswan to Elephantine. There are three Nubian villages on the island, and on the left is a museum housing finds made at Yebu, the name of the ancient city that occupied the southern end of the island. Beyond the island the desert spills into the Nile.

Bottom right: The Mausoleum of Aga Khan II, the spiritual leader of the Ismailis and an important international figure in the 1930s, when he became president of the League of Nations. The mausoleum lies above the villa where, until his death in 1957, he spent the winter months.

Aswan

Aswan is where the valley closes upon the river, no more buffer of cultivation on either side, instead a universe of desert sundered by the pulsing Nile flowing out of Africa. The layer of sandstone covering Upper Egypt from Edfu southward is ruptured here by the thrust of underlying granite which the river has hewn into the rocks and islands of the First Cataract. Even before completion of the first dam in 1902, and the giant hydroelectric dam in the 1960s, this was where traffic on the Nile stopped. Camels transported cargoes around the rocks while lightened boats took their chances through the granite passage. Aswan has always been where Egypt proper ends. Beyond lie Nubia and Sudan and the traditional routes of invasion and trade.

Tourism together with the High Dam, which regulates the water supply for Egypt and provides the country with electricity, have brought growth and development to Aswan and an influx of workers. Cruise boats are tied up all along the Corniche where the façades are new and concrete. But a few streets back from the Nile, the surviving parts of the picturesque older town deserve exploration, especially when the heat of day slackens.

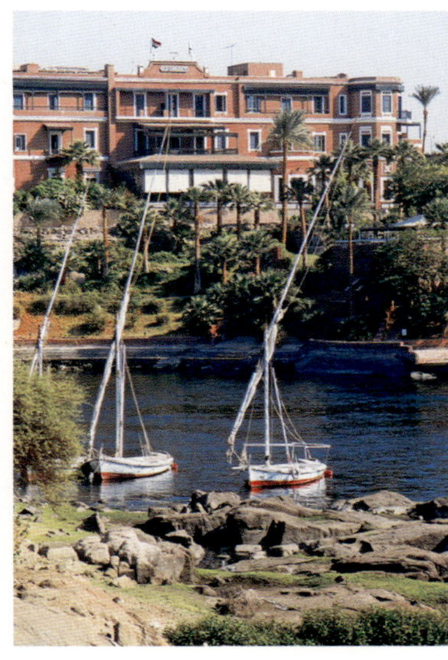

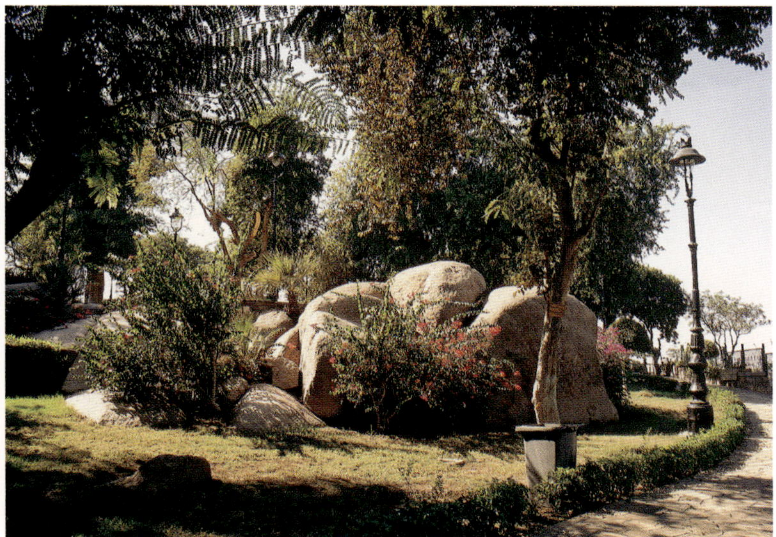

Above: The Old Cataract Hotel seen from Elephantine Island. The hotel dates from 1902 and is one of the grand hotels of Egypt. Its gardens and terrace enjoy beautiful views along the Nile and across to Elephantine, the Mausoleum of the Aga Khan, and the old monastery of St. Simeon on the distant desert horizon.

Above right: Granite outcrops at the Ferial Gardens. Some of these, like many others around Aswan, bear inscriptions left by the ancient Egyptians.

Right: Aswan town seen from Elephantine.

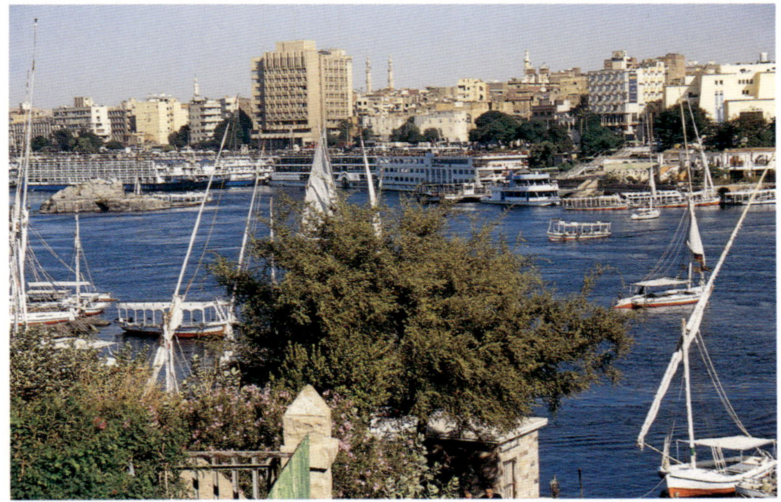

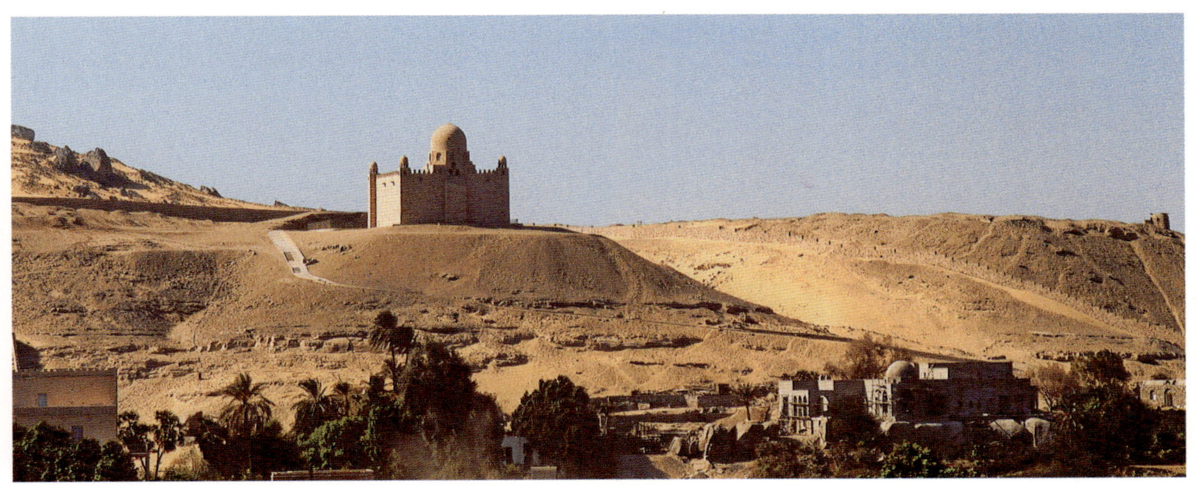

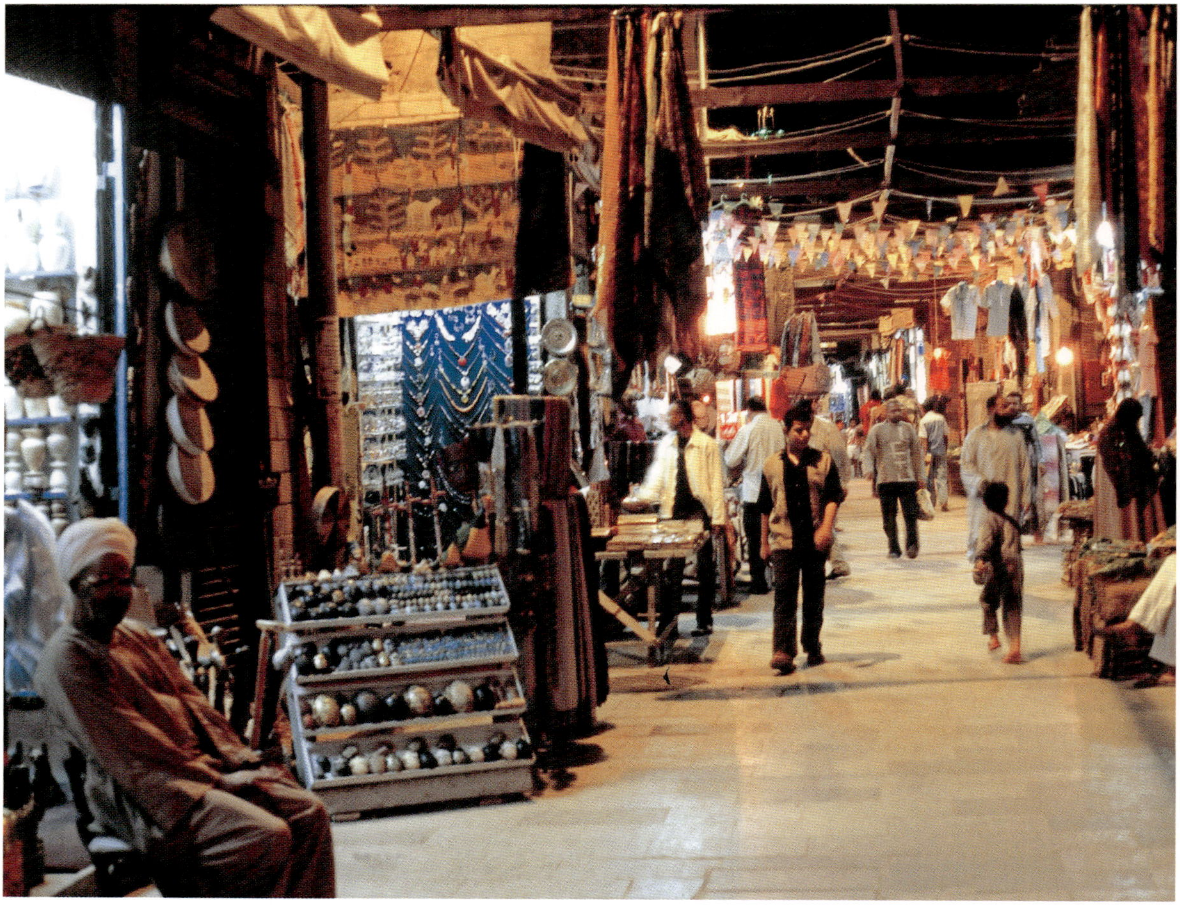

Above: Aswan's market street, al-Souk Street, is the best bazaar outside Cairo. It is liveliest at night when the heat of the day has passed. Aromatics, spices, ebony, and other exotic goods are sold, as well as local weaving, for which Aswan is famous.

Right: Young women shopping for gold jewelry along al-Souk Street.

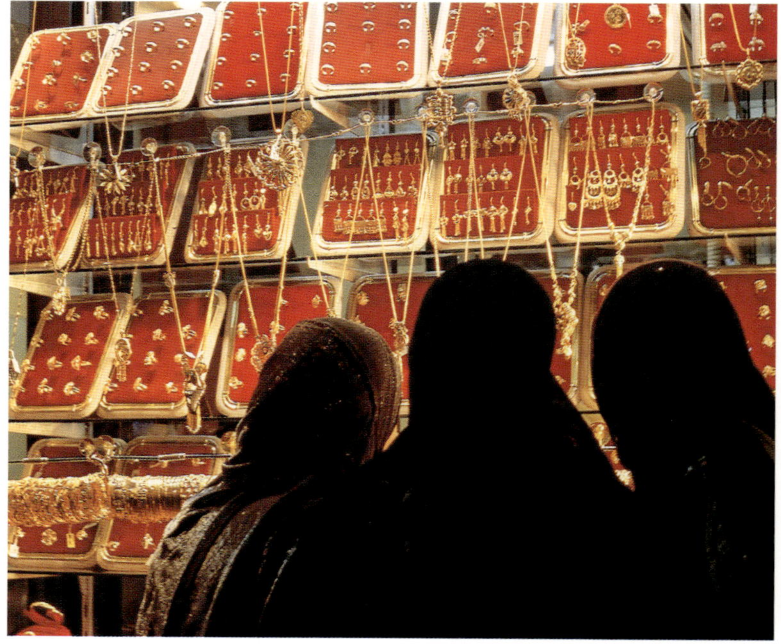

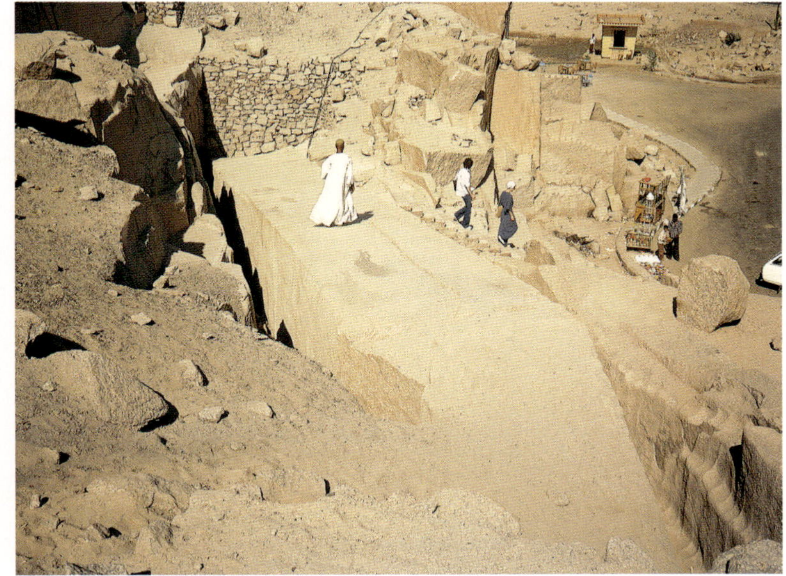

Left: The prized red granite used for statues, columns, obelisks and many other kinds of monument throughout the ancient world came from Aswan's quarries. This unfinished obelisk was probably commissioned by Thutmose III for erection at Karnak until a flaw was discovered.

Aswan can be very hot in the summer, but the close proximity of the desert means that it is also extremely dry, and so the climate is never oppressive. In winter the nights can be cool, but summer nights are the perfect time to enjoy the town. In the evening you can take a stroll along al-Souk Street, Aswan's sinuous market street. You can visit the Nubian Museum, which stays open late, and you can enjoy a meal at a restaurant overlooking the Nile. You may notice Nubian spoken, or if not here then when you are floating on a felucca and hear the boatmen calling to one another.

In ancient times this area on the east bank was known as Syene and was famous for its nearby quarries of red granite, but it was always secondary to the main commercial and administrative settlement of Yebu, which stood at the southern end of the long island opposite the Corniche. The ancient Egyptian name for the town was Yebu, meaning elephant; it owed its name and much of its importance to the ivory trade from the south. The Greek translation was Elephantine, the name by which the island is still known today.

About the most purposeful thing to do at Aswan is to take the motor launch to the island of Philae and visit its Temple of Isis. Otherwise you can hire a felucca or motorboat for a lazy visit to Elephantine Island and the Botanical (Kitchener) Island hidden behind it, and then land on the west bank to visit the tombs of the Nobles and St. Simeon's Monastery. For sheer pleasure, nothing beats sailing about aimlessly in a felucca and visiting nothing at all, or sitting on the terrace of a hotel overlooking the river and letting the world float peacefully past. The greatest delight of Aswan is to know that when morning comes there is so little to do. Those who insist on doing it can easily do it all in a day or two. Those who want to do nothing will want to stay far longer.

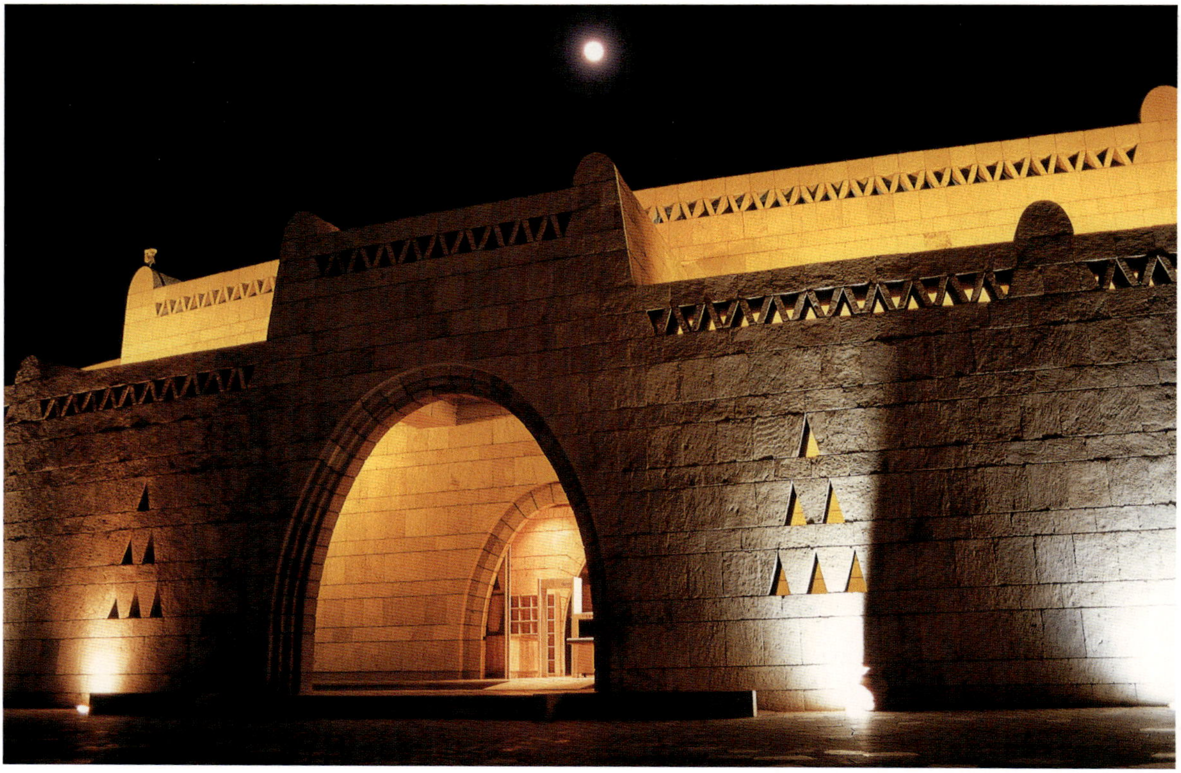

Above: The Nubian Museum is a striking modern sandstone building on the slope of a granite outcrop at the southern end of town. Its façade is decorated with traditional Nubian architectural motifs.

Right top and bottom: Music and dancing, children at their lessons, and other scenes of traditional Nubian village life are illustrated by dioramas in the ethnographic section of the museum.

Below: A mummified ram with golden mask, one of a number found in the ram cemetery adjacent to the temple of Khnum on Elephantine Island.

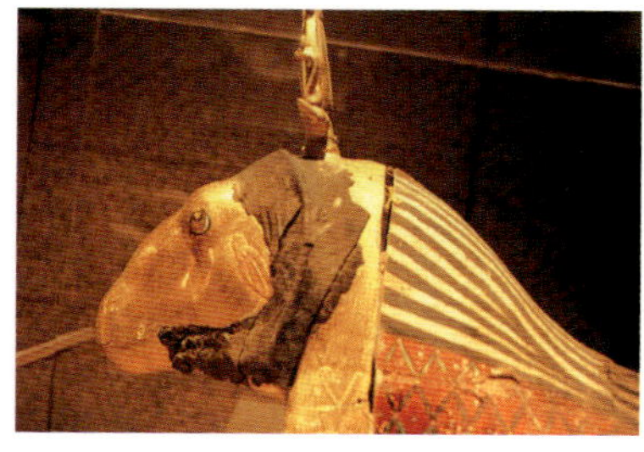

The Nubian Museum

The exhibits in the Nubian Museum run the gamut from prehistoric rock art to scenes of village life in the twentieth century before the completion of the Aswan High Dam drowned the whole of Nubia beneath Lake Nasser. The Nubians admired and mimicked the ancient Egyptians, but Nubian culture has always been most stimulating and entertaining in its folk art, as in the tiny ceramic frogs used as playthings during the Greco-Roman period, the boldly painted murals of saints of the Christian period, or the domestic architecture. Reconstructed houses in the ethnographic section show how Nubians expressed their strong decorative sense by setting china plates into the façades of their houses and painting their exterior walls in brightly colored geometric patterns. Combining the decorative with the functional, they pierced the walls of their houses with a characteristic latticework of triangles to catch the slightest breeze.

The ancient land of Nubia extended south from Aswan into Sudan, but with the construction of the Aswan High Dam in the 1960s all of Egyptian (Lower) Nubia has been completely submerged beneath the waters of Lake Nasser. Effectively Egyptian Nubia has ceased to exist, though Nubians continue with their lives in Aswan, around Kom Ombo, and elsewhere in Egypt, while the museum preserves what has been salvaged of their past.

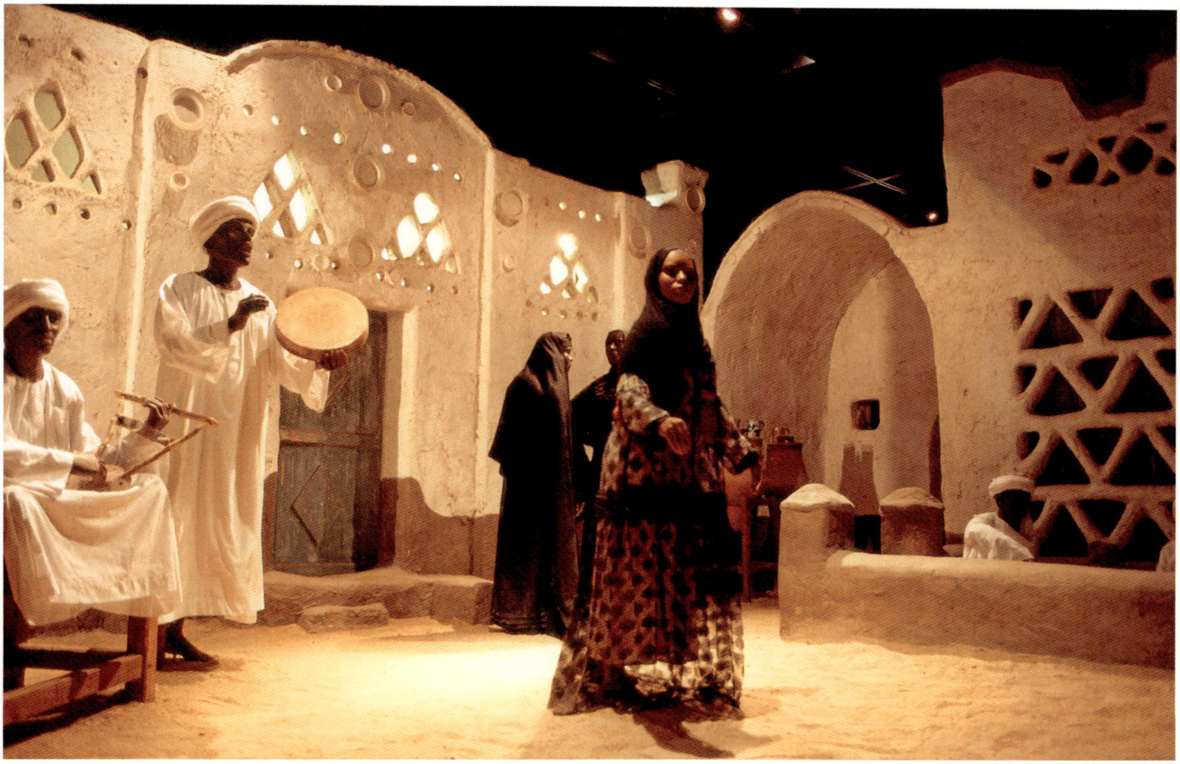

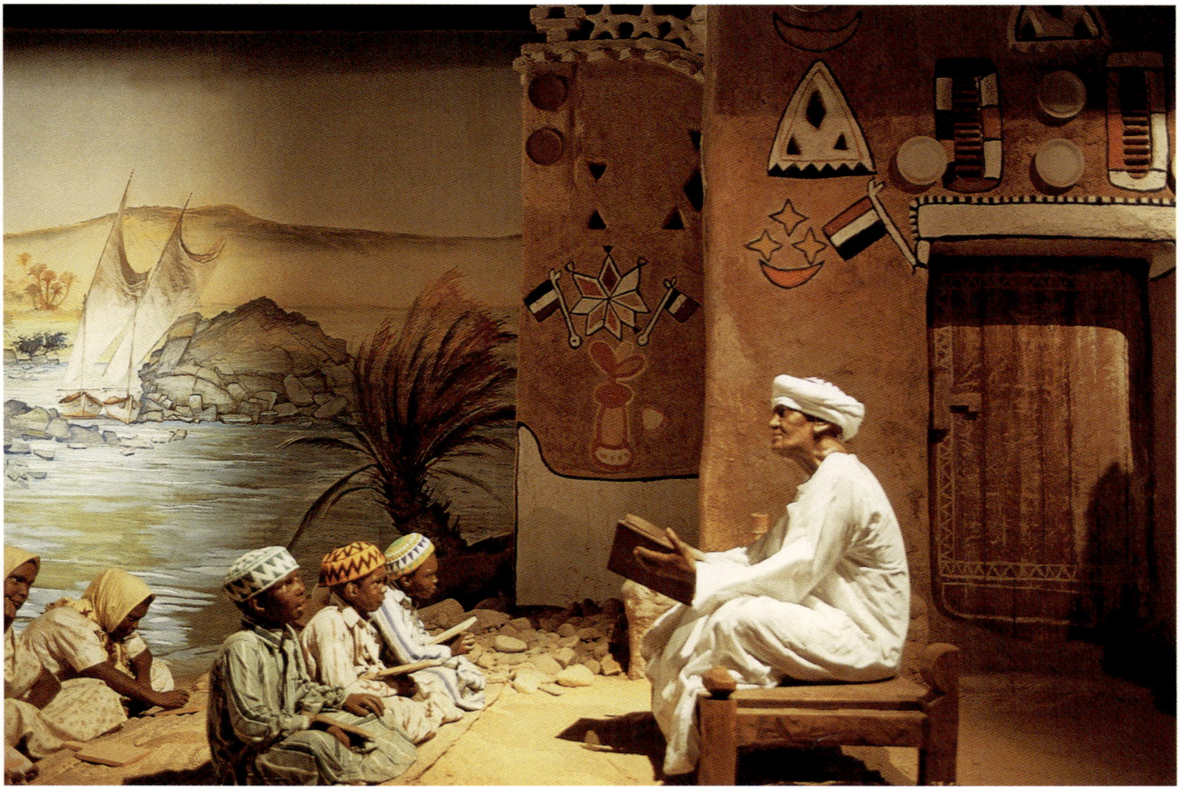

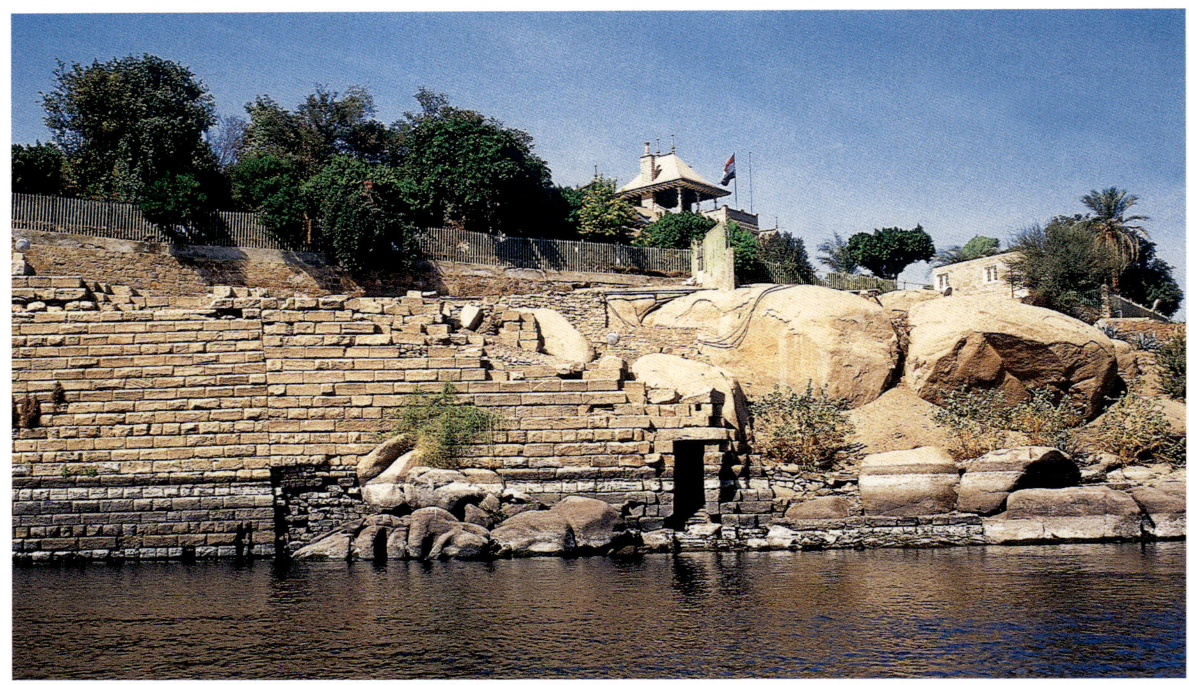

Above: The museum on Elephantine and, below it, the Nilometer, which can be entered directly from the river or down steps from above. Originally associated with the New Kingdom Temple of Satet, the Nilometer was rebuilt by the Romans, who marked the scales in Greek. The first century AD Greek geographer Strabo records that "on the side of the well are marks, measuring the height sufficient for the irrigation and other water levels. These are observed and published for general information. This is of importance to the peasants for the management of the water, the embankments, the canals, etc., and to the officials on account of the taxes. For the higher the rise of water, the higher are the taxes." The High Dam put an end to the annual inundation.

Right: A few boat lengths south of the Nilometer, the granite embankments of Elephantine bear hieroglyphs, which stretch from the Eighteenth Dynasty down to Psamtik II of the Twenty-Sixth Dynasty (shown here).

Yebu

The ancient town of Yebu stood at the southern end of Elephantine Island; some artifacts recovered here are on display in the adjacent Aswan Museum. There is also a Nilometer, dating from the New Kingdom. The island was home to Khnum, a ram-headed creator god of the cataracts who fashioned man on a potter's wheel. Excavations have revealed several temples, including one to Yahweh as there was a sizable Jewish colony here in the sixth century BC.

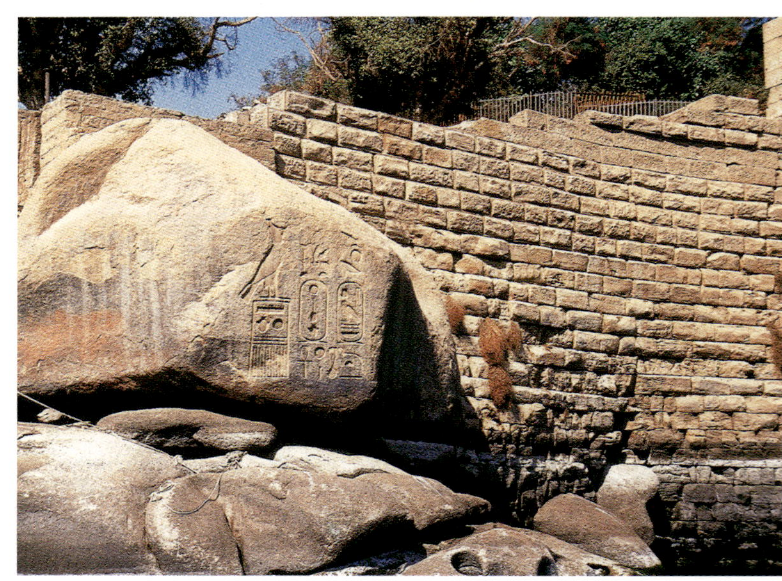

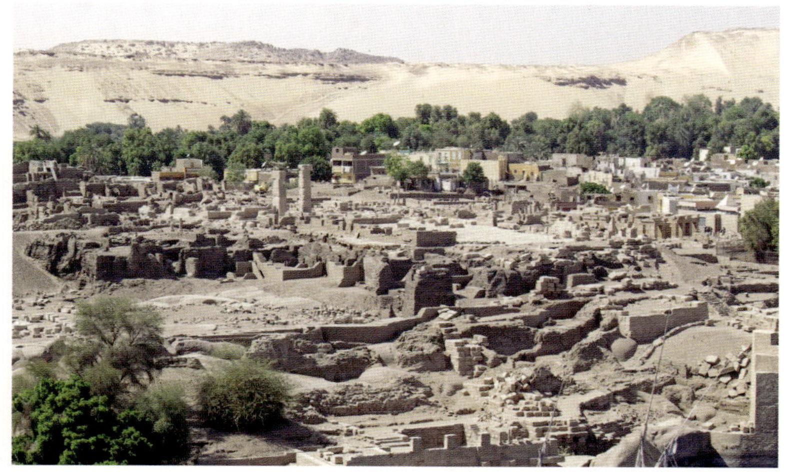

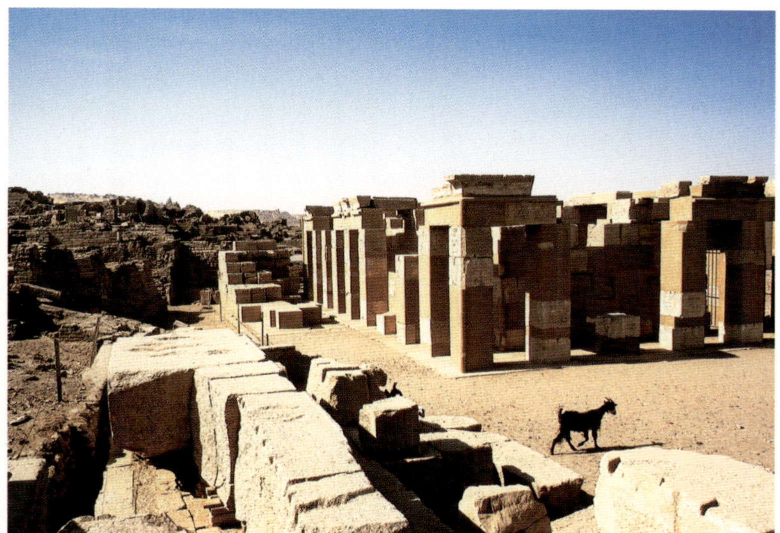

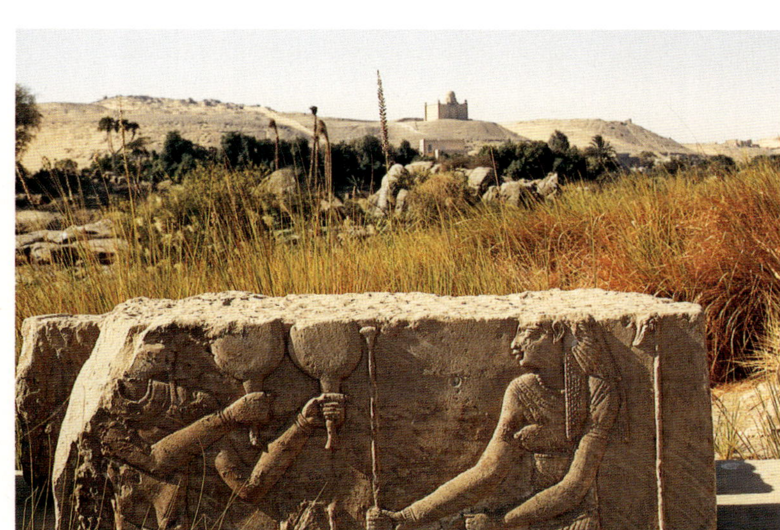

Left: Worship of Khnum on the island of Elephantine went back to the Old Kingdom, but the most prominent remnant of his temple, the gateway in the center of this photograph, is a re-erected gate of the time of Alexander IV, son of Alexander the Great. Khnum was believed to control the annual inundation of the Nile and therefore was associated with procreative powers, so that he was often depicted as the god who formed man on his potter's wheel. Rams sacred to Khnum were mummified, adorned with gilded masks, and buried in stone sarcophagi on the island, to the right of the temple ruins; fine examples are on display at the Nubian Museum.

Left center: The reconstructed remains of the Temple of Satet lie to the west of the island's museum. Satet was a war goddess worshiped here as protector of Egypt's southern frontier and as the consort of Khnum. From at least the Old Kingdom a series of temples were built to the goddess on this spot; the reconstruction is of the New Kingdom version, built by Thutmose III.

Below: A fragment of a Ptolemaic relief amid the ruins of Yebu. In the background, on the west bank of the Nile, is the Aga Khan's mausoleum.

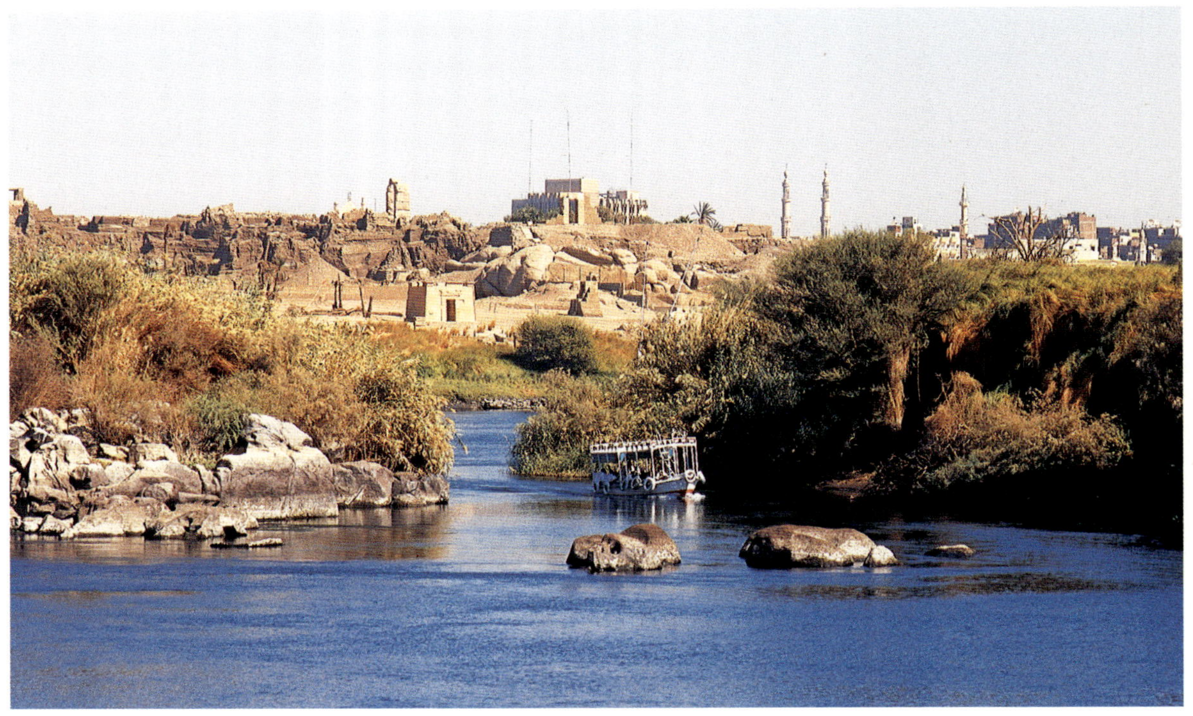

Above: A launch heading upriver from Elephantine Island. The ruins of Yebu are at the southern end of the island; some of the minarets and higher buildings of Aswan may be seen beyond.

Below: There are three Nubian villages on Elephantine Island; some houses have kitchen gardens.

Below right: A Nubian house on Elephantine.

River and islands

One of the magical pleasures at Aswan is to sail among the islands in the river aboard a graceful swallow-sailed felucca. The Nubian boatmen call out to one another in their native tongue, and as they pass in their feluccas there is the ancient sound across the waters of singing and beating drums. Taking advantage of the current and the prevailing wind, your boatman can explore the channels between Elephantine and the Botanical Island and then tack upriver to Sehel at the First Cataract.

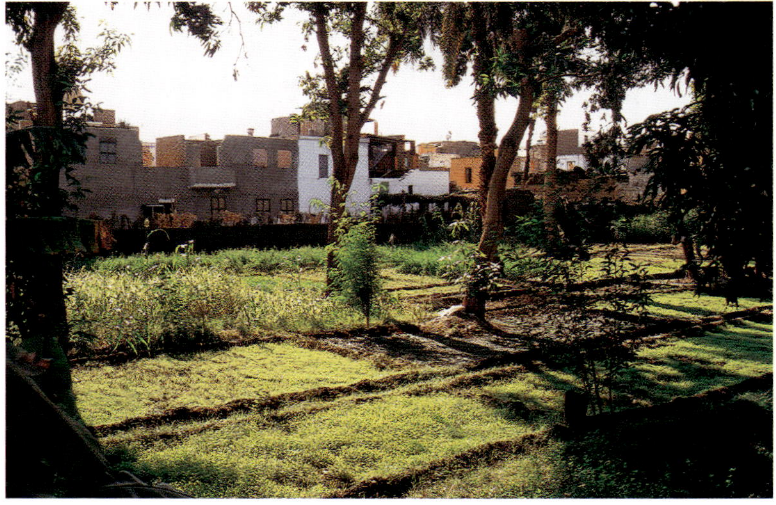

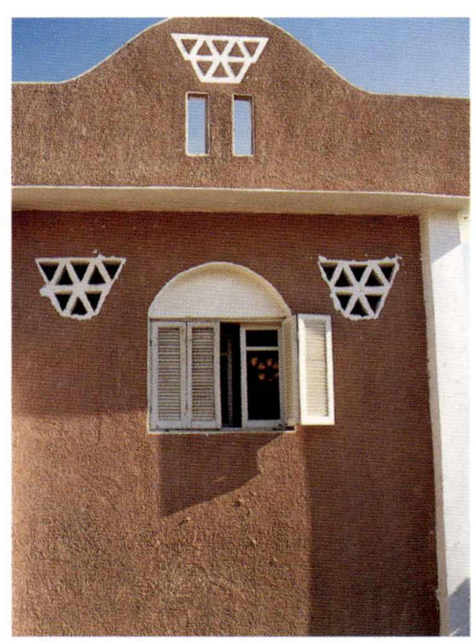

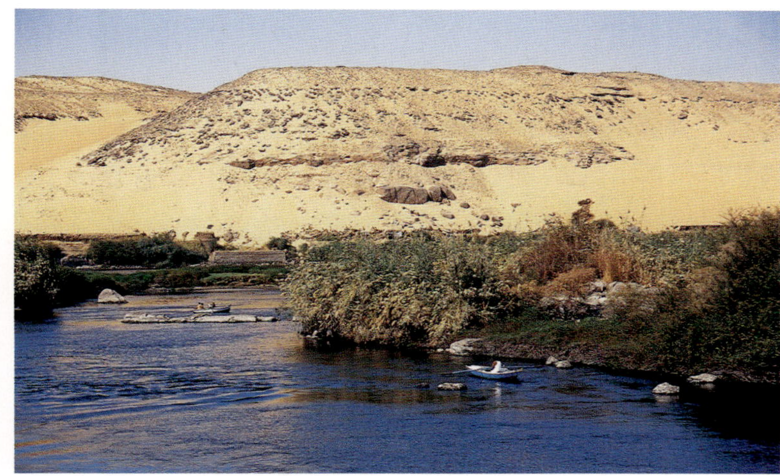

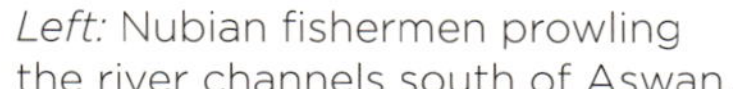

Left: Nubian fishermen prowling the river channels south of Aswan.

Left center: The island of Sehel is just below the First Cataract, and even at the north end of the island the boat is shoved about by turbulent whirlpools. Walking across the sands to a granite outcrop at the south end of the island gives you a view of the rocks and swirling waters of the cataract, but the pounding Nile and foam passed into history at the beginning of the twentieth century with the construction of the original Aswan dam, which can be seen in the distance.

Below left: In the faint blue of sunset, the sail of this felucca catches the last glimmer of light off the horizon and glides like a crescent moon against the darkening desert.

Below: The boatmen at Aswan are Nubians. They are darker and have lighter builds than Egyptians, and among themselves they speak Nubian rather than Arabic.

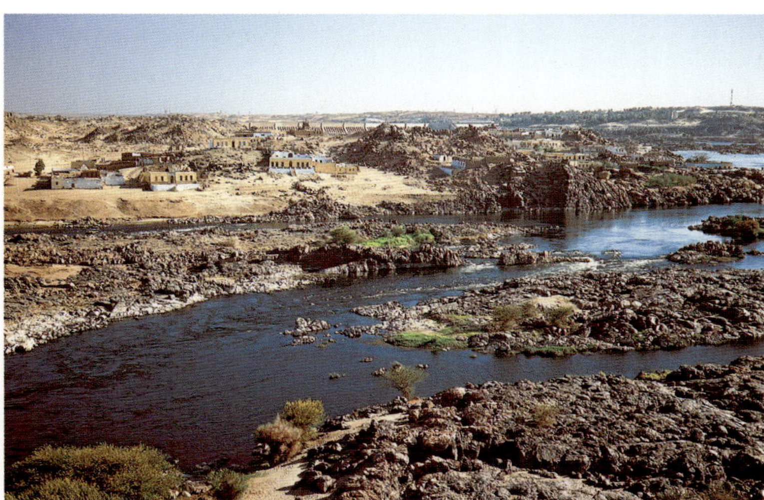

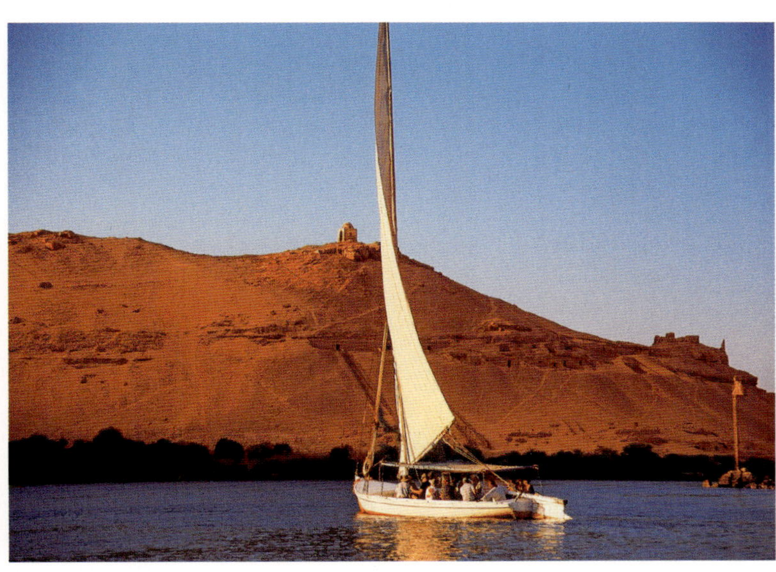

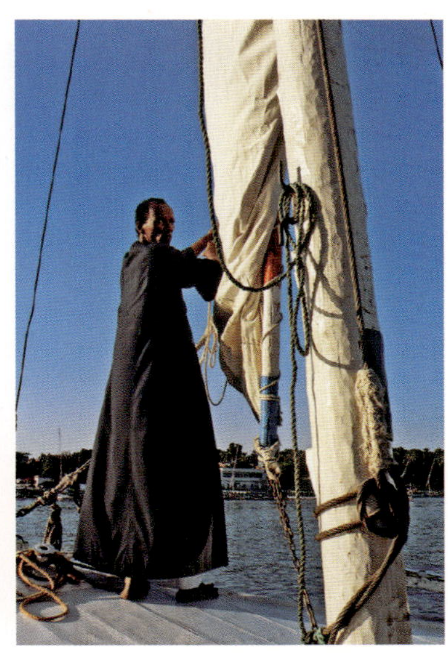

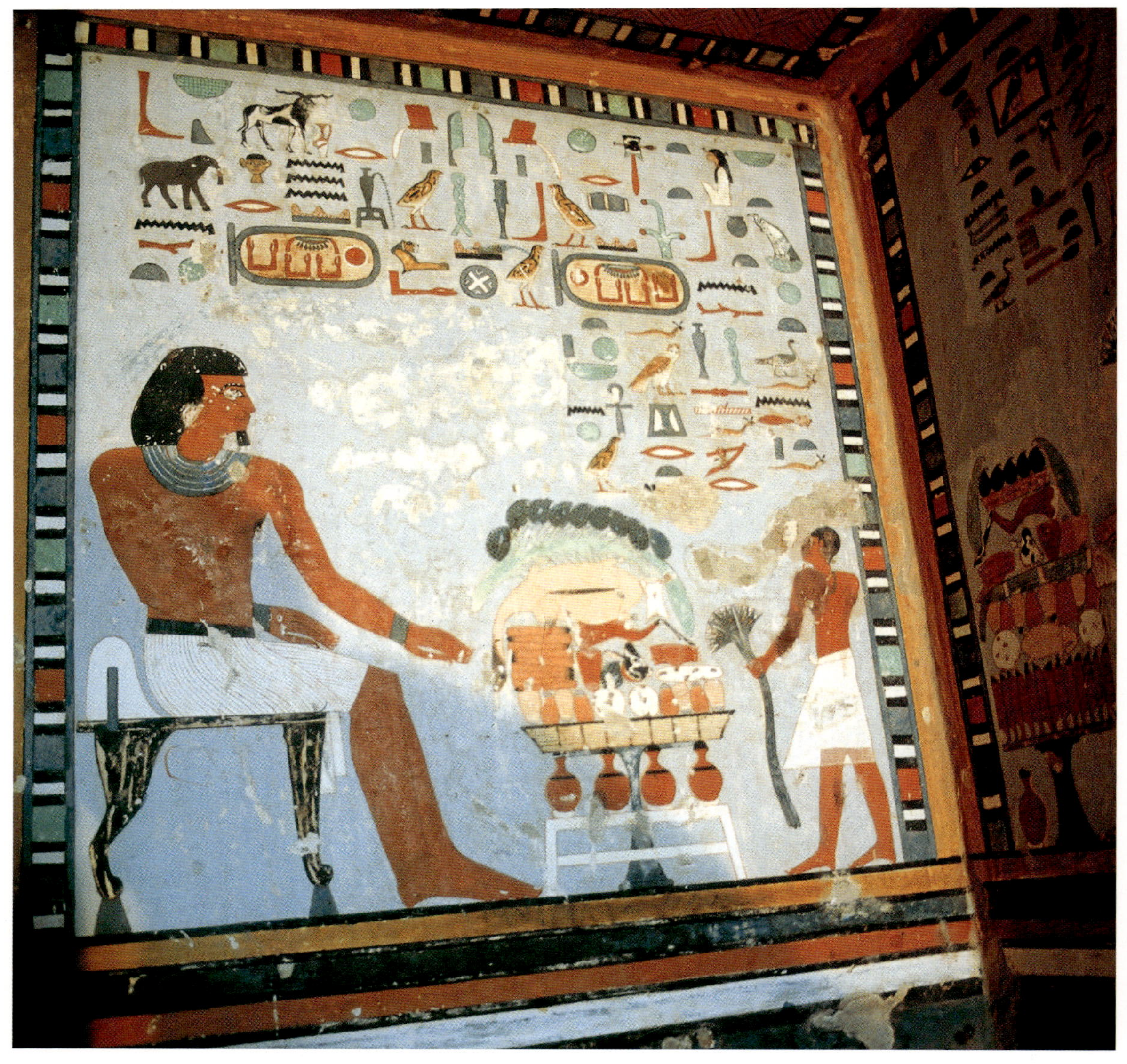

The Nobles' Tombs

The Nobles' Tombs, at Qubbet al-Hawa on the west bank of the Nile opposite the north end of Elephantine Island, were the burial places of governors, princes, and priests whose lives revolved around the Nubian trade, the defense of the southern frontier, or the divine rising of the waters. The tombs date mostly from the late Old Kingdom and the Middle Kingdom. A ferry or felucca brings you to the landing stage from where you trudge up a sandy path to the lines of tombs cut into the cliff face. Some of the tombs were originally approached by the steep causeways you see etched into the hillside. At night the whole cemetery area on the flank of the hill is illuminated by floodlights and can be seen from all over Aswan.

Left: This painting is at the back of the innermost shrine of the tomb-chapel of Sirenput II, Governor of Aswan under the Twelfth Dynasty king Amenemhat II. It shows his son, holding flowers, standing before him and a groaning table of food offerings. The hieroglyphs are beautifully detailed and colored, and include birds and animals and, unique to this tomb, an elephant.

Right: The tombs across the Nile from Aswan. The summit of the hill is crowned with the Qubbet al-Hawa, the Dome of the Winds, an old lookout tower. It commands a magnificent view of the Nile valley, the cataract, and the desert that more than compensates for the difficult climb. A path runs from here across the desert to St. Simeon's Monastery, about forty-five minutes by foot.

Bottom right: The stepped ramps, leading up from the river, that formed part of some of the tomb-chapels had a flat surface in the center for hauling up the coffin.

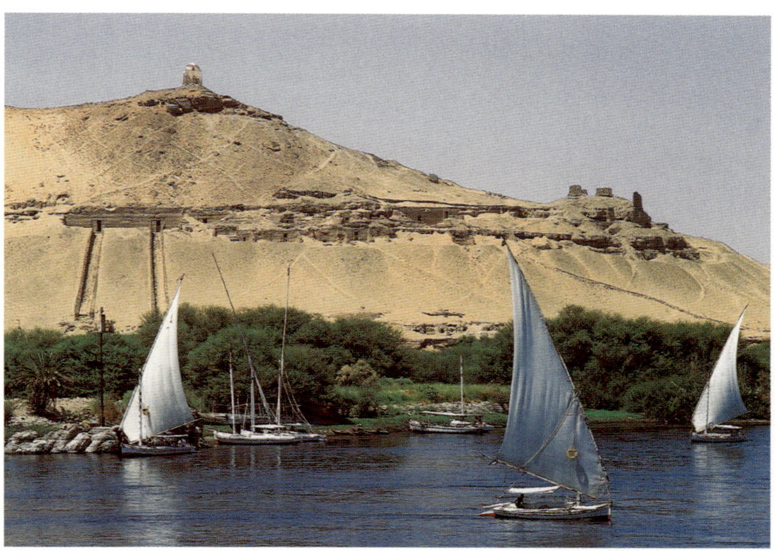

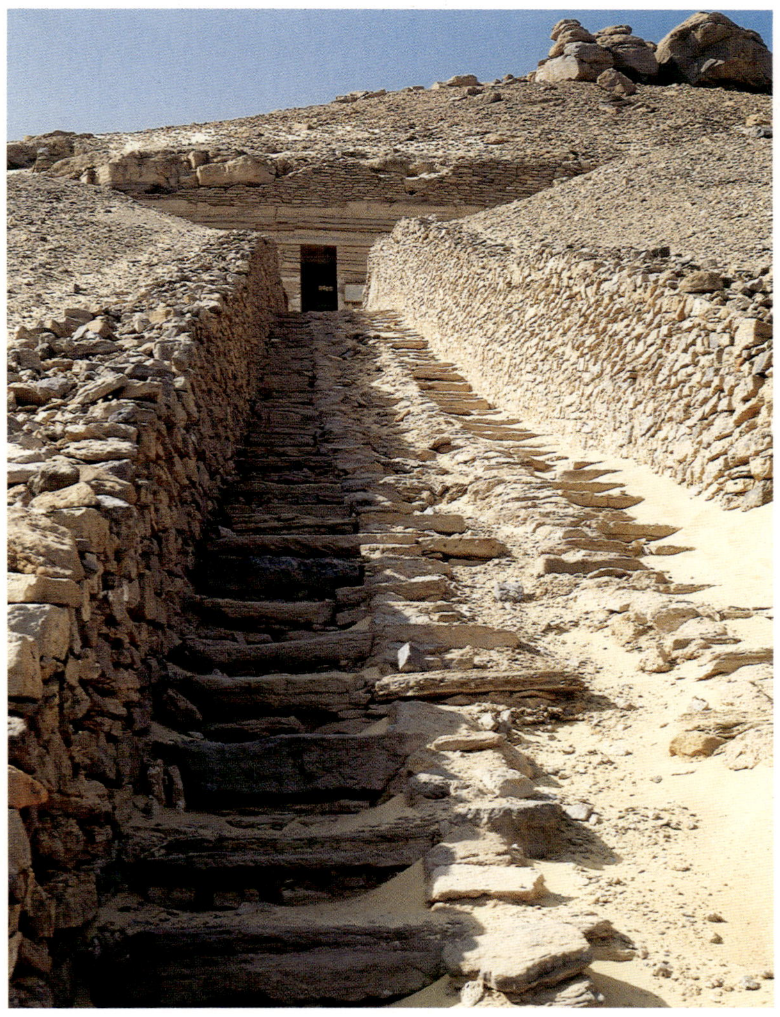

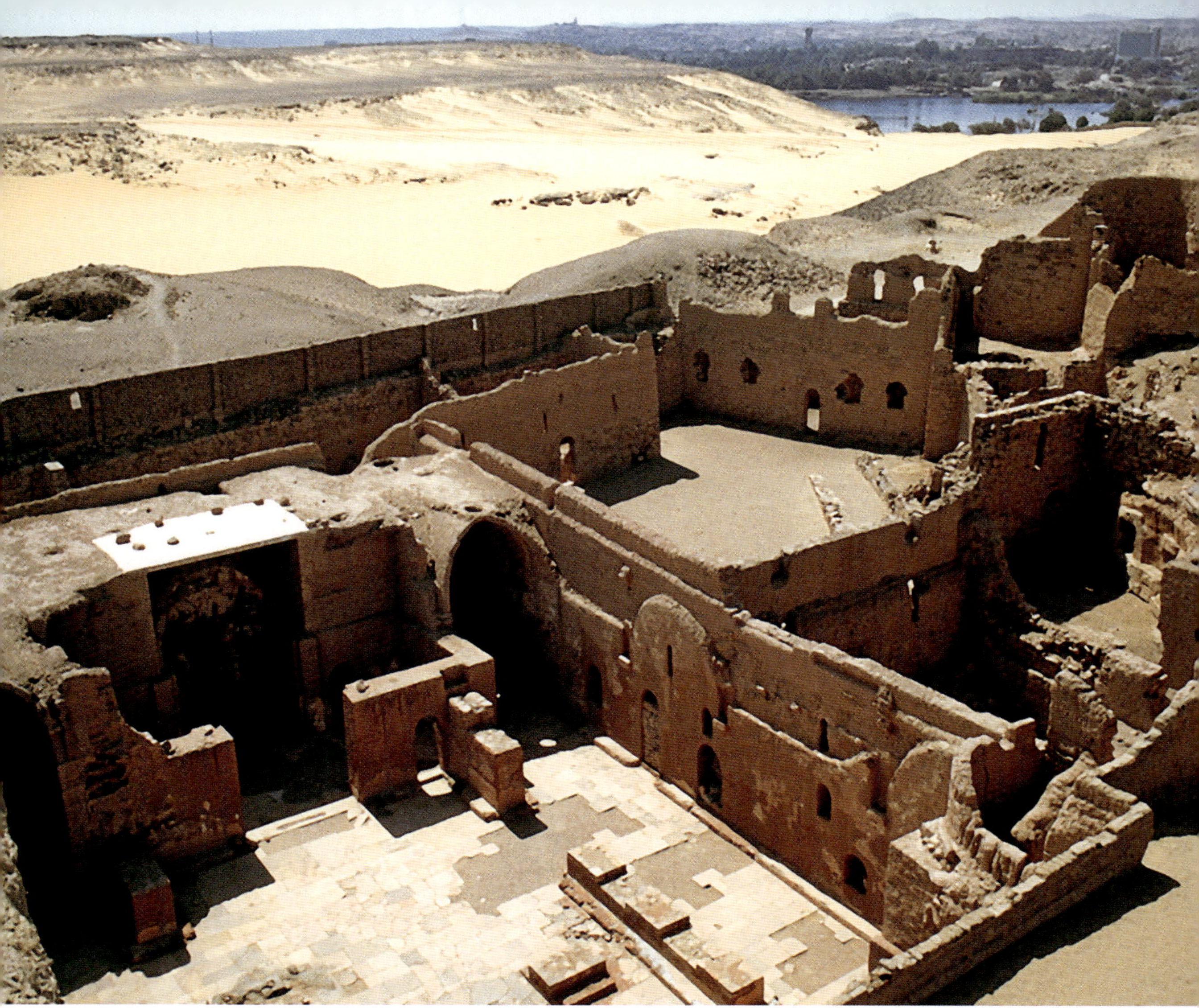

Above: From the tops of the walls there is a glimpse of Aswan, and of green amid the universe of sand. Yet when the monastery was flourishing this valley was cultivated with fields and gardens down to the Nile.

Monastery of St. Simeon

The Monastery of St. Simeon, Deir Amba Samaan in Arabic, is the finest example of an original Christian monastery in Egypt. Built in the seventh century, it was destroyed in 1173 when Saladin sent his troops against Christian Nubia. St. Simeon was built on a grand scale. A small city built on several levels was enclosed within thirty-foot-high walls, with cells for 300 monks and dormitories for several hundred pilgrims, as well as bakeries and workshops to provision the community. Portions of frescoes have survived the centuries, including a nearly complete Christ Pantocrator in the basilica church near the entrance. The surrounding desert, with its hills and caves, offered solitude and communion with the divine for thousands more monks and hermits.

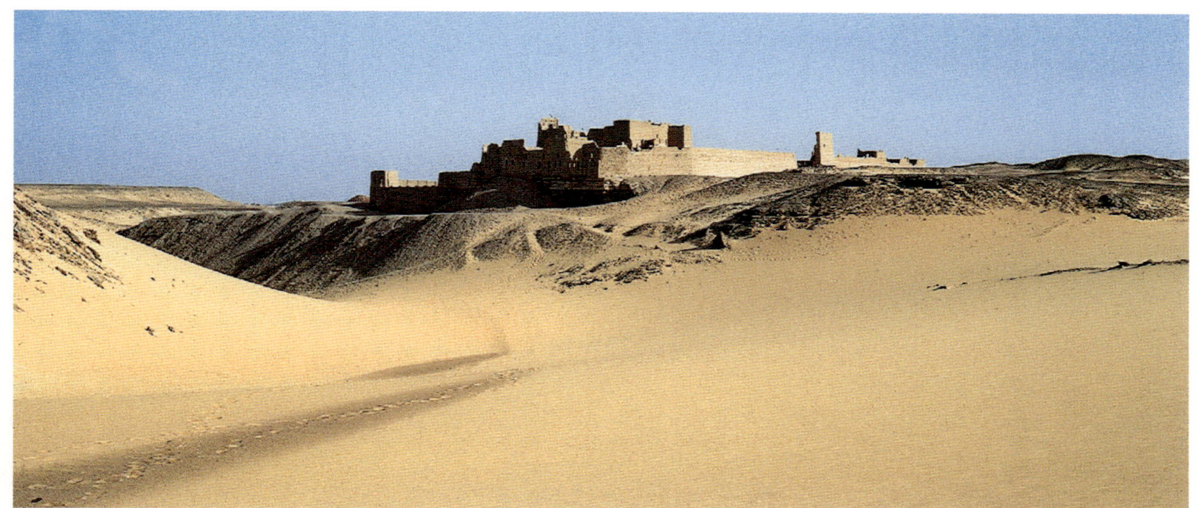

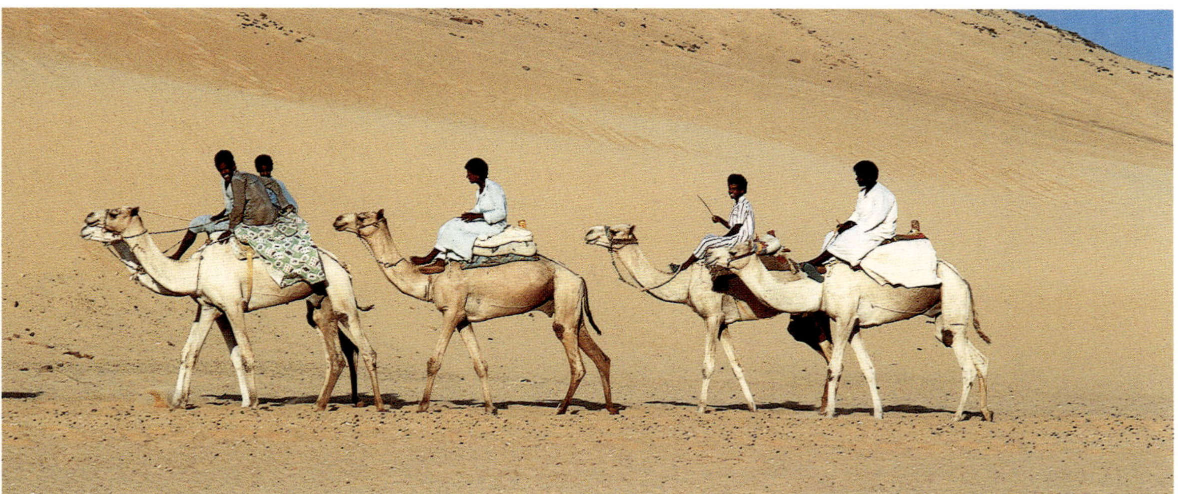

Top: With its towers and walls, the monastery looms like a desert fortress. The lower stories are stone; the upper are mud brick, and it is these that have most fallen into decay or vanished altogether.

Center: Camels can be hired to take you from the boat landing on the Nile up to the monastery and also for longer rides across the desert.

Right: The monastery was a comforting bastion against the fierce landscape. Monks' cells were kept cool by shadow, the thickness of the walls, and the evening breezes.

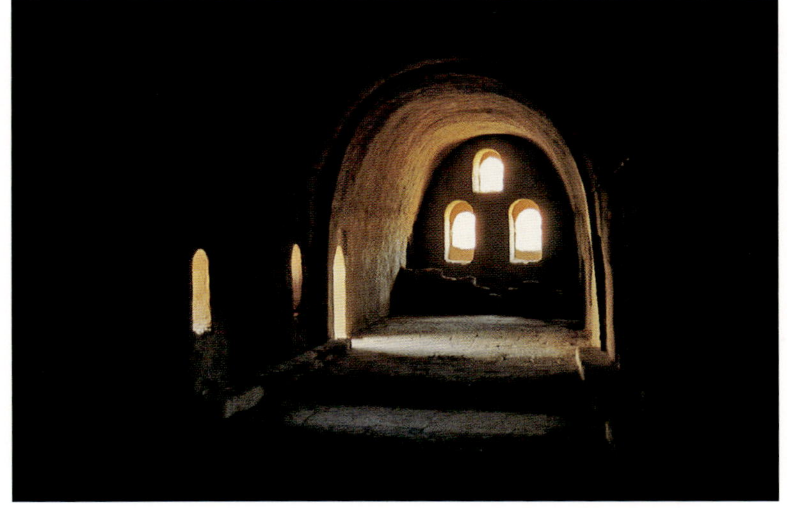

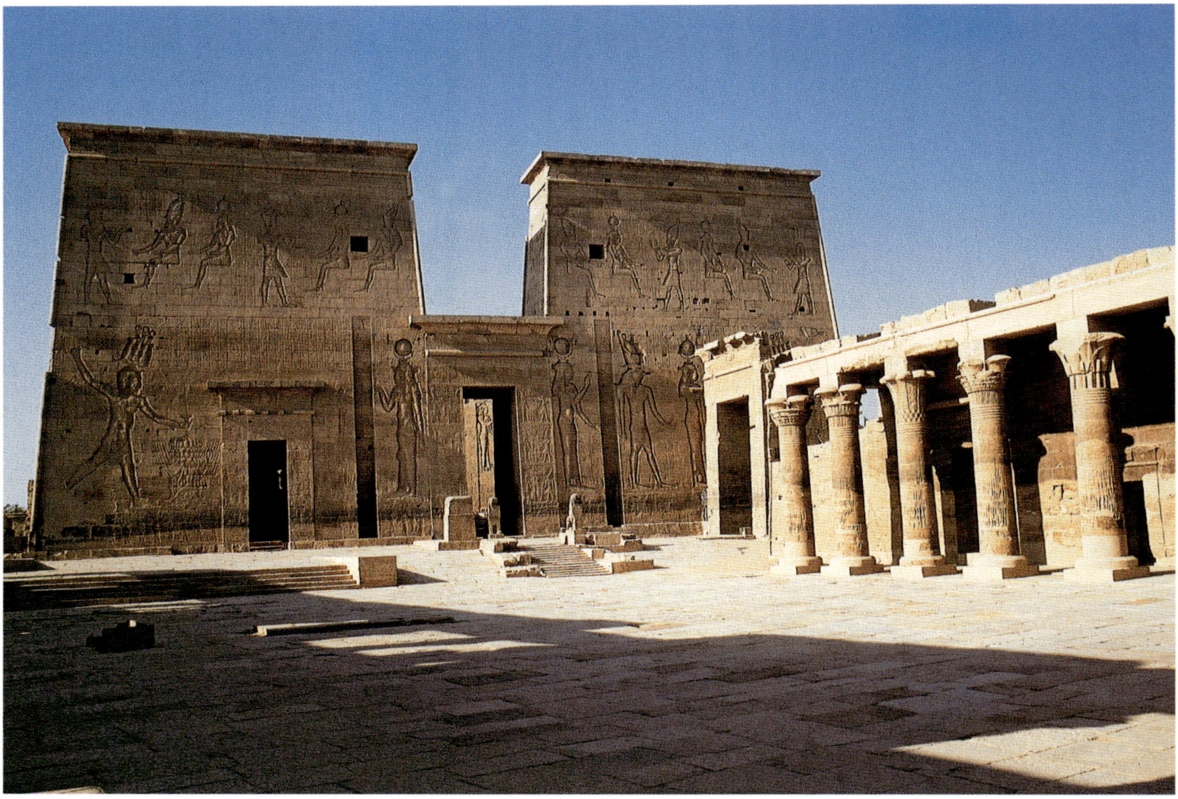

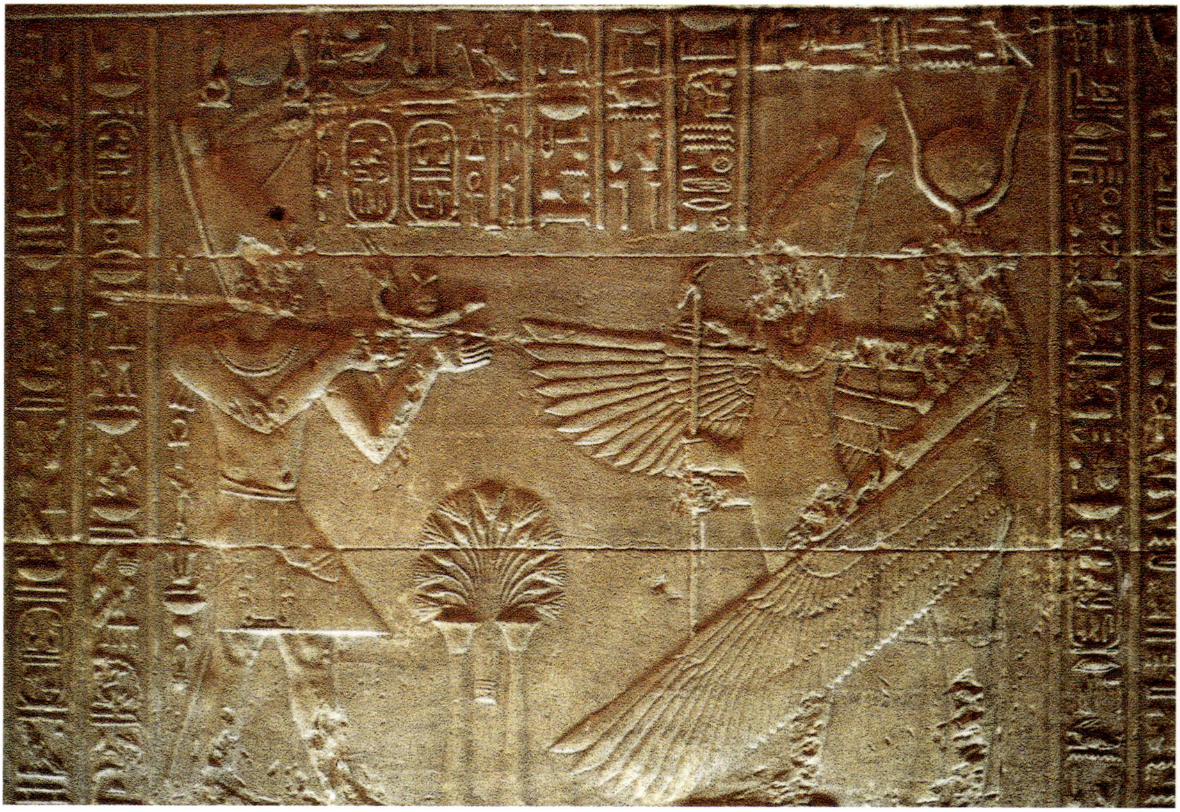

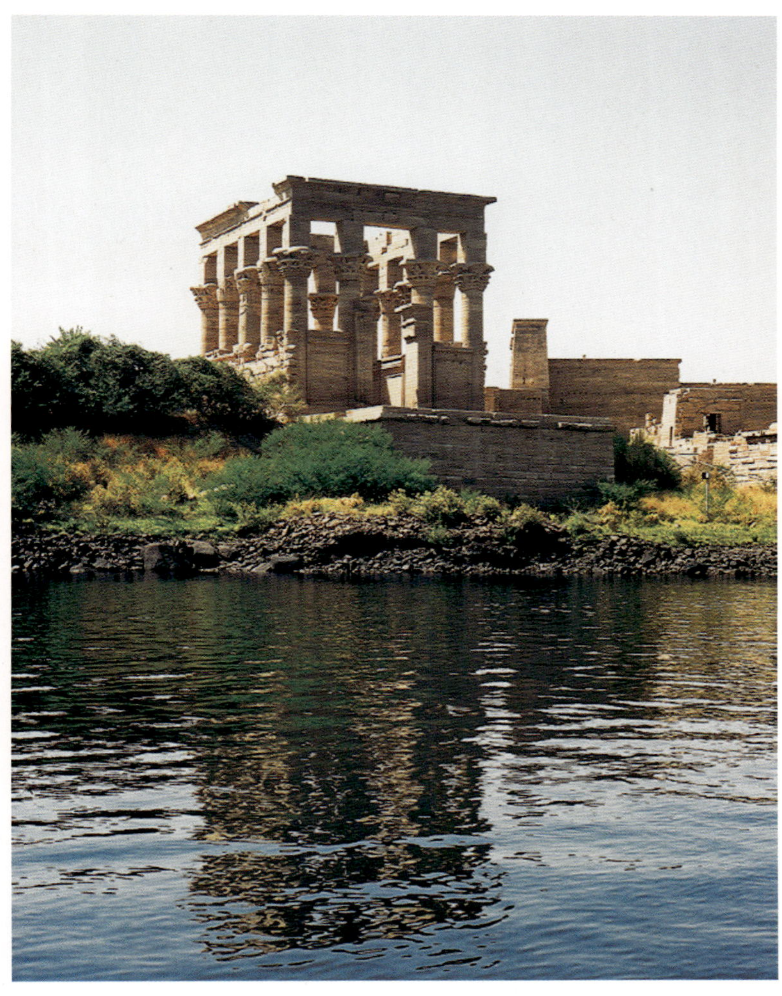

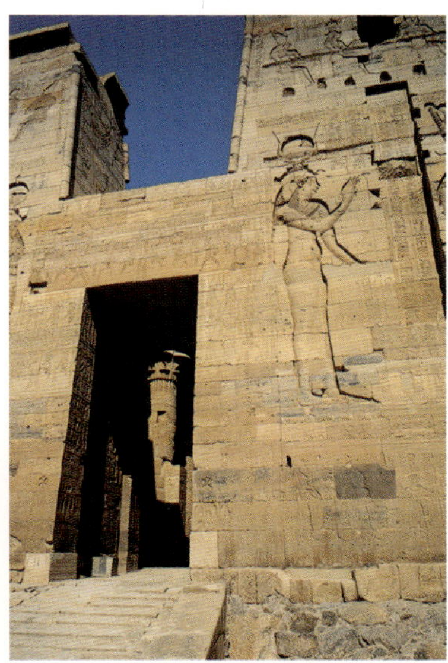

Far left top: The first pylon of the Temple of Isis is decorated with reliefs of Ptolemy XII Neos Dionysos, smiting his enemies, in the same way as he does at Edfu; he does so in the presence of Isis, Hathor, and Horus. His daughter, the great Cleopatra VII, closely identified herself with the goddess, and called herself the "new Isis."

Far left bottom: In the sanctuary of Isis, a relief shows Ptolemy II offering to Osiris and Isis, the latter protecting her brother-husband with outstretched wings.

Above left: The Kiosk of Trajan overlooks the water as you make your approach to Philae. It is decorated with scenes of the emperor Trajan offering incense and wine to Isis, Osiris, and Horus.

Above: The second pylon marked the entrance to the temple proper, the goal of pilgrims from all over the Mediterranean world. The walls of the antechamber are covered with reliefs of Ptolemaic kings and Roman emperors.

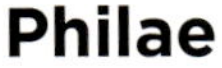

Philae

Through her suffering and joy Isis offered an emotional identification so powerful and satisfying that for some centuries before and after the advent of Christianity she was the greatest deity of the Egyptian, Greek, and Roman worlds. As the wife of the murdered and dismembered Osiris, and as the mother of Horus whom she conceived after she had restored Osiris to wholeness, Isis was revered as the Great Mother of All Gods and Nature, Victorious over Fate, and the Promise of Immortality. She was passionately worshiped by men and women alike, and Philae was the great center of her cult. Isis was worshiped here at Philae until AD 543, when the emperor Justinian closed her temple, imprisoned her priests, and removed her statues to Constantinople. Ten years later her temple was turned into a church.

When the High Dam was built in the 1960s the island of Philae became almost completely submerged. So a nearby island, standing higher out of the water, was carved to replicate the original Philae and

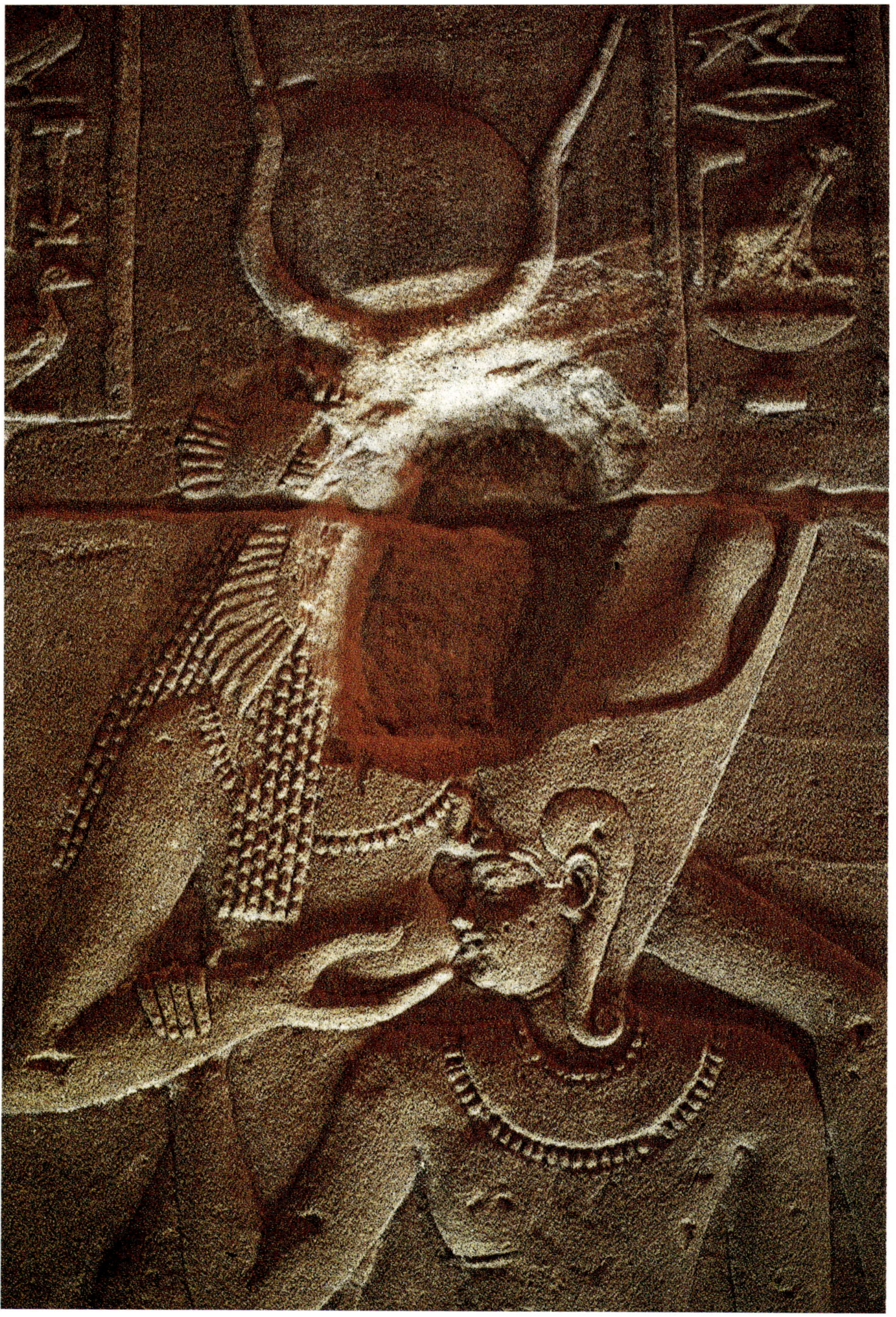

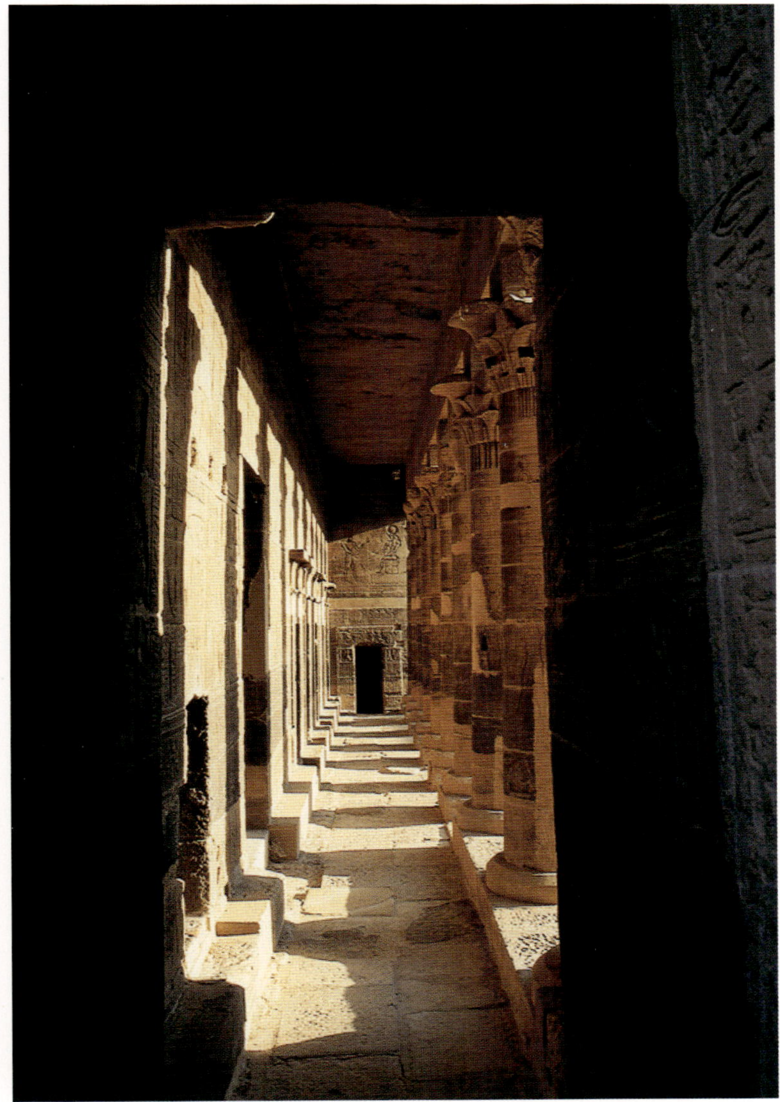

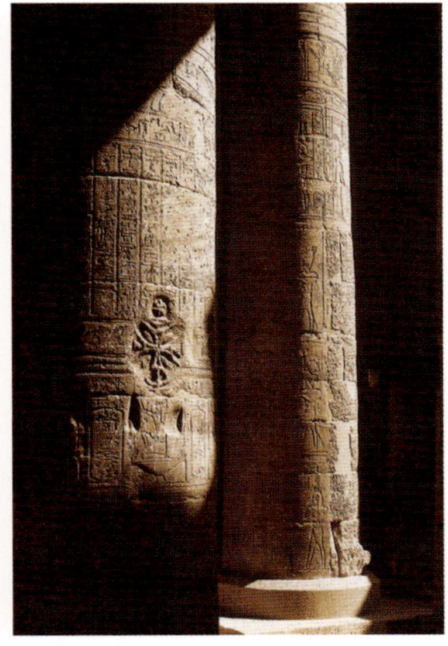

Far left: A relief within the sanctuary, showing Isis nursing Horus. Her face was hacked out by Christians, but they perpetuated the iconography in their images of Mary with the infant Jesus.

Left: A colonnade running along the outer court of the Temple of Isis.

Above: A Christian cross cut on a column of an antechamber to the sanctuary of the goddess. The temple became a church in AD 553.

has been given its name, and the Temple of Isis and the other monuments have been placed in positions corresponding as nearly as possible to their previous relationship.

Visitors to Philae land at the ancient quayside and mount stairs to a gateway built by Nakhtnebef of the Thirtieth Dynasty. A processional way leads to the Temple of Isis, passing through an outer court lined with colonnades. These and almost everything else on the island date from the Ptolemaic and Roman periods. After passing through two pylons and successive antechambers you arrive at the sanctuary of the goddess with a pedestal on which stood the sacred boat with the image of Isis. The walls are decorated with reliefs showing Isis suckling the infant Horus, and receiving offerings from a pharaoh while protectively embracing Osiris with her outstretched wings.

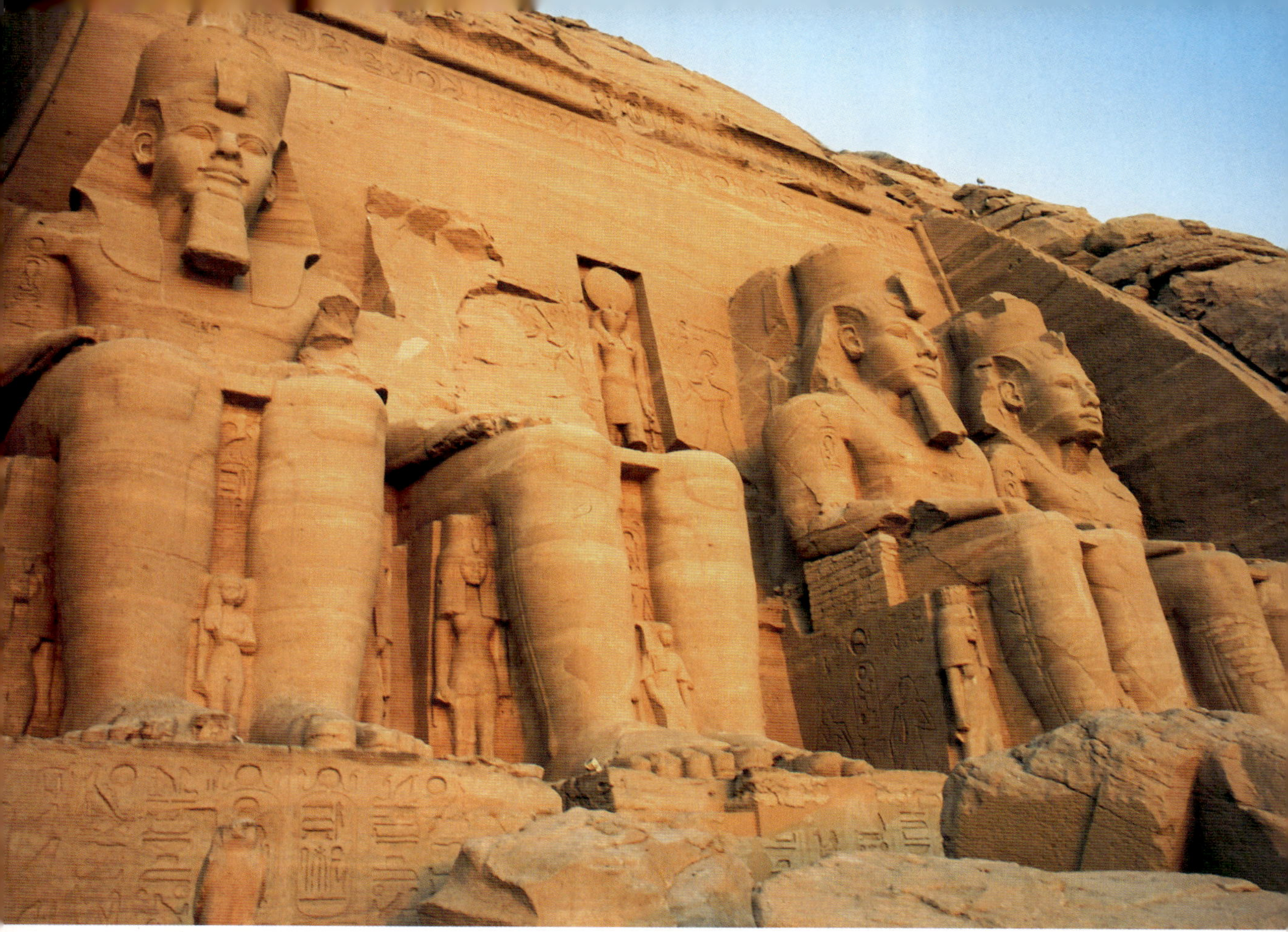

Above: Four colossi of Rameses II sit enthroned before his Temple of Ra-Horakhty where they have witnessed well over a million dawns. Rameses identified himself with Horakhty, the god of the midday sun. The head and torso of the second colossus fell in an earthquake seven years after the dedication of the temple.

Abu Simbel

The rock-cut temples of Abu Simbel stand on the west bank of Lake Nasser deep in Nubia, only forty kilometers north of the border with Sudan. With the construction of the High Dam at Aswan in the 1960s, the temples faced drowning beneath the rising waters of the lake; instead they were reconstructed at this higher elevation. The larger of the two is the Temple of Ra-Horakhty with four colossal statues of Rameses II seated before the cliff-face pylon; nearby is the smaller Temple of Hathor, with its striding colossi of Nefertari and Rameses seeming to emerge from the rock. Before the creation of the lake, the temples overlooked a bend in the Nile and dominated the landscape. This was in part their purpose. Travelers between Africa and Egypt would have seen the imposing colossi, an assertion of Egyptian power and a warning to the Nubians. The most dramatic approach is still by boat, but the temples can also be reached by air and road.

Rameses identified himself with Ra-Horakhty; Ra is the quintessence of the sun god in all his manifestations, while Horakhty is Horus of the Horizon (the midday sun); so the Temple of Ra-Herakhty is effectively the

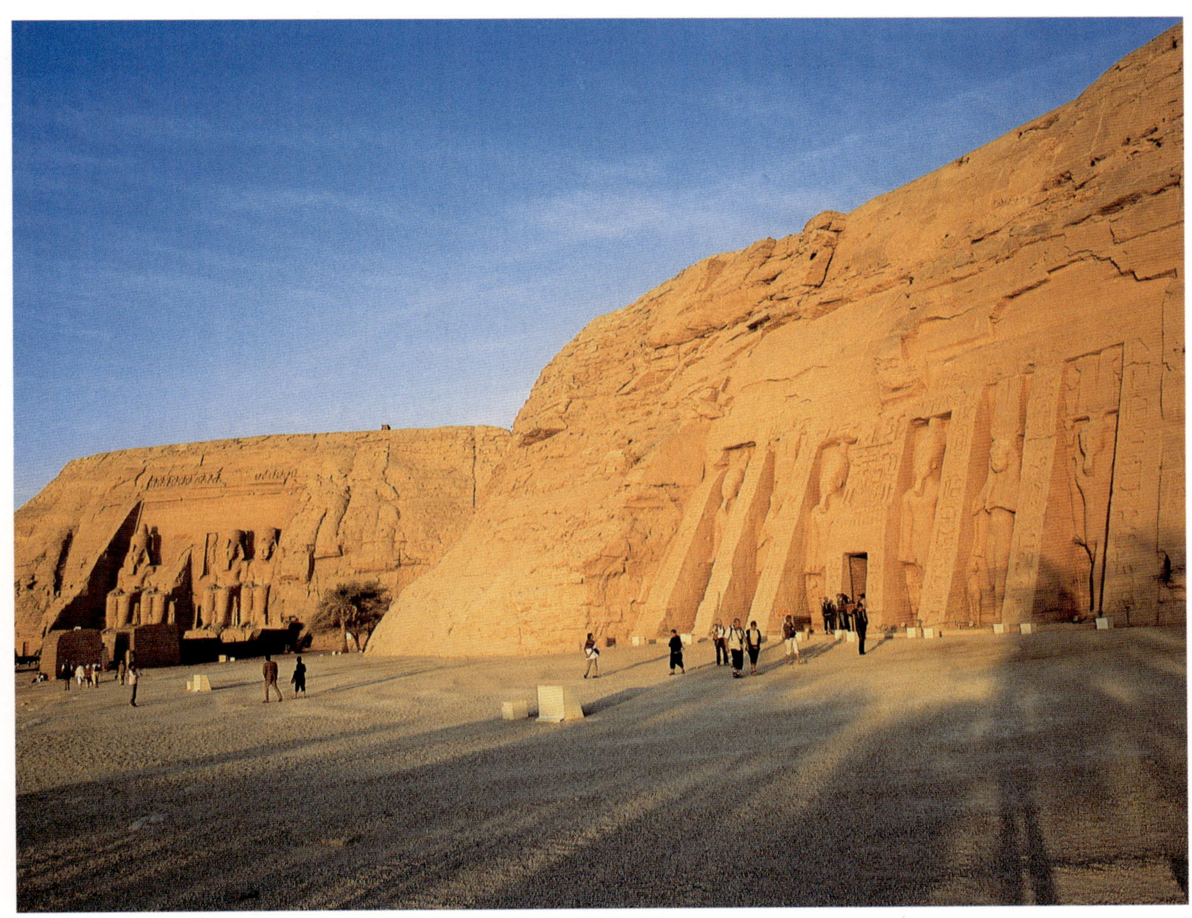

Above: Rameses's Temple of Ra-Horakhty on the left, and Nefertari's Temple of Hathor on the right.

temple of the deified Rameses himself. The point is driven home within the temple by the four great figures of Rameses set against the pillars of the hypostyle hall, and again by the four seated figures in the sanctuary beyond: Ptah, god of Memphis, Amun, god of Thebes, Ra-Horakhty, god of Heliopolis, and the divinized Rameses himself, each the equal of the others, united as one. Taken together with the reliefs around the walls of the hypostyle hall, which show Rameses heroically beating back his enemies at the battle of Qadesh, the message of Abu Simbel is clear: Rameses is proclaimed conqueror, hero, and then god.

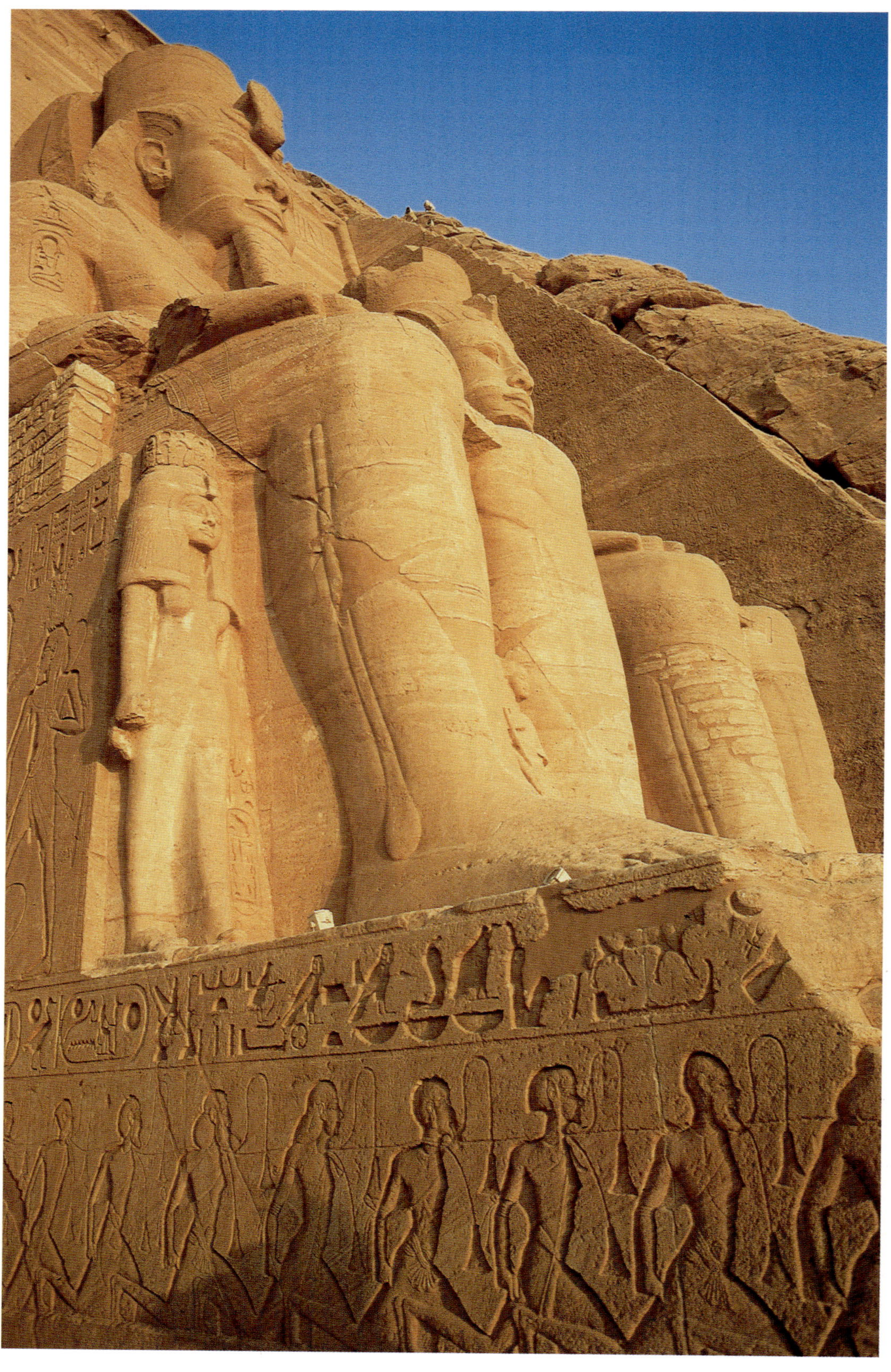

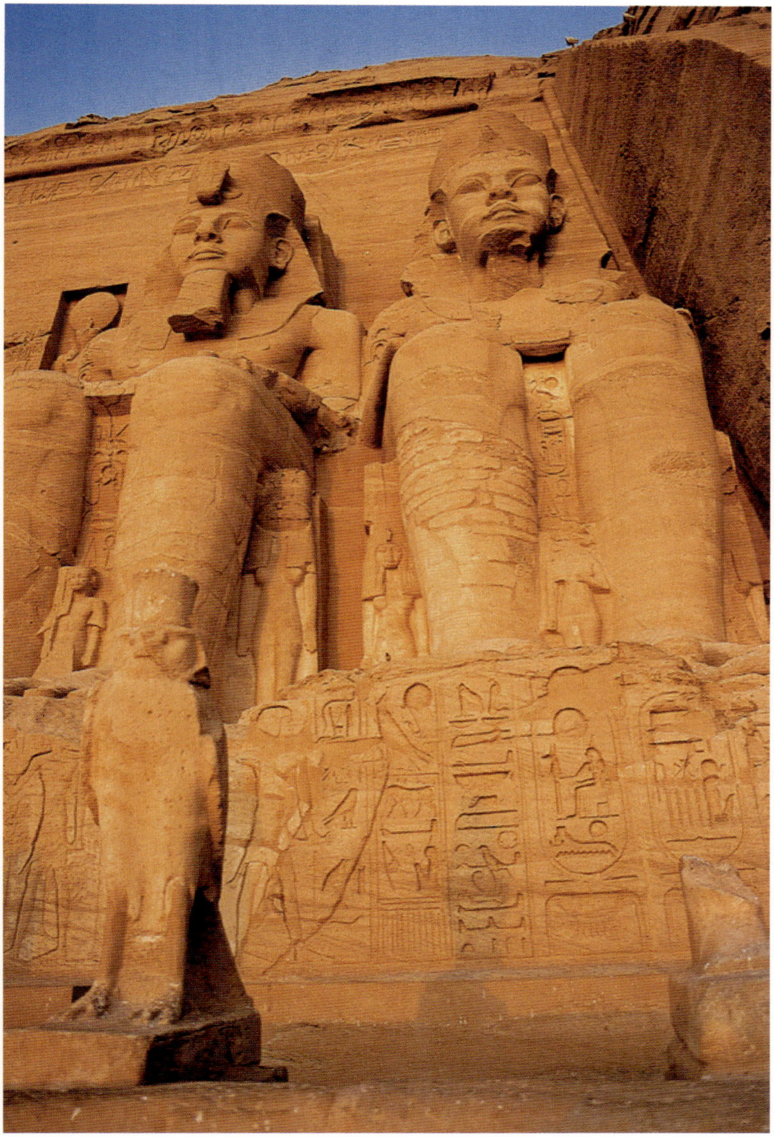

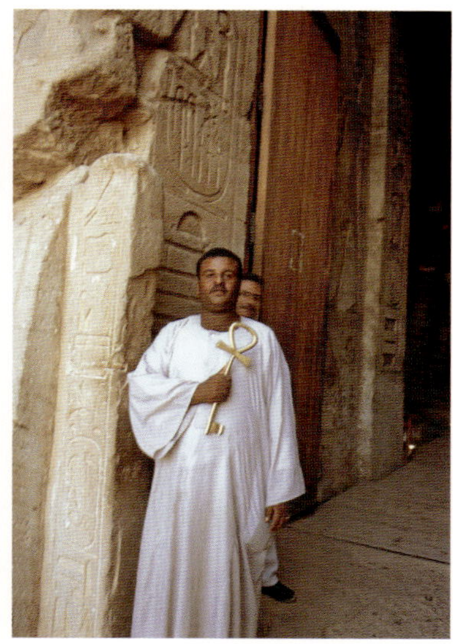

Above: The doorkeeper at the Temple of Ra-Horakhty.

Left and above: The sands of centuries rose as high as the faces of these colossi until finally cleared away just over a hundred years ago. The base below Rameses's feet has been carved with Nubian and Syrian prisoners.

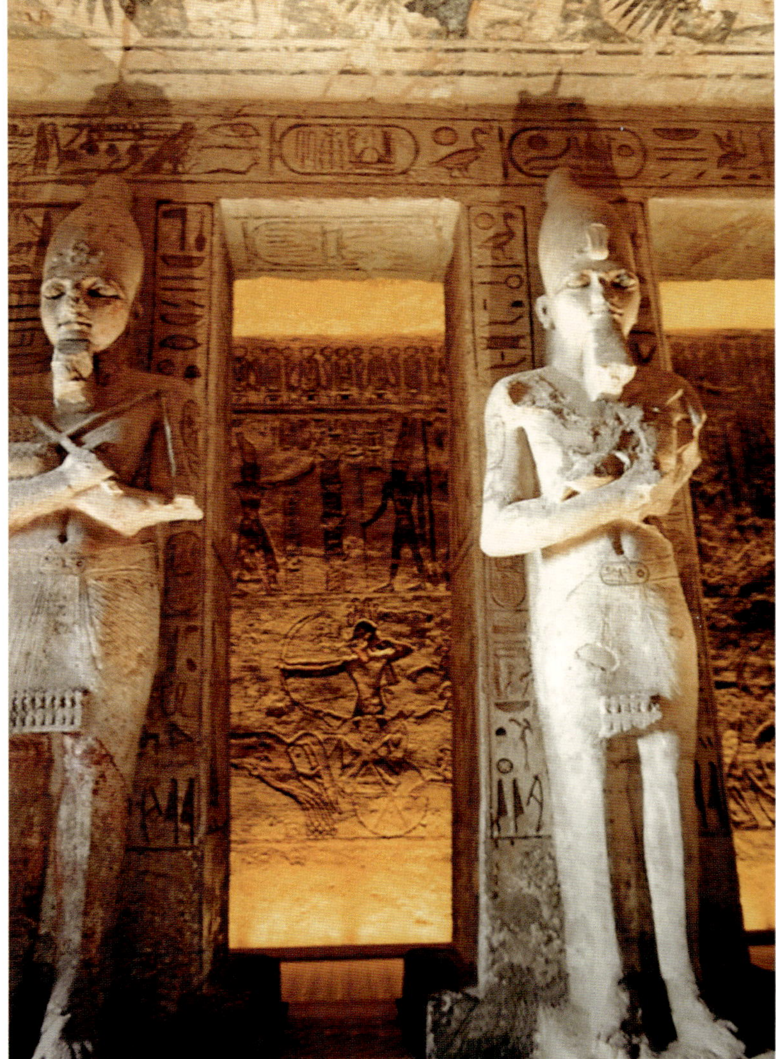

Right: The interior walls of the Temple of Ra-Horakhty feature extensive depictions of the battle of Qadesh in Syria, in the fifth year of Rameses's reign. It was a battle Rameses endlessly boasted about, and boast he needed to do, as he nearly met with disaster after falling into a Hittite trap. The Poem of Pentaur, inscribed on the temple walls, gives a vivid account of the battle; when all looks lost, Rameses desperately beseeches Amun: "What ails you, my father Amun? Is it a father's part to ignore his son? Have I done anything without you? Do I not walk and halt at your bidding? I have not disobeyed any course commanded by you... what does your heart feel, O Amun, for these Asiatics so vile and ignorant of God?... What will men say if even a little thing befall him who bends himself to your counsel?" Through considerable personal courage and with the help of Amun, Rameses cut himself free from his enemies, though he failed to take Qadesh.

Bottom: Rameses in his chariot storming a Syrian fortress. Flying above his head is a protective vulture.

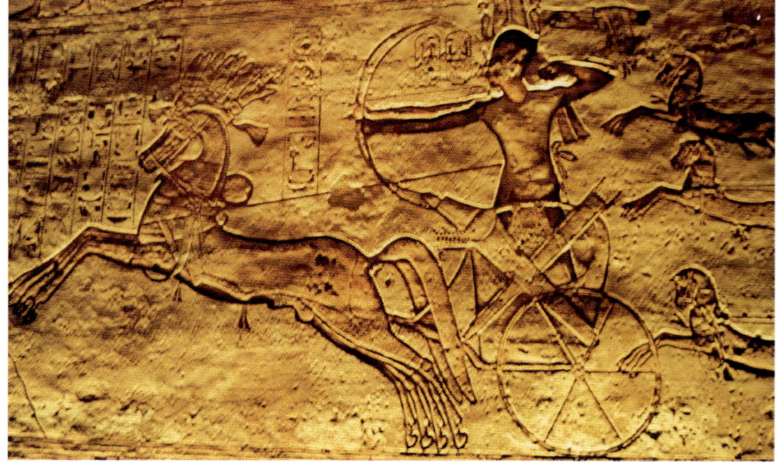

Far right: The hypostyle hall within the Temple of Ra-Horakhty. The ceiling is painted with flying vultures, protectors of royalty. Gigantic statues of Rameses stand against the four pillars on either side. The central aisle leads to the sanctuary of the gods, with their figures carved out of the living rock: Ptah of Memphis, Amun of Thebes, Ra-Horakhty of Heliopolis, and Rameses II himself, who was regarded as a fully fledged god in Nubia.

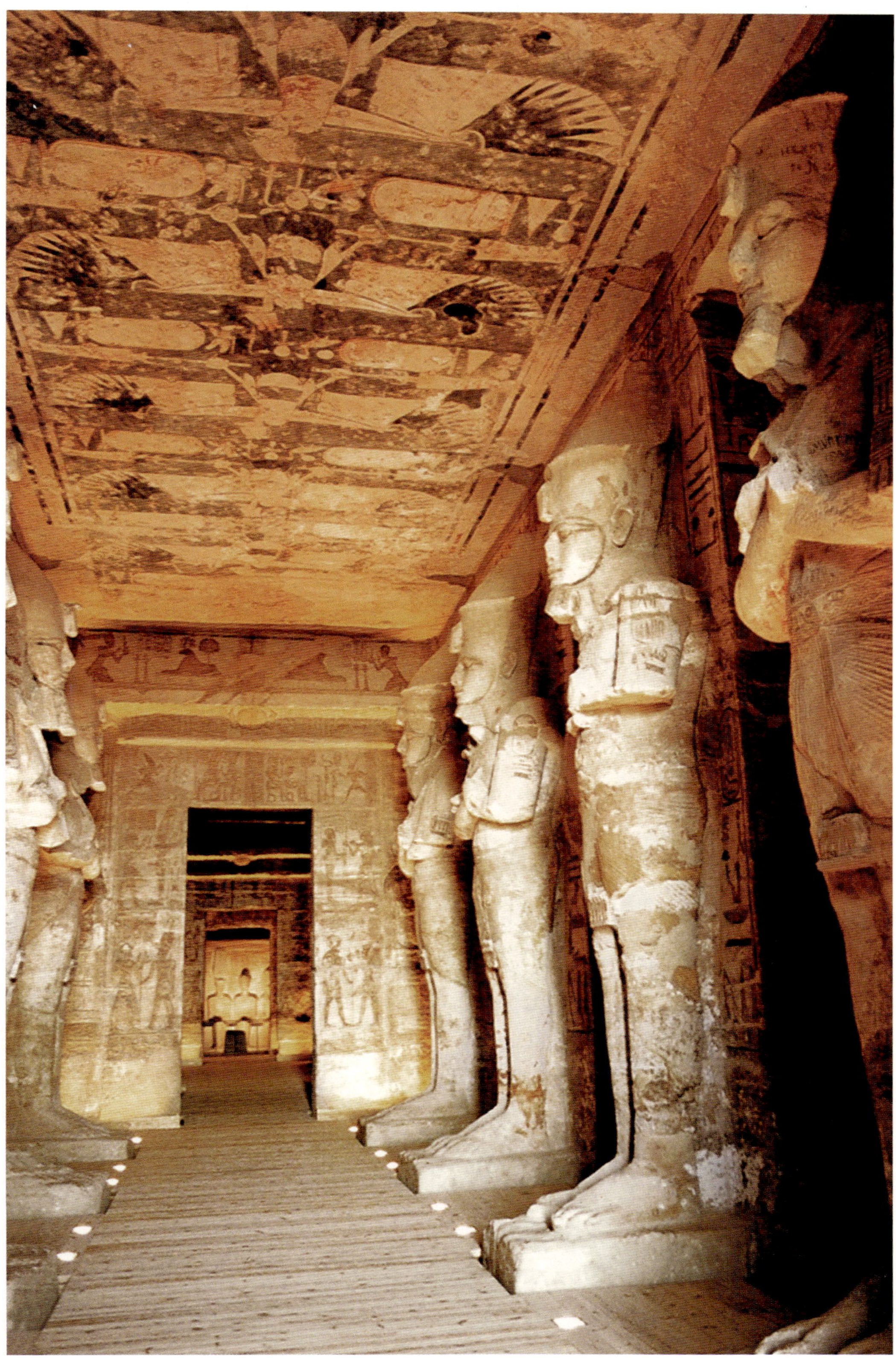

Right: At the Temple of Hathor, the colossal figures of Rameses and his wife Nefertari seem to emerge from the mountain, liberated from the imprisoning rock by the divine force of the rising sun. Here as elsewhere throughout the temple, Nefertari cuts a delightful figure, a slender form in flowing dress, appealing, graceful, dignified. But when Rameses came to Abu Simbel in about 1256 BC to inaugurate the rock-cut temples, he came without his queen, and she died the following year. For once setting aside his royal bombast, the inscription he cut into the façade of Hathor's temple is touched with the poignancy of his regard for his wife: "Rameses has made a temple, excavated in the mountain, of eternal workmanship, for the Chief Queen Nefertari Beloved of Mut, in Nubia, forever and ever, Nefertari for whose sake the very sun does shine." The small figures represent children of Rameses and Nefertari.

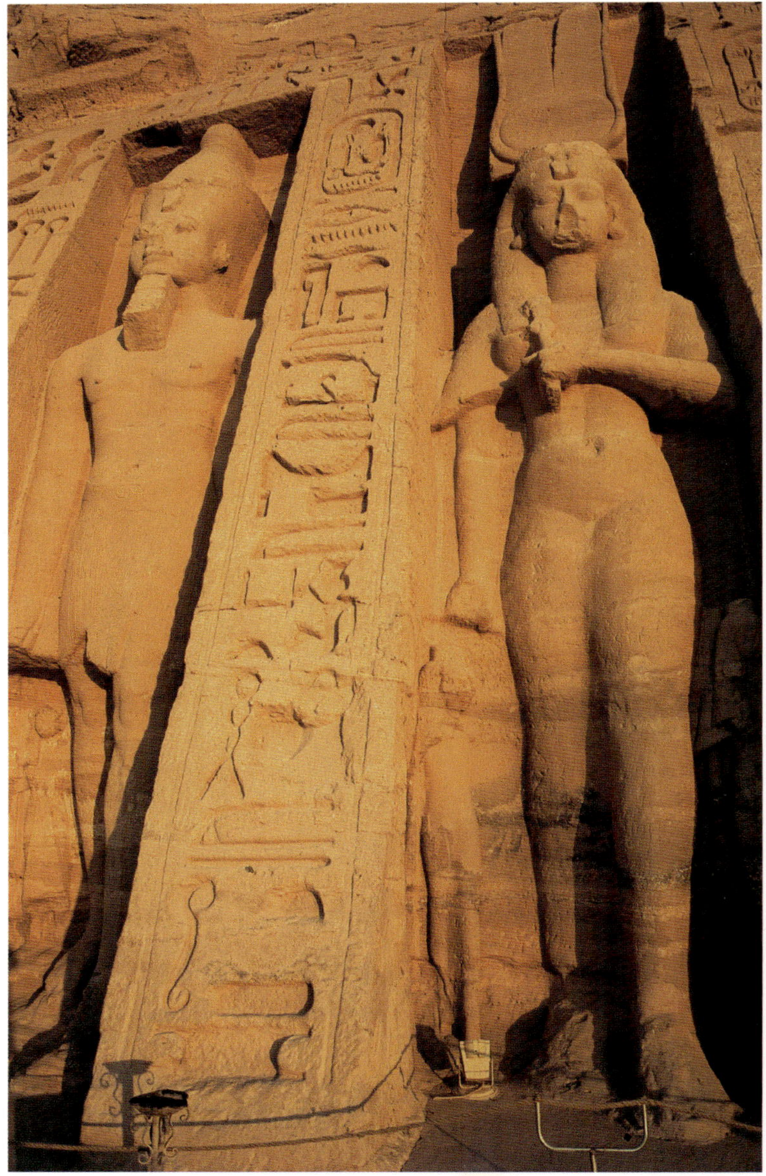

The Temple of Hathor complements the larger Temple of Ra-Horakhty. Hathor was wife to the sun god during his day's passage and mother to his rebirth. As Rameses is identified with Ra-Horakhty, so his wife Nefertari is identified with Hathor. Six colossal statues of Rameses and his queen fill the façade of Nefertari's temple, accompanied by smaller images of their children. They give the uncanny impression that they are striding free from the rock, and at any moment will stride out toward the sunrise. In the sanctuary within the temple Hathor the divine cow emerges from the rear rock wall, a suggestion of the world beyond where her milk brings life to the souls of the dead.